SPAIN AND THE JEWS

ELIE KEDOURIE
General Editor

Spain and the Jews

The Sephardi Experience 1492 and After

With 44 illustrations

THAMES AND HUDSON

For Michael

Designed by Sue Ebrahim

Any copy of this book issued by the publisher as a paperback is sold subject to the condition that it shall not by way of trade or otherwise be lent, resold, hired out or otherwise circulated without the publisher's prior consent in any form of binding or cover other than that in which it is published and without a similar condition including these words being imposed on a subsequent purchaser.

© 1992 Thames and Hudson Ltd, London

First published in the United States in 1992 by Thames and Hudson Inc., 500 Fifth Avenue, New York, New York 10110

Library of Congress Catalog Card Number 92-80566

All Rights Reserved. No part of this publication may be reproduced or transmitted in any form or by any means, electronic or mechanical, including photocopy, recording or any other information storage and retrieval system, without prior permission in writing from the publisher.

Printed and bound in Yugoslavia

Contents

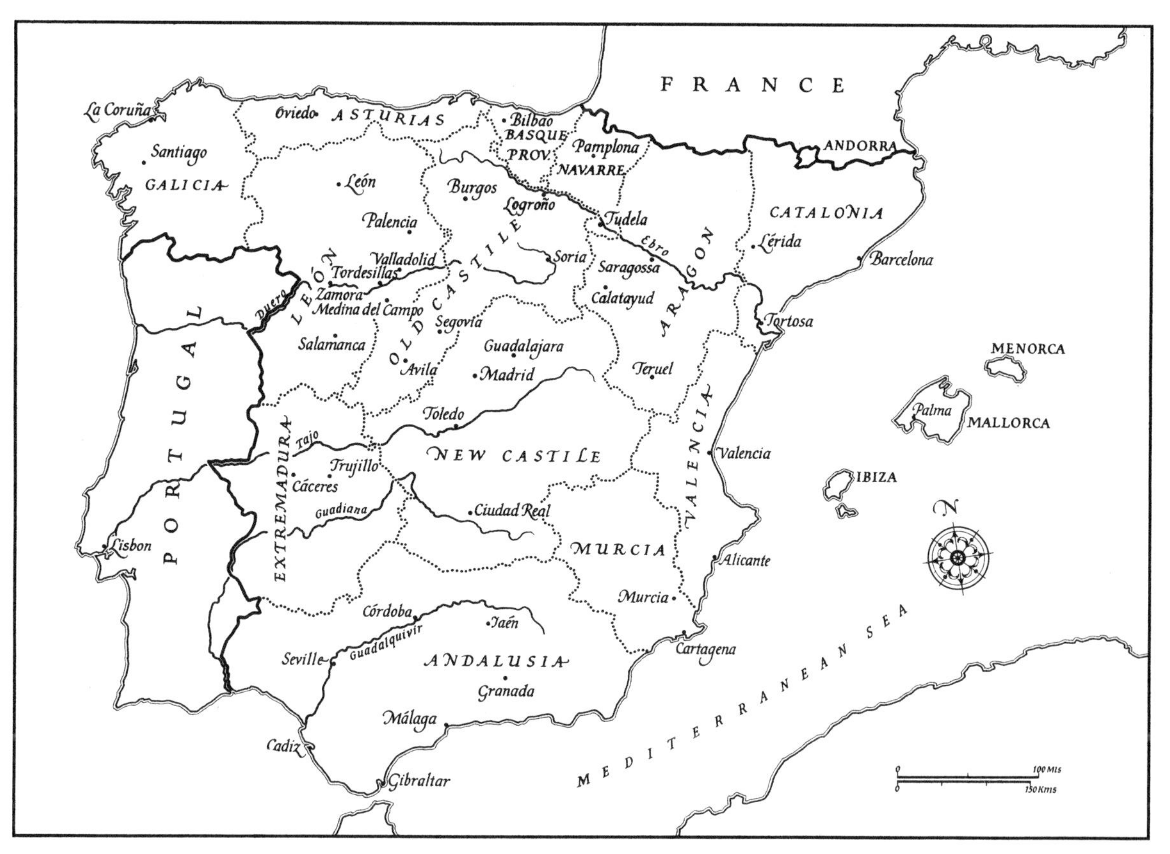

Spain at the time of the expulsion

Introduction

ELIE KEDOURIE

The year 1992 marks the five-hundredth anniversary of the expulsion of the Jews from Spain. Shortly thereafter they were also expelled from Portugal. Had they not been expelled, they would by now have had two millennia of continuous presence in the Iberian Peninsula. When Ferdinand and Isabella decreed their expulsion, Jews had lived continuously in the Peninsula under the Romans, the Visigoths, the Muslims, and in the Spanish kingdoms which vied and fought with the Muslims, and ended by defeating them. Only Babylonian Jewry, which lived for two and a half millennia in the territory now called Iraq, has a longer record of continuous existence in one country.

As is well known, the Jews had a prominent position in the Iberian kingdoms. They played a central role in fiscal administration as providers of funds and supervisors of tax collection. They played their part in the general life of the society and were to be found in most walks of life, in both town and country, until the very eve of the expulsion. The situation of the Sephardim (*Sepharad* being the traditional Hebrew name for Spain) was thus quite different from that of the Ashkenazim (*Ashkenaz* traditionally designating, in Hebrew, Germany and areas to the East where Jews were to settle) from the time of the Crusades onwards. In these regions the Ashkenazim may be said to have been on the whole frozen out of the general society and subjected to unremitting exclusion, persecution and massacre. They thus became of necessity self-enclosed and inward-looking.

We may illustrate this difference by quoting a passage which occurs in Arnold Toynbee's *Study of History* (vol. II, p. 246). There he records an observation he made while travelling in the Near East in 1921, which surprised him a great deal, accustomed as he was to thinking of the Jews as they had been widely portrayed in England, in particular following the immigration from Eastern Europe, which had led to the passage of the Aliens Act of 1905. In common with most people, Toynbee, who in any case disliked Jews, tended to look upon these immigrants, and hence upon all Jews, as outlandish, rough, illiterate and uncultivated, as shady, shifty and subservient. In 1921, he found himself on a train going from Salonica to Vedona. In his carriage were three Jewish schoolteachers and a Greek officer. The schoolteachers, from Salonica – which became a main centre of Sephardic life following the expulsion – were in high spirits

> and gave vent to their mood by breaking into song. They sang in French: the 'culture language' in which the modern Near Eastern Jew has found the necessary supplement to his hereditary Castilian vernacular.

After they had been singing for some time the Greek officer broke his silence and asked, 'Won't you sing in Greek for a change? This country is part of Greece now, and you are Greek citizens.'

> But his intervention [Toynbee went on] had no effect. 'We prefer French,' the Jews answered, politely but firmly, and fell to singing in French again, while the Greek lieutenant subsided. There was one person in the carriage, however, who was even more surprised at the Jewish teachers' reply to the Greek officer than the Greek himself, and that was the Frankish spectator. Seldom, he reflected, would a Jew have shown such spirit in such circumstances in France, or England or America.

Toynbee thought that the behaviour of the Salonica schoolteachers 'bore witness to the relative humanity with which the Jews in the Ottoman empire had been treated by the Osmanlis'.

In this Toynbee was no doubt right. Those Sephardim who found refuge in Ottoman lands did experience relief from the persecutions to which Jews had been intermittently, and at times ferociously, subject in Christian Spain and which culminated in the decree of expulsion. Their position in the Ottoman polity was the same as that of other, longer-established, Jewish communities. As a non-Muslim People of the Book, their status, inferior as it was to that of Muslims, was legally well-defined and fairly securely established. They did not have, as under the Christians, to labour under the ever-present imputation that they had been offered, and had spurned, salvation; and under the perpetual accusation that they had been guilty of the death of Jesus. This advantage the newcomers to Salonica came to share with their other correligionists under Ottoman rule. It made for a self-assured stance, free of the necessity to justify their beliefs and sometimes even to apologize for their very existence. Further, living in Ottoman lands, the Sephardim could renew a connexion with communities with whom they shared those religious traditions and practices which originated in Babylonian Jewry and served to distinguish them from the Jews of Ashkenaz. These traditions and practices, adopted by the Jews of the Iberian Peninsula at least from the time of the Muslim conquest, explain why, today, those Jews of the Arab world dislodged from their ancestral homes by the Arab-Israeli conflict immediately find a familiar and congenial home within congregations which the refugees from Spain and Portugal established in London, New York and elsewhere.

In explaining the behaviour of the Salonica schoolteachers, Toynbee was, however, mistaken in ascribing it solely to the benefits of Ottoman rule. What we know about the history of the Sephardim before and after their expulsion would lead us rather to think that their ethos and attitudes, exemplified in this incident, are older than their ancestors' settlement in Ottoman lands. In spite of intermittent attacks and persecutions – which became gradually more severe in the century between the horrific outburst of 1391, which led large numbers to convert to Christianity, and the expulsion decree of 1492, it does remain the case that Jews were still to be found in all walks of life, both humble and exalted. Two well-known, albeit exceptional, examples may give an idea of the place of the Jews in Spanish society. Abraham Senior (*c.*1412–*c.*1493) was the chief tax-farmer of Castile. He threw his influence in Spanish politics on the side of King Ferdinand of Aragon and Queen Isabella of Castile, who in turn were very favourably inclined towards him. They made him, for instance, treasurer of the Santa Hermandad, or Holy Brotherhood, a body of armed men established by them to ensure law and order in their territories. Senior endeavoured to avert the decree of expulsion, but of course failed. The King and Queen succeeded in persuading him to convert, and he did so, together with his family, in June 1492, the two rulers serving as his godparents.

Don Isaac ben Yehuda Abravanel (1437–1508) was Senior's contemporary and colleague in the financial administration of the Kingdom, and worked together with Senior to deflect Ferdinand and Isabella from their purposes. He was of Spanish origin, but after 1391 his family left Spain for Portugal, where it attained a most prominent position in the Court. Don Isaac had been treasurer of Alfonso V of Portugal, and a highly influential figure in the Court and among the aristocracy. When Alfonso was succeeded by his son, Abravanel became involved with the aristocratic opposition to him, and had to flee to Castile when the King gained the upper hand over his enemies and was determined to destroy Abravanel. The former treasurer attributed this misfortune to having served an earthly ruler, and resolved to devote his life to religious study, writing commentaries on Joshua, Judges and Samuel. In 1484, however, he took up government service once more, this time under Ferdinand and Isabella. Unlike Senior, he refused to apostasize in 1492, and took the road of exile. He went to Naples where he took service with its King, in the meantime completing a commentary on Kings. When the French occupied Naples, Abravanel's house and library were sacked. He went to Corfu, then returned to Italy in 1496, completing a commentary on Deuteronomy which he had begun many years earlier in Lisbon. Aside from these commentaries, Abravanel was the author of a formidable corpus of philosophical and religious writings which show that he was at home equally in Jewish and in secular learning. In 1503 Abravanel settled in Venice, took part in diplomatic negotiations between Venice and Portugal, and also finished commentaries on Jeremiah, Genesis and Exodus.

Abravanel lived and died as a Jew, and combined a career of learning with the practice of public affairs in more than one country and at the highest level. Conversos, too, played a leading part in European business and politics, before and after their return to Judaism. Solomon Abenaes (1520–1603) was born Alvaro Mendes to a New Christian family in Portugal. He farmed diamond mines in India and, returning to Portugal, took a prominent part in politics. He lived successively in Madrid, Florence, Paris and London. In 1585 he went to Istanbul and reverted to Judaism. He farmed the Ottoman customs revenues, was made duke of Mytilene, and was architect of an Anglo-Ottoman alliance directed against Spanish expansionism.

The careers of Abravanel and Abenaes show the extent to which rulers, whether Christian or Muslim, valued the knowledge, experience and international connexions of such figures. The history of the Nasi family – Gracia Nasi (*c.*1510–69) and her nephew and son-in-law Joseph Nasi (*c.*1524–79) – is even more striking. Born Beatrice de Luna to a New Christian family in Portugal, she married Francisco Mendes, also from a New Christian family who, together with a brother established in Antwerp, ran a business which combined banking and precious stones. In 1537, having become a widow, she left Portugal for Antwerp to join her brother-in-law. Here she moved in aristocratic circles, also aiding her brother-in-law in his efforts to facilitate the flight of conversos and New Christians being pursued by the Inquisition. When he died in 1543, Beatrice had to flee from Flanders, leaving much of her property behind. She settled in Venice, where she was denounced by her sister-in-law as a judaizer. The Ottomans, moved by her nephew, João Micas, who had accompanied her when she left Portugal, intervened in her favour and she was allowed to leave Venice unmolested. She went to Ferrara where the ruling House of Este was hospitable to Jews. Here, she openly professed Judaism, taking the name Gracia Nasi, perhaps because the family was descended from the ancient Spanish Jewish family of this name. In Ferrara, too, she was busy organizing the flight of New Christians from Portugal. In 1553 she settled in Istanbul and was there the head of the family firm which engaged in large commercial and banking operations. She was active in establishing *yeshivot* and synagogues in Istanbul, and notably in Tiberias, then a ruin, which she secured from the Sultan for an annual payment of 1000 ducats. In 1556–57 Gracia Nasi attempted to organize a boycott of the port of Ancona in retaliation for the holocaust of twenty-six conversos who had been condemned as renegades from Christianity.

The career of her nephew, the son of a royal physician and professor of medicine at the University of Lisbon, is quite as remarkable. After his aunt's departure from Antwerp, João Micas was in contact with the Emperor Charles V, and is said to have been the jousting partner of his nephew, the future Emperor Maximilian. Failing to save the family property from confiscation, he fled Antwerp in 1547. He established himself in Istanbul in 1554, professed Judaism openly, was circumcized and took the name Joseph Nasi. In the struggle for the succession to Sultan Suleiman, he favoured Selim over his brother. Selim II made Joseph Nasi duke of Naxos and count of Andros. He played a prominent part in the conduct of Ottoman foreign affairs, in 1569 encouraging the revolt of the Netherlands against Spain. Following his aunt's death, he obtained confirmation and extension of the Tiberias concession, and in 1564–65 rebuilt its ruined walls.

The decree of expulsion was issued by Ferdinand and Isabella on 31 March 1492. It offered the Jews of their realms the choice either to convert, or to leave by 31 July. Though the possessions of those Jews who chose exile were not to be confiscated, yet the short period allowed between the publication of the decree and the stipulated departure necessarily meant that those who chose exile either had to dispose of their assets at distress prices, or to abandon them if they could not readily be liquidated. Furthermore, were any Jew who left to come back, he would suffer capital punishment.

As the decree made clear, the authorities had two main objects in mind: that all Jews should convert; but that if they did not, then these should cease to be an organized Jewish community to act as a magnet attracting the large number of conversos who had, under duress, ostensibly abandoned their faith during the century which began with the riots of 1391, and which similar outbreaks thereafter periodically punctuated. The authorities had sought to prevent this judaizing by physically isolating the Jews in separate quarters. This policy, however, failed to prevent contacts between the two groups, hence the drastic measure edicted in March 1492.

This measure, and the forced conversions which had preceded it, exemplify a powerful and abiding tendency in European history since soon after Constantine's conversion to Christianity. Previous to this, the Roman empire had never sought to enforce religious uniformity on its subjects, and Constantine himself disclaimed any desire to do so. However, a century after his death, in 438, one of his successors, Theodosius II, issued a statute defining Jews as 'enemies of Roman laws and of the supreme majesty'. A century later, edicts by Justinian I worsened further the position of the Jews within the Roman empire. His *Corpus Juris* was accepted as a legal authority not only in the Byzantine empire, but also in the lands which had formed the Roman empire in the West, and the

Corpus Juris made Judaism a kind of crime, effectively removing Jews from the general society. Henceforth, the drive towards uniformity of belief becomes manifest as a powerful tendency in European politics. The tendency was not confined to political and ecclesiastical leaders, but penetrated deep in society. The edict of 1492 was indeed a royal edict, but it had been preceded by a century of sporadic persecution in which clerics and burghers played a prominent part, with the mob following their lead, even against the wishes of rulers and their advisers who disapproved of such violent proceedings.

The drive towards uniformity in members of the body politic has taken many forms in European political thought and practice. The citizens of Rousseau's *Social Contract* undertake all to be bound by the tenets of a civil religion, to depart from which lays them open to capital punishment. In our own times, the Bolsheviks, in the USSR and elsewhere have penalized those who, in their estimation, belong to the wrong social class; while the Nazis exterminated Jews because they did not belong to a presumed Aryan race. Paradoxical as it may seem, the Nazi criterion for membership in the body politic, namely race, was also invoked in fifteenth-century Spain against the conversos who had converted precisely in order to escape the exclusions and persecutions to which Jews were subjected on grounds of religion. In 1449 anti-converso riots broke out in Toledo and elsewhere in Castile, and the municipal authorities decreed that conversos, being descended from Jews, were forbidden to hold any municipal office in which they might exercise jurisdiction or authority over those of pure Christian descent. Scandalous though this stipulation seemed to some ecclesiastical authorities, purity of blood eventually became a requirement for holding office in all of Spain and Portugal, and in their overseas dependencies, to be abolished in Portugal only in 1773, and in Spain as late as 1860.

It is not known exactly how many Jews chose to leave rather than abandon their religion: the figures are still subject to controversy, which is reflected in the contributions that follow. As may be seen, Professor Beinart's figures are higher than those suggested in Dr Kamen's chapter. Professor Beinart considers that the contemporary documents would support his view. The disagreement cannot be resolved in these pages, but readers should take note of it. Whatever the true statistics, a great many Jews went over the land frontier to Portugal, only to be forcibly converted five years later. Sephardim who left in 1492 for other destinations did succeed in reconstituting their communities, some in North Africa, others here and there in the Italian Peninsula and in other places, most notably in the Ottoman empire. Later, conversos or New Christians who had remained secretly faithful to their religion, or perhaps loyal to their origins, or driven to flight when the Inquisition pursued and harried them, also re-established Sephardi communities, most notably in Amsterdam. If one had been writing a hundred years ago, one would have simply recorded that the descendants of those who had been expelled or had to flee were able, generation after generation, freely to practise their religion and preserve their traditions, and continue to live in modest prosperity under the protection of the laws. However, a hundred years later one has to record that the two great communities of Salonica and Amsterdam, and the smaller communities which had taken root elsewhere in the Low Countries and in Ottoman areas now part of Bulgaria, Greece and Yugoslavia suffered, between 1940 and 1945, almost complete extermination at the hands of the Nazis – a scourge which, in some of its characteristics, was prefigured by the Inquisition, but was infinitely more methodical, savage and pitiless than anything imagined or inflicted by its tribunals.

The international situation no doubt facilitated the resettlement of Sephardi communities outside the Iberian Peninsula. The Ottomans were in rivalry and contention with Spain, while the Protestant Reformation created new political centres in northern Europe inimical to Spain, a Catholic Great Power. Within these centres, particularly the Netherlands, the Sephardim were able to secure a lodgement. These opportunities would, however, have availed little if the Sephardim had not had the spiritual and intellectual resources which would enable them to subsist as a community aware of itself, committed to its beliefs, and able to take up and develop traditional organizing principles, in a way such as to be able to continue making sense of a world in which they had suffered such a great and sudden catastrophe.

Don Isaac Abravanel's commentaries and his reflections on religious and political life, written in the midst of great adversity and successive upheavals are a case in point. Another, much more important figure whose work had a lasting influence on Judaism and Jewish life everywhere is Joseph Caro (1488–1575). Caro was possibly born in Toledo, and was taken to Istanbul as a child. Before settling in Safed, in Galilee, he lived in other Ottoman cities with Sephardi congregations: Adrianople, Nikopolis, Salonica. At the age of thirty-four, in 1522, he began a new codification of Jewish law, *Beit Yosef*, which he completed twenty-four years later, the digest of which, the famous *Shulhan Arukh*, came to be accepted as authoritative by both Sephardim and Ashkenazim. Caro's object was to introduce order into a body of law which had come to include a great and confusing variety of laws and customs. A large enterprise of this kind serves to show that the catastrophe of 1492 did not dry up the well-springs of intellectual and religious vitality, and may even have served to make them flow more copiously.

The Safed where Caro settled and lived the rest of his life was a centre of Sephardi religious life, and particularly the study of the Kabbalah. Kabbalists, or mystics – to use a vague general term – existed both among

Sephardim and Ashkenazim. In Safed, where a great number of Sephardi religious figures had settled, practice and study of the Kabbalah continued a tradition in Iberian Jewry which by then was very old. The *Zohar*, which purported to unveil to its qualified students the esoteric secrets which hold a key to the mysteries of the Godhead and the universe, was a product of Sephardi religious speculation in Spain. As with Caro's enterprise, the Kabbalah in Safed shows a new vitality in its practitioners. Caro himself practised Kabbalah, and the most influential kabbalists sat at his feet, and became in turn masters at whose feet disciples sat. Moses Cordovero (1522–70) was Caro's disciple, and his student was Isaac Luria Ashkenazi (1534–72) whose teaching, later interpreted or distorted in a particular way, was to have far-reaching consequences in Jewish history.

For the kabbalist, to make sense of the world with all its imperfections and shortcomings, it is not enough to study the world of appearances. The veil hiding reality must be penetrated, and when it is, after arduous practice and study, it will be seen that our world is part of a cosmic divine drama unfolding according to its own dialectic. In this drama, God, in order to reveal Himself, conceals and contracts Himself. His concealment is the coming into being of His emanations which are scattered all over the universe, overlaid with impure and evil matter. This contraction and concealment are the necessary prerequisite for God revealing Himself.

In this vein, Luria propounded a doctrine of the restitution or restoration of the cosmos. This restoration will depend on the deeds of men, of ascetics who, through mystic labours and prayers, will extinguish the world's blemish, redeem the exile of Israel and the world's exile from God. A distorted form of this doctrine was used by Sabbetai Sevi (1626–76) and by his devotees, to show that he himself was the Messiah who, by deliberately breaking the law and plumbing the depths of sin, at last makes possible the abolition of all sin, and brings about the manifestation of God who will reveal Himself in His glory. Whether Sabbetai was himself a Sephardi or not, the fact is that he was active throughout Sephardi communities in Smyrna (Izmir), where he was born and brought up, in Jerusalem, Salonica and elsewhere in the Balkans. Belief in his (false) promise that the Jewish people were soon to be redeemed through him spread to the four corners of the Jewish world, and was by no means confined to Sephardim.

The expulsion decree was the culmination of a long train of events which began with the riots of 1391. In fear and under duress large numbers of Spanish Jews converted. It is the situation of these conversos in Spanish society, and the suspicion, whether genuinely entertained or deliberately fomented, that many of them were not sincere in their conversion, that they continued to adhere in secret to Judaism, which led ecclesiastical authorities, as well as Ferdinand and Isabella, to take action, even more severe and stringent, to prevent the backsliding occasioned by the presence of former correligionists who kept alive Jewish teachings and practices, and who had synagogues to which conversos could resort. Physical isolation of the Jews was tried and was believed to have failed. Expulsion was the next step, leading either to the conversion of the Jews or their departure. Either way, the danger of conversos backsliding would have been practically removed.

Measures dealing with Jews as such were judged, however, not to be enough. More than a decade before the expulsion, in 1478, the Catholic Monarchs requested and received Papal permission to establish an Inquisition, the task of which was to extirpate judaizing heresy among the conversos. The Spanish National Inquisition – its motto *Misericordia et Justitia* – carried on by the Church under the authority of the State, was aimed at the conversos, not the Jews. It quickly established a network of tribunals under the oversight of a Supreme Council equal in rights with the other Councils of Castile and Aragon.

The tribunals heard evidence and deliberated in secret, the accused having no way of confronting and cross-examining his accusers. Sentences were very severe. Conversos found guilty could be sentenced to death. Those so sentenced were 'relaxed' to the secular authority who executed them by burning at the stake – the Church abhorring the shedding of blood. If the guilty escaped the death sentence, they might be punished by imprisonment either for life or for an indefinite term, or for a fixed one. Or again, a guilty converso might, by an act of abjuration, purge his guilt and be 'reconciled' to the Church. In all cases, however, condemnation meant confiscation, to the benefit of the State, of the condemned person's property. 'Reconciliation' was not as mild and merciful as it sounded, since the 'reconciled' were debarred from civil or ecclesiastical benefices and honours, and debarred from becoming, *inter alia*, doctors, notaries, public scribes, tax farmers or collectors, stone masons or tavern owners. Alongside them, their sons and grandsons were debarred from holding any public office. They might not, also, ride or travel in carriages and carts. They might not wear jewelry or silk and brocade. They were forbidden to bear arms or ride horses. They were also, of course, to have no intercourse of any kind with Jews, or observe Jewish customs, or keep Jewish books. Quoting a contemporary chronicler, Haim Beinart (*Conversos on Trial*, Jerusalem 1981, p. 34) states that in Seville, where the Inquisition began, between 1481 and 1488 over seven hundred conversos were burned at the stake and over five thousand 'reconciled' to the Church. The Spanish Inquisition was not finally abolished until 1834, and it has been estimated that up to 1808 some 32,000 heretics, of whom the great majority would have been conversos, were burned at the stake.

The horror conveyed by these figures is prodigiously enhanced if we keep in mind their effect on those conversos who were spared the attentions of the Holy Office. Year in year out, decade after decade, they had to live with the numbing fear that some denunciation, perhaps lacking all foundation, made by a person unknown, would lead to interrogation, incarceration in the prisons of the Inquisition, condemnation following deliberation in secret conclaves, and most probably at best ruin for oneself and one's family. Yet as the records of the Inquisition show, again and again men and women in all walks of life, whether lettered or illiterate, whether humble workmen or doctors renowned in their profession, or powerful financiers, braved these dangers in order to take part in secret ceremonies to celebrate the Sabbath and the Festivals, to keep the Fasts, and to avoid eating unlawful foods. There were also some who, in spite of the obvious danger, had themselves circumcized or even performed the operation themselves. As the decades went by, knowledge of Judaism, its practices and rituals, necessarily became gradually more vague and hazy. This does not seem to have extinguished the fidelity of the crypto-Jews to their proscribed religion, or their loyalty to the Jewish people. These crypto-Jews became, in the striking words of a modern historian, Carl Gebhardt, 'Catholics without faith and Jews without knowledge, albeit Jews by their will'. For a great many, the will to remain Jewish, even after many decades of living as Catholics in a Catholic country, obviously remained very strong.

A striking expression of this loyalty occurs in the writings of Orobio de Castro (1617–87). Born in Braganza in Portugal as Balthazar de Orobio, descendant of four generations of New Christians, Orobio left Portugal with his parents for Spain, in order to escape the Inquisition which had tried and sentenced his paternal and maternal grandparents for the crime of judaizing. In Spain Orobio became a well-known doctor and a professor of philosophy at Salamanca. He, however, fell foul of the Inquisition, was arrested, tortured and imprisoned for three years. He fled to France, where he taught medicine at the University of Toulouse. He finally made his way to Amsterdam in 1662 where he openly professed Judaism, taking the name Isaac. He became a notable and acute defender of traditional Judaism against Deism, Spinozism and Sabbateanism. Indeed as a philosophical writer he came to have a European reputation and audience. In one of his writings during his Amsterdam years, Orobio declares:

> ... in Spain I presented a Christian appearance, since life is sweet; but I was never very good at it, and so it came out that I was in fact a Jew. If, then, whilst I was there [in Spain], confronted with the risk of [losing my] freedom, status, property, and indeed life itself, I was in reality a Jew and a Christian merely in outward appearance, common sense shows that in a domicile of freedom, a true Jew is what I shall be. (Quoted in Yosef Kaplan, *From Christianity to Judaism: The Story of Isaac Orobio de Castro*, 1989, pp. 329–30).

Orobio, as has been seen, was born in Portugal. It was in order to escape the Portuguese Inquisition that his parents left for Spain in 1623. The Portuguese Inquisition was established much later than the Spanish, in 1537. When it got into its stride, however, it was just as, if not more formidable than, Ferdinand and Isabella's engine of persecution. It can also be said that the task of the Portuguese inquisitors was more arduous than that of their Spanish colleagues. When expulsion was decreed in 1492 and those who clung to their Judaism departed, the Spanish conversos would have little or no contact with their former correligionaries, and knowledge of Judaism, Jewish rites and traditions would become progressively hazier. A great many of the Spanish Jews went to Portugal which was by far easier of access than any other destination, where the King allowed the refugees, against payment, freedom to practise their religion. Five years later, however, his successor, seeking through a dynastic marriage to unite under his rule the Kingdoms of Spain and Portugal, acceded to a condition made by Spain that Portugal should be emptied of Jews. The Portuguese King finally decided that this condition would be met by forcibly converting the Jews *en masse*. The whole of the Portuguese community thus became, at a stroke, New Christians. This instant change of religion meant that the social connexions, the traditions, the knowledge of Judaism remained, although under a blanket of proscription and secrecy. The fact, also, that the Portuguese Inquisition did not start in earnest until the 1540s meant that crypto-Judaism could subsist among the New Christians, without attracting the horrendous punishments inflicted by its tribunals, and without perpetual fear of being informed against and the secrecy in which the tribunals operated. The New Christians were forbidden to leave the Kingdom without permission, but over a period numbers were successful in effecting their escape and joining older-established Sephardi communities, or in founding communities of their own. This was most notably the case in Amsterdam where, from the end of the sixteenth century, Portuguese Jews were allowed to establish themselves and practise their religion without molestation. The newcomers began to play a prominent part in the worldwide Dutch commerce which the independence of the Netherlands from Spain and its rise as a naval power made possible. These crypto-Jewish refugees from Portugal, after living for a century or more as New Christians, succeeded in re-establishing a Jewish community on authentic Jewish lines, its numbers continuously augmented by a flow of refugees from Portugal and Spain, and in integrating themselves once more in the main line of the historic Jewish tradition. From the start, the Amsterdam community also showed an openness to the world which has been a distinguishing mark of Sephardi Jewry. Professor Yosef Kaplan writes that the Jews of Amsterdam anticipated central European Jewry by a century in realizing the ideals of *haskalah* or enlightenment:

> They created a rich literature in Spanish and Portuguese, and in the educational institutions which they established these languages were formally taught. Both by private teachers and by those in congregational employ, the youth were taught Latin and other European languages. Their schools were amongst the most modern in Europe both in regard to organization and pedagogical method. Particular emphasis was placed on learning the Hebrew language grammatically, and study of the Bible preceded study of the Talmud and other literature of Jewish Halakhic self-regulation. The economic activities of the members of the congregation and their social connections induced them to study the local vernacular literature, to cherish the cultural values of their environment, and to achieve a new appraisal of relations with the non-Jewish world, attempting to fit into its society successfully.

Professor Kaplan is, however, careful to point out that in contrast to the *haskalah* in Germany, and later on in Eastern Europe,

> This seventeenth-century Sephardi type of Judaism had no ideology with a professed programme of 'enlightenment' intended to engineer changes in Jewish society. The syntheses that these Sephardi Jews fashioned grew up so to speak organically, as part and parcel of their unique form of Jewish social and spiritual life. (Kaplan, *op. cit.* p. 382.)

Those New Christians in Portugal and conversos in Spain who were unwilling to abandon their loyalty to Judaism of necessity had, as noted, a progressively hazier notion of the religion they had been forced to abandon. They also, very naturally, came to be increasingly influenced by the Catholicism in which they were brought up, so that their notion of the Judaism to which they wished secretly to remain faithful was a kind of mirror image of the Christianity with which they were being made familiar in Church, school and university. If they objected to the teachings of the New Testament and disbelieved in them, it was because they had become convinced that the divine revelation recorded in the 'Old Testament', to which they could not be prevented from having access, was authentic, while the New was fake and to be rejected. Judaism came thus in their minds to consist exclusively of what was set down in the 'Old Testament'. It may well be, even, that some of these judaizers invented for themselves a religion which was neither Judaism nor Christianity, but an amalgam of elements taken from the two religions. Judaism, in any case, was much more than what the Bible, the Written Torah, contained. Equal in authority was the Oral Torah which is traditionally believed to have been revealed to Moses at the same time on Mount Sinai, and to have been transmitted by him to Joshua, and thereafter to the Prophets and 'to the Men of the Great Synagogue'. Its guardians and expounders, generation after generation, were the sages whose decisions and conclusions constitute an unbroken chain, which began with 'Moses our teacher'. The Talmud, the Midrash, the codes of law, the responsa and the commentaries succeeding one another: it is all these which made up Judaism as it gradually came to be in the centuries following the Babylonian exile and the later clash with Rome.

The case of Uriel da Costa (1585–1640) is instructive in this respect. Born in Porto in Portugal, his parents were of New Christian origins. His father was a pious Catholic, while his mother was a secret judaizer. It may be that it was under her influence that the young Gabriel – this being his baptismal name – became disaffected towards Catholicism and believed that the true faith was to be found in the 'Old Testament'. It would seem that the Inquisition began to suspect the family of judaizing tendencies and set in train an investigation. Gabriel, his mother and brothers succeeded in escaping, and eventually reached Amsterdam where they professed Judaism openly, and joined the Portuguese congregation. Gabriel now adopted the name, Uriel. The traditional Judaism practised in Amsterdam, however, Uriel found unsatisfactory, even shocking. Here were so many departures from the Bible, the sole authentic source of genuine Judaism. The Judaism professed in Amsterdam, for instance, in accordance with the traditional teaching, believed in the resurrection of the dead and the immortality of the soul. This, Uriel da Costa considered, was contrary to the word of the Bible where neither resurrection nor immortality are spoken of. These beliefs could therefore form no part of Judaism, as he argued in a treatise which proved that immortality of the soul was a false belief. One thing leading to another, Uriel da Costa came to be convinced that the Torah, far from being a divine revelation, was in reality a human invention. God, the undoubted author of Natural Law could not also be the author of a revelation so much at variance with it. From being a secret judaizer, and then a member of a Jewish congregation, Uriel da Costa became a deist. His beliefs were utterly incompatible with Judaism and the congregation twice excommunicated him. Twice he recanted in humiliating public ceremonies. His reason, as he said in a brief autobiographical essay, was that in a country where he was a stranger, and the language of which he did not speak, it was best to submit to the wishes of the congregation he had escaped from Portugal in order to join, and conform to their behaviour: as he wrote, to act the monkey among monkeys. Da Costa was, in effect, practising here the same dissimulation which judaizers practised in self-protection under the Inquisition. Amsterdam, however, was not Porto and its Portuguese congregation was not the Portuguese Inquisition. Possibly in order to escape the intolerable strain occasioned by the quest for an authentic religion which his reason could approve, Uriel da Costa ended by taking his own life.

Another case in point is that of Dr Juan de Prado (*c.*1615–70). He was a contemporary and a friend of Orobio's at the University of Alcalá. Like Orobio he was a student of medicine, and the two, as Orobio confessed to the Inquisition under torture many years later, had then entered secretly into a covenant of judaizers. A relative of his also confessed under torture at about the same time that Prado had persuaded him to abandon Christianity and embrace Judaism:

He began by telling me that God had given Moses the written Law on Mount Sinai and miraculously parted the waters of the Red Sea so that the Hebrews could pass through it on dry ground ... he said that the true Law, the one in which one can be saved, is the ancient Law. Consequently I should observe and practise this Law, for in it I shall find my salvation.

Prado, this relative also declared,

said that no one had led him to convert to the Law of Moses and no one had taught him this Law. He had learnt by himself, through his books and his university education. (Quoted in Yirmiyahu Yovel, *Spinoza and Other Heretics: The Marrano of Reason*, 1989, pp. 58–99.)

Prado effected his escape from Spain and reached Amsterdam about 1655 where he made public profession of Judaism, took the name Daniel, and joined the congregation. But like Uriel da Costa, he found it difficult to submit to traditional Judaism with its rites and practices based on the authority of Halakhah as expounded by generation upon generation of rabbis. As he told his relative, he had learnt his Judaism all by himself, a Judaism, then, which was the conclusion, as it were, of a ratiocinative exercise. What reason, however, could establish, reason could likewise demolish. When he was being questioned by the Inquisition, Orobio disclosed another detail about Prado's religious opinions. A few years after their intercourse at the university, Orobio declared, he met Prado once more who told him that in his view all religions were equal. Whether this meant that their respective practitioners could attain salvation each in their own way, or that they were different ways of knowing God, it remained that these religions were all derived from the Law of nature. From this to Deism is obviously but one step.

When Prado was openly professing Judaism in Amsterdam, he began privately to express scepticism about Judaism and indeed other revealed religions. A student to whom he was teaching Latin reported that Prado asked him whether he believed in rewards and punishments in the next world. When the student expressed astonishment at anyone doubting what was one of the Thirteen Articles of the Faith, Prado 'replied sarcastically that up to now no one has returned from the next world to ask for our help.'

He especially mocked [reported the student] the wisdom of the sages saying that such a thing is impossible and defies common sense, so that everything that has been said about the resurrection of the dead is sheer nonsense. He also says that the world was not created but has always existed in the same form and will continue to exist forever. (Quoted in Yovel, *op. cit.*, p. 72.)

Like Uriel da Costa, Prado in Amsterdam was a crypto-deist or a secret libertine. As his old friend Orobio put it:

It is only to you that it so happened, to be a fake Christian and a true Jew where you could not be a Jew, and to be a fake Jew where [finally] you could be truly Jewish. (Quoted in Yovel, *op. cit.* p. 63.)

A year after his arrival in Amsterdam, Prado's opinions were investigated by the authorities of the congregation. They were found to be heretical and Prado was excommunicated. He recanted publicly, promising never to repeat his error. A year later, the community heard that Prado had relapsed. He was condemned once more. All through, Prado was unwilling to cut his relations with the synagogue and did his best somehow or other to persuade the authorities to allow him to remain within the fold. Uriel da Costa did the same, but his biting words about acting the monkey when consorting with monkeys indicate the cold resolve of a solitary stranger to seek some kind of protective camouflage. Prado seems more ambivalent, torn between conclusions deemed to be made mandatory by reason, and loyalty to a community with which, however ambiguously, he identified himself.

The passage from Orobio just quoted above occurs in an *Epistle against Prado* which he wrote *c.* 1665. Earlier, Uriel da Costa's opinions had provoked a similar rejoinder by Semuel da Silva, who published in 1623 a *Treatise on the Immortality of the Soul.* It is thanks to the long passages from da Costa's writings which da Silva included in his own treatise that we are at all able to form some idea of these opinions. The rejoinders which da Costa's and Prado's opinions elicited are indication enough of the perils of Deism, which were a direct outcome of crypto-Jewish life in the Iberian Peninsula, to which the Amsterdam community found itself exposed, and which it took determined steps to combat.

Another peril against which the community had to guard was that of Sabbatean Messianism which began to be rife after Sabbetai Sevi proclaimed himself to be the awaited Messiah in 1665. Sabbateanism attracted devoted followers all over the Jewish world. Its appeal to Sephardim, forcibly converted, practising a secret religion, expelled from ancestral homes, and pursued by the Inquisition, is understandable. Messianic yearnings and hopes flared up here and there over the decades among Jews, conversos, New Christians in Spain and Portugal. None, however, seems to have been so influential or so widespread as Sabbateanism. The very fact of Sabbetai's apostasy to Islam evoked powerful echoes, seeming to speak to the condition of those who were outward Christians and secret Jews. Queen Esther, it may be recalled, was to these crypto-Jews a figure of special significance: she married an idolater and hid from him the fact that she was Jewish; yet she was not considered a sinner but, on the contrary, an instrument of salvation. That Sabbetai turned Muslim was, likewise, considered a proof that he was indeed the Messiah. Miguel Cardoso, who had escaped from Spain in 1648 and taken the name Abraham, became a convinced Sabbatean, to such an extent that he quarrelled bitterly with his elder brother, Isaac, a distinguished doctor, poet and philosopher who had left Spain at the same time, and who was to write a notable work in defence of Judaism, *Las excelencias de los Hebreos* (Amsterdam 1679). As Abraham Cardoso saw it, Sabbetai was destined to become a Marrano (i.e. a crypto-Jew) like him, and take upon himself the sins of the children of Israel who had abandoned the Torah: by his transgression Sabbetai was able to intercede for the transgressors who had been obliged to abandon their faith. Abraham Cardoso went further, using an argument in defence of Sabbetai which shows how much some crypto-Jews in the Iberian Peninsula were influenced by the Christianity they were obliged outwardly to profess. The triumph of the new Messiah comes about following the suffering and degradation he has to undergo, and because of them, exactly like Jesus. As he wrote in a letter attacking his brother and Isaac Orobio:

> And in another place it is implied that twice he shall be incarcerated, having to exclaim, *My God, my God, why hast thou forsaken me*, for all of Psalm 22, and the end of 89, refer to him; that they shall have to curse him; that God must bring him under severe sentences and troubles never imposed on the ancient fathers; that the enemies must oppose him, and that woe to him who shall be present at that time, because of the great disorders and doubts which there must be concerning the belief [in him]; and that many shall have to abandon the Law; and that afterwards he shall ascend to be supreme and elevated with the spirit of the Lord, and with that of his mouth he shall slay evil, cast down isolatry and triumph in the world. (Quoted in Yosef Hayim Yerushalmi, *From Spanish Court to Italian Ghetto*, 1971, p.337.)

Sabbateanism posed an obvious danger to traditional Judaism and to the stability of communities and communal institutions. Like Deism, it had to be combated. Its most forceful opponent was Jacob Sasportas (1610–98), the first Haham of the newly established Portuguese congregation in London, and some decades later Haham of the Amsterdam congregation. *The Fading of Sevi's Flower*, in which he collected his rejoinders to, and refutations of, the Sabbateans, powerfully confronts the spiritual peril which Sabbateanism represented. Sabbetai's claim to be Messiah, Sasportas argued, was manifestly false, since there was no possible resemblance between the Messianic era as described in the Bible and Sabbetai's own times. Sabbateanism was a revolt against the rabbinical norms which were bound up with, and vital to, the survival of Judaism. It was a deliberate attempt to make lawful that which had been forbidden as unlawful and sinful, in the evil belief that only through sinning can salvation be attained, and that Sabbetai's apostasy was its necessary prelude.

It is appropriate to conclude by evoking the memory of another outstanding Sephardi figure who, in his outlook and career, exemplified some abiding characteristics of the Sephardi ethos, open to the world while holding on firmly to tradition – an ethos which can be discerned in Spain and Portugal and has remained manifest to the present day. David Nieto (1654–1728) served as Haham of the Spanish and Portuguese congregation in London from 1701 until his death. Nieto studied medicine at Padua, and he came to have many connexions with the non-Jewish learned world. He was an authority on calendrical studies, dedicating a book on this subject to a Medici cardinal. He believed indeed that it was the duty of a teacher to make children familiar not only with religious texts, but also with general literature. In a well-known reply to a sermon preached at an *auto de fe* by the Archbishop of Granagor in Portugal, Nieto declared that Jews do not prohibit books like the Inquisition, but rather explain them to their children.

Nieto was aware of the spiritual and intellectual perils which life in a fairly open society entailed for the Jews of his day, and in his various writings attempted to counter the very same seductive ideas with which Orobio, Isaac Cardoso and Sasportas had to contend, rejection of the Oral Torah, Deism and Sabbatean antinomianism. In the words of a modern student of his thought,

> Nieto set the tone for the totality of Anglo-Jewry, this curious combination of full participation in the life of the environment with conservatism in Jewish belief and practice which has remained characteristic of the Anglo-Jewish Community as a whole to this day (J.J. Petuchowski, *The Theology of Haham David Nieto*, 1954, p.132).

This judgment applies not only to Anglo-Jewry in which Sephardim set the tone at its modern beginnings, but also to Sephardi communities everywhere.

The Alba Bible, commissioned in 1422, represents a high point of Jewish-Christian co-operation. Here the patron, Don Luis de Guzmán, sits enthroned in the centre and below is seen receiving the manuscript from Rabbi Moses Arragel of Guadalajara.

: comer. beuer. calçar. vestir. visitar. consolar. enterrar.

The Jewish Bible was translated from the Hebrew by Rabbi Moses and illustrated by Christian illuminators. Above: Ezra reads the Law to the assembled Jews.

Above: Rabbi Moses pays homage to King John II. In spite of his expertise, he was subject to guidance by two theologians of Toledo; one of them, the Franciscan Brother Arias, is shown (right) instructing him.

The Tabernacle from the Alba Bible, with ritual objects used in Jewish worship. Here the advice of Rabbi Moses must have been particularly vital. We see the High Priest within the Holy of Holies, the Ark of the Covenant, the Menorah and a sacrificial altar.

אחת משלש המצות

443

A page from the Golden Haggadah, one of Spanish Jewry's most exquisite books. The upper right picture shows Miriam's dance, part of the story of Exodus. The other three show episodes from the Passover, which commemorates that event: the distribution of unleavened bread, the sacrifice of the Paschal lamb; and the search for leavened bread on Passover eve.

Left: illustrations from two manuscripts of the 14th century. At the top, a family assembled for the Seder meal. Below, a page from the Kennicott Bible, completed in 1476, with a border showing an army of cats storming a castle defended by mice.

The synagogue of El Tránsito at Toledo is the most outstanding monument to the Jewish presence in Spain. It was built in 1366 at the expense of Samuel Halevi, Treasurer of King Don Pedro, probably by Muslim craftsmen. Its stucco frieze (top) carries inscriptions in Hebrew and Arabic glorifying the God of Israel, the King of Spain, and Halevi himself, plus the arms of Castile and León.

Another relic of Judeo-Spanish harmony: a Hebrew inscription in the royal chapel of Seville Cathedral.

In Portugal the Jewish community enjoyed considerable prestige. Nuño Gonçalves included the judicial head of Portuguese Jewry in his St Vincent Altarpiece of 1465 (right).

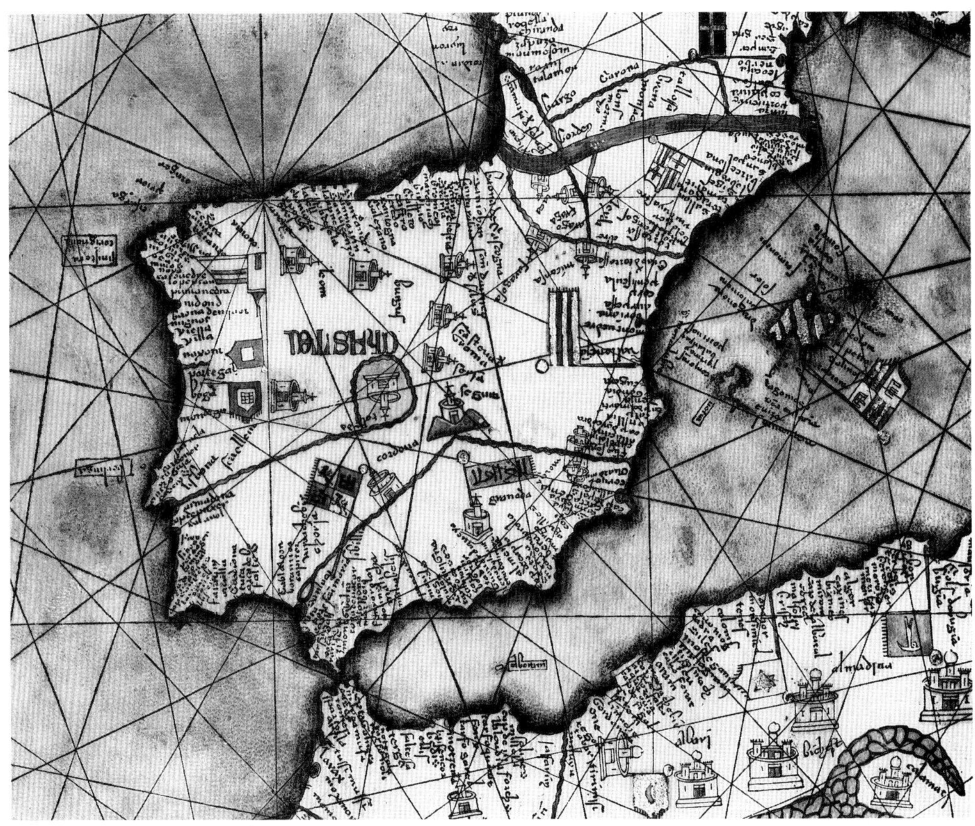

Jewish intellectual achievements included the maps of Abraham Cresques (top) and Maimonides' very influential Guide for the Perplexed *(above: Aristotle, sitting on a throne spangled with six-pointed stars, demonstrates the astrolabe). Right: a rabbi (the great Talmudic teacher Gamaliel) instructs a group of young people.*

Chapter One

The Jews in Spain during the Middle Ages

ANGUS MACKAY

Convivencia

The history of the Jews in Spain during the Middle Ages was a chequered one. Subsequent chapters will concentrate on those momentous events which were the causes and consequences of the expulsion of 1492, but this one will devote considerable attention to the twelfth and thirteenth centuries, a period of relative tolerance to which some Spanish historians have applied the term *convivencia*. The word *convivencia* literally means 'living together with others', and in general terms it has been taken to denote a context of coexistence characterized by Christian respect for Jewish and Islamic culture. But the concept of *convivencia* is also one which must be understood in medieval terms. At all times the fundamental religious issues which divided Christians and Jews were present, and a more precise definition of *convivencia* would stress that the Christians combined hostility towards the Jews with a certain degree of grudging tolerance. Moreover towards the end of the thirteenth century and during the fourteenth century *convivencia* broke down, and a rising tide of intolerance and persecution culminated in widespread and horrific massacres in 1391.

Although the available evidence is notoriously difficult to interpret, a necessarily cautious estimate would suggest that there were some 100,000 Jews in thirteenth-century Spain and that they constituted just under two per cent of the total population.[1] Subsequently, after the Black Death of 1348 and the large number of conversions due to persecution, the total number of Jews would decline. Yet for several reasons this minority of Jews always figured prominently in the documents, chronicles, and literature of the medieval period. In part this was due to the fact that they naturally tended to form their own communities, rather than live in dispersed isolation, in order to avail themselves of such vital services as those provided by the synagogues or by Jewish butchers. But this tendency was reinforced by the way in which the Christian authorities tried to segregate the Jews by, for example, assigning to them specific and separate areas within the towns. In general terms it was felt that Jews should not be able to use their wealth or occupations in order to acquire power over Christians. Jews were to be easily distinguishable from Christians by wearing special emblems on their clothing, they were not allowed to have Christian servants, and they were to be confined to their own easily identified communities known as *aljamas*. These communities varied in size to a considerable extent. Towns such as Saragossa, Barcelona, and Valencia, in the Crown of Aragon, Toledo, Burgos, and Segovia in the kingdom of Castile, and Tudela and Pamplona in the kingdom of Navarre had large Jewish communities, but the 'visibility profile' of any particular *aljama* might depend not so much on its own size as such but on its size relative to that of the town in which it was located. Many towns, for example, were hardly more than villages with a rural rather than an urban pattern of life. Then, too, the thirteenth century witnessed massive strides in the reconquest of Muslim Spain, and as such places as Mallorca (1229), Córdoba (1236), Valencia (1238), and Seville (1248) fell to the Christians, so too were Jewish as well as Christian settlers encouraged to move south and set up their *aljamas*. In Jerez de la Frontera, for example, some ninety Jews were assigned houses in an intra-mural area which was separated off from the rest of the town by a wall, with a gate providing access to the *aljama* and its synagogues and shops.[2] In this way important Jewish communities would slowly come into existence in the reconquered regions of Valencia, Murcia, and Andalusia.

How did these Jews make a living? The stereotype of the medieval Spanish Jew as a rich towndweller, moneylender, financier, or tax farmer is misleading. Many Jews owned or leased rural properties in the form of small farms, large estates, vineyards, and orchards; others were beekeepers; still others owned large flocks of sheep. The documentation for thirteenth- and fourteenth-century Calahorra, for example, reveals a lively land market in which Jews participated actively by selling, buying, and leasing grain lands, vineyards, and orchards, and in doing so dealing with cathedral canons, parish clergy, and Christian landowners. The Jews, then, were active in the rural economy even if, as was not unusual, they owned town dwellings as well. As for those who did live and work in an urban environment, their occupations were very varied. The men could be found working as weavers, tailors, cobblers, blacksmiths, chemists, butchers, dyers, silversmiths, doctors, small shopkeepers, grocers, and jewelers; the women working as laundresses, midwives, weavers, and spinners. In Murcia in 1407, for example, there were thirty Jewish tailors, seven weavers, and three dyers. The 'typical' Jew in Murcia was a tailor, in Logroño a leather worker. A few Jews were relatively rich and influential; many others were humble and poor.

But if the stereotype is misleading, it is for all that not unimportant. Perceived reality, as distinct from 'real' reality, could be of great importance. A few Jews did play a significant role as financiers, tax collectors, and moneylenders, and bearing in mind their numbers relative to those of the Christians and Muslims who also lent money and collected taxes, their contribution was proportionately larger. Don Solomon ibn Zadok, for example, was the chief collector of taxes for Alfonso X of Castile (1252–84) and acquired extensive landed properties in the region of Seville; when he died in 1273 his son, Don Isaac ibn Zadok, became equally influential in the royal court. Round about the same time in the crown of Aragon the Ravaya family were farming the royal revenues, lending money to Peter III (1276–85), for whom Joseph Ravaya acted as royal treasurer, and introducing important reforms in the central administration. Nor should these examples give the impression that Jewish financiers were only important in the thirteenth century or that their acumen served only the interests of the Crown. In the fourteenth century, for example, the great Jewish financier Samuel Halevi acted as the chief treasurer of Peter I of Castile (1350–69), and Jewish financiers and tax collectors were to be found in the service not only of the noble houses of Spain but of individual archbishops and bishops, as well as religious institutions, such as cathedral chapters.[3] How are such extraordinary success stories to be explained? Sometimes historians have been tempted to think in terms of an innate talent which Jews possessed for finance and banking, or to argue that since Christianity condemned usury and since there were many careers which were prohibited to the Jews, the latter naturally tended to gravitate to money-lending and finance. But such arguments fail to convince. There were Jews who had no financial talent at all, and Christian money-lenders certainly existed. One pragmatic explanation suggests itself. Jews, as such, were no more possessed of an innate financial talent than Christians. But, operating on a family basis, once they acquired expertise, this became part of the family inheritance. Right down to the expulsion of 1492 it is possible to detect veritable family dynasties of such financiers both among the Jews and the conversos.

In addition, while we must not allow ourselves into being deluded that the Jews controlled the major share of fiscal and financial transactions (in fact the opposite was the case), it nevertheless seems true that at the very highest levels individual Jews possessed a technical competence and a genuine talent which could not be rivalled. The proof of this can be seen in the outcome of the civil war in Castile between King Peter I and his bastard half-brother, Henry of Trastámara. Henry relied heavily on anti-Jewish propaganda, stressing in particular the evil presence of Jewish financiers and tax collectors at the royal court. But, after he had won the war and usurped the throne, he too found that he had to rely on Jewish financiers like Joseph Picho, who became the chief royal financial official (*contador mayor*), and tax farmers like Samuel Abravanel of Seville.[4]

The Jews were envisaged as being 'slaves of the king' (*servi regis*).[5] For the Church this 'servitude' derived from the part that the Jews had played in the crucifixion, but for the Crown it emphasized royal jurisdiction over all Jews as against any competing claims of noble, ecclesiastical or municipal authorities. The Jews as 'slaves', therefore, could often benefit from royal protection, and Jewish communities were allowed a considerable degree of autonomy in the running of their own affairs. Yet paradoxically these communities developed in ways which bore striking resemblances to trends in the Christian municipalities. For example, just as Christian municipalities became 'legal persons' or corporate entities distinct from the individuals who lived in them as a result of the revival of Roman law principles, so too did the legal writings of the halakhic scholars (experts in Jewish law) also transform the *aljamas* into legal personalities in the thirteenth century. To some degree this was due to the fact that during Alfonso X's reign royal officials began to apply the concepts of Roman law to the *aljamas* in the same way as they did to the towns. But the rabbis too had a vested interest in securing this transformation which replaced a 'democratic' partnership of all the members of a community, based on unanimity, with a corporation whose leaders or representatives derived their authority from the 'greater and wiser part' (*maior et sanior pars*). Thus, as Yom Tov b. Abraham Ishbili put it:

> My teacher Solomon ibn Adret, may his memory be blessed, used to say that any *taqqanah* (communal statute) which the majority of the community, the power of which lies in its numbers and wisdom, agrees upon, even though a minority oppose it, is nevertheless binding upon all.

Inevitably, however, 'wisdom' was attributed to an elite few and hence, just as in the Christian towns, oligarchies emerged to dominate the Jewish communities. The *taqqanot* or communal statutes of Tudela of 1305, for example, stated that:

> No *taqqanah* enacted by the community from the festival of *Sukkoth* onwards shall be valid unless signed by eight men from the eight families that regularly assemble at the meetings of the community as well as the *mukademin* (community officials) holding office at that time . . . And these families are: the Falaquera, the Abbasi, the Pesad, the Shaib, the David, the Menir, the Camis, the Ora Buena. And no *taqqanah* shall be enacted in their absence.[6]

The existence of oligarchies and powerful families caused problems within the Jewish communities and led to conflict. A family's prestige tended to be based on wealth and power, and its wealth in turn frequently derived from tax exemptions and privileges granted by kings in return for services rendered. Many felt that 'the wisdom' which justified honour, prestige, and power within a community should instead be defined in terms of learning and piety. And, as conflicts developed, so all manner of issues were brought into dispute. Many examples could be cited, but it is perhaps better to examine one in detail in order to see the extraordinary ramifications to which such disputes gave rise, especially since light will be thrown on other major issues affecting medieval Hispano-Jewish civilization.

Piety and learning

The powerful family of the Alconstantinis in mid-thirteenth-century Barcelona enjoyed immunity from the *aljama*'s jurisdiction and exemption from all the taxes which the rest of the community had to pay. But when they tried in addition to secure a concession from James I (1213–76) which would accord them supreme rabbinical and judicial authority over all the Jewish communities of the realm, a violent controversy broke out, with the Alconstantinis and their allies being opposed by a coalition of rabbis led by the famous Nahmanides (Rabbi Moses b. Nahman). But the controversy was not simply about power. Nahmanides accused his opponents of corruption, immorality, and irreligiosity, alleging that they did not pray and even desecrated the Sabbath. Stressing a combination of social protest and piety, Nahmanides was to win this particular struggle but not before it had widened to include a bitter polemic about the rationalist works of the great Jewish philosopher Maimonides (1135–1204). Social, economic, religious, and philosophical issues had become completely entangled.[7]

But what did Maimonides have to do with this and other similar controversies? From the twelfth century onwards many Spanish Jews were attracted to the ideas of Aristotle, and of these scholars Maimonides was the greatest. In his most famous work, *Guide for the Perplexed*, he set out to reconcile religion and reason, using arguments derived from Aristotle in order to provide rational arguments for fundamental religious beliefs, such as monotheism and freedom of the will. He did not claim that all aspects of revealed religion were accessible to reason: for example, he held that although the creation of the world, as described in *Genesis*, was philosophically probable, it could not be demonstrated by means of reason and had to be accepted as a matter of faith. Yet despite his caution, many were outraged by what they regarded as an attempt to create a faith of reason which would undermine some of the fundamental tenets and observances of Judaism. After all, once this kind of thing started where would it all end?[8]

In fact, even before Maimonides, one of the greatest Hebrew poets of Spain, Judah Halevi (*c.*1075–*c.*1150), had launched an attack on Jews who studied philosophy.[9] During his life Halevi travelled widely among the Jewish communities of both Christian and Muslim Spain, and he became passionately convinced about both the special relationship between God and the people of Israel and the unique role of the Jews in history. According to him, no amount of reasoning or philosophical speculation could ever get to the heart of genuine religious experience, which was none other than a knowledge of God through revelation combined with the precepts of proper conduct. The idea that the redemption of the people of Israel was close at hand and that the Jews should return to Jerusalem and Palestine obsessed him. He referred to 'the goodness' of Spain, but his heart was in the East:

My heart is in the East, and I in the depths of the West.
My food has no taste. How can it be sweet?
How can I fulfil my pledges and my vows,
When Zion is in the power of Edom, and I in the fetters of Arabia?
It will be nothing to me to leave all the goodness of Spain.
So rich will it be to see the dust of the ruined sanctuary.[10]

Halevi witnessed the suffering of Jews caught between the warring Christians (Edom) and Muslims (Arabia). He also witnessed the attempts of some Jewish leaders who tried to secure their own safety and that of other Jews by gaining influence at the courts of Christian and Muslim rulers. But the Jews of this courtier class who fawned on their rulers were, according to Halevi, idol-worshippers and men who used their learning and wealth to the detriment of the true faith. Disillusioned and convinced that the Messianic Age was at hand, Halevi decided to leave Spain and return to the home of his ancestors. He went to Alexandria and subsequently set out for the Holy Land. Legend has it that he reached Jerusalem, knelt down to kiss the stones of the Wailing Wall, and was then trampled to death by a horse.

Although the controversies aroused by Maimonides' rationalism continued into the thirteenth and fourteenth centuries, new issues came into play. In the dispute between the Alconstantinis and Nahmanides, for example, the former and their allies, notably Judah and Abraham ibn Hasdai, tried to protect their political position in Barcelona by denouncing the mystical zeal of their opponents. It was this predilection for mysticism which had led Nahmanides and his supporters not only to attack Maimonides' *Book of Knowledge* and *Guide for the Perplexed* but also, so the ibn Hasdai brothers alleged, to try to enlist the help of the Franciscans and Dominicans in order to have the books condemned.[11] Whatever the truth about this particular allegation, the development of the mystical movement of kabbalism during the thirteenth century added a new dimension to the controversy over rationalism and, as Yitzhak Baer pointed out a long time ago, provided striking parallels to some of the attitudes and beliefs expressed by the Franciscan Spirituals.[12]

The homeland of kabbalism was Castile and, in particular, the small towns to the north of Toledo, such as Guadalajara, which seem throughout the centuries to have been particularly prone to intense religious fervour. It was there that the great teachers of the Kabbalah lived and wrote – men like Todros b. Joseph Halevi Abulafia of Toledo and Moses ben Shem Tob of León.[13] It was the latter who wrote the fundamental treatise of the Kabbalah, *Sefer ha-Zohar* (*The Book of Splendour*), usually referred to simply as the *Zohar*. The kabbalists received the support of many religious Jews who were renowned for their piety.

Just as St Francis (d. 1226) had laid a special emphasis on humility and poverty, so Rabbi Moses of León made it clear in the *Zohar* that he was on the side of the humble and the poor.[14] The poor man is closer to God than other people because the poor and humble are God's vessels and their prayers reach him before those of others. Religious wisdom does not depend on learning, and indeed learning can be an impediment: 'Behold, the fear of the Lord, that is wisdom; and to depart from evil is understanding' (*Job* 28:28). Moreover, if prophetic powers are to be gifted by God to certain individuals, then these will certainly not be arrogant intellectuals but rather the humble and unlearned, even the illiterate or children.

It followed from all this that power, wealth, learning and authority were corrupting agencies which could even become satanic. For the Spiritual Franciscans, for example, Rome was the opposite of what it seemed. Rome was in fact Babylon, the Roman Church was the Babylonish whore, and the pope was anti-christ. Analogous attacks on the wealthy, corrupt, and irreligious Jewish aristocracy were made by Rabbi Moses of León in the *Zohar* and by an anonymous late thirteenth-century kabbalist in a work entitled *Ra'aya Mehemna* (*The Faithful Shepherd*). The leaders of the Jewish communities are attacked for neglecting the Torah and for being Averroistic in outlook. This latter accusation was serious and was to have important implications for the future. The 'Averroists' appear to have been basically irreligious and they would eventually become associated with views which were expressed in a variety of ways, most of which were to the effect that 'We live and die like the beasts.'[15] According to their opponents such men, of course, were also the corrupters of morals and they subverted justice to their own profit and to the detriment of the poor. Assuredly the charges and counter-charges relating to 'mysticism' and the rationalist works of Maimonides made during the Alconstantini controversy in Barcelona involved very serious issues.

It would be perverse, however, to accept the denunciations of the pietists and kabbalists at face value, and in fact Jewish scholars and intellectuals made a profound contribution to Spanish and European civilization. To a large extent this was due to the fact that they were the mediators between the two great civilizations of Christianity and Islam. Rarely did Christian or Muslim scholars visit the cultural centres of the opposing faith, but there were many Jews who, like Judah Halevi, travelled extensively. Moreover when Jews conversed with Christians or Muslims they had to use the language of the people they were talking to. The result was a formidable linguistic proficiency, even at non-scholarly levels. The surviving account book of a relatively humble fourteenth-century Jewish merchant of Barcelona, for example, reflects the languages of his customers. It is written in Hebrew characters but the dominant language is Arabic, although there are also a large number of words and expressions in Catalan, Castilian, and Hebrew.[16] Jews, therefore, made excellent diplomats and ambassadors for kings and princes. More importantly they played a vital role in the translation of scholarly works and in the transmission to Europe of Arabic-Greek learning.

During the twelfth century Jewish scholars with a good command of Arabic helped in the process of translating into Latin the works of Avicenna, Solomon ibn Gabirol (Avicebron), al-Ghazzali, and treatises of medicine, astrology, astronomy, alchemy and geomancy.[17] The preface to the Latin translation of Avicenna's *De Anima* tells how this process of translation and transmission of learning was carried out. The Jewish scholar Ibn Daud, who describes himself as *israelita philosophus*, translated the Arabic text into Castilian, and then his Christian collaborator, the archdeacon Domingo González, translated the Castilian into Latin. In the thirteenth century Jewish scholars at the court of Alfonso X of Castile continued the task of translating, concentrating particularly on scientific works. For example, working with their Christian counterparts, Jewish scholars like the physician Rabbi Judah ben Moses ha-Kohen, the astronomer Abraham Alfaquim, and Rabbi Isaac ibn Zadok, translated a whole series of astronomical and astrological works from Arabic into Castilian. These included the famous *Alfonsine Tables*, a compilation of the movements of the planets originally carried out by an eleventh-century Arabic astronomer but revised in the light of observations effected by the king's scholars in Toledo (the *Libros del saber de astronomía*), a collection of astronomical treatises, two astrological works, the *Libro de las cruzes* and the *Libro de los juicios de las estrellas*, and the richly illustrated treatises on the properties of stones known as the *Lapidario*.

Next in importance to the Jewish scholars at the court of Alfonso X of Castile were those who worked to promote the astronomical, astrological, and cartographical interests of Peter IV (1336–87), ruler of the Crown of Aragon.[18] The astronomer Isaac Nifoci, for example, was commissioned by the king to make astrolabes, quadrants and clocks, and two brothers, from a prominent Mallorcan family, Belshom and Vidal Ephraim, were asked to translate astronomical treatises.

The Jews of Mallorca, who were already well known as makers of astrolabes and other instruments, acquired even greater fame as cartographers. They produced the portolan charts, of which by a royal decree of 1354 each Aragonese galley had to carry at least two.[19] These charts were practical aids to navigation, and the information they gave about coastlines, ports, and distances was the direct result of extensive trading contacts throughout the Mediterranean. In addition to the portolan charts, however, the Jewish cartographers also produced world maps, the most celebrated of these being the illustrated 'Catalan world atlas' of 1375 by Abraham Cresques which was subsequently given to Charles V of France. This atlas displays a quite unexpected range of knowledge, particularly with respect to the interior of Africa, the information probably being acquired from Jews in North Africa, merchants and, in the case of Asia and China, travellers returning from the East. Cresques, for example, was certainly aware of the trans-Saharan caravan routes and the sources of gold in the western Sudan. His map includes the cities of Sijilmasa, Timbuctu, and Mali, a picture of a veiled man on a camel, and another of Mansa Musa, the ruler of the kingdom of Mali, holding a nugget of gold, with the following explanatory inscription: 'This negro lord is called Musa Mali, Lord of the Negros of Guinea. So abundant is the gold which is found in his country that he is the richest and most noble king in all the land.'[20]

Apart from philosophy, and those subjects which might loosely be termed 'the sciences', such as astronomy, medicine, and cartography, Jewish scholars made a profound contribution in terms of religious scholarship. Halakhic scholars (rabbis expert in Jewish law) were forever having to deal with every conceivable kind of religious, social, and even economic problem. This might involve the systematic codification of the Law, as in Maimonides' famous *Mishneh Torah*, in which he did not allow his 'rationalism' to interfere with the basic principles of the Halakhah, Talmudic commentaries, or even the most apparently mundane problems which had to be dealt with by means of rabbinical *responsa*. The *responsa* were almost a form of literature, rather like the *exempla* of the Christians: they addressed specific problems which either did not seem to have a solution or had contradictory solutions. When such a problem arose a rabbi, famed as a halakhic scholar, would be asked for his opinion. Descending from the heights of philosophy, the great rabbis of Spain, men like R. Nissim b. Reuben Gerondi or R. Isaac ben Sheshet (Ribash), had to deal with practical matters and, in so doing, created what may be termed case law. On one occasion, for example, R. Isaac ben Sheshet was consulted on how debts were to be repaid after Henry II of Castile had debased the coinage and devalued the money of account.[21] Famed for their learning, the rabbis might be consulted on some matters by Christians as well as Jews. The Bible, for example, was a text which many Christians, with good reason, felt should be translated into the vernacular via Hebrew, not Latin. As late as 1422, Don Luis de Guzmán, master of the Military Order of Calatrava, commissioned Rabbi Moses Arragel of Guadalajara to prepare a translation and commentary of the Old Testament. The task took some ten years to perform and he worked in collaboration with Christian artists, the end result being a magnificently illustrated work of scholarship which is known today as the Alba Bible.[22] Christians and Jews could still work together in *convivencia*, but such examples were now rare. By this date thousands of Jews had already been massacred or forced to convert.

The optimistic view

It would be idle to pretend that, even at the best of times, relationships between Christians and Jews were not characterized by important differences. Both Christians and Jews concerned themselves much with doctrines of exclusivity based on 'their' version of the truth. In the case of the Jews the special and exclusive relationship between the people of Israel and God was perceived as marking them off from the other inhabitants of Spain. Not without some justification did Abraham ibn Ezra observe that while the Muslims were renowned for their love poems and luxuries, and the Christians for their wars and vendettas, the Jews spent their time in singing the praises of God.[23] For both Jews and Christians alike mixing with 'the other side' was potentially dangerous, intermarriage unthinkable. Yet within this context of suspicion and exclusivity the emphases changed over time. The splendidly illustrated *Cantigas de Santa María* of Alfonso X of Castile, for example, may serve to convey what might be termed 'the optimistic view' of the Jew held by thirteenth-century Christians.[24]

The stories recounted in the *Cantigas* include several of the standard anti-Jewish themes which were prevalent during the medieval period in Europe: the Jew as the Devil's disciple, as the enemy of Christianity, as the archetype of avarice, as a traitor, as a sorcerer, and as a child murderer. *Cantiga* 3, for example, relates one of the most widely known medieval legends, the story of Theophilus who, with the help of a Jew, sold his soul to the Devil. *Cantiga* 4 tells how a Jewish father tried to murder his own son because the boy had taken communion with other, Christian, children, and in *Cantiga* 6 a Jew kills a child because he is irritated by his songs in praise of the Virgin Mary. More ominously in *Cantiga* 12 the Jews are depicted as crucifying the wax image of a Christian child.

The reader at this point may well ask: 'How on earth do such stories constitute "the optimistic view" of the Jew held by Christians?' The answer to such a question depends on comparing the Jews as they appear in the *Cantigas* and how they were to be depicted later, and looking at those subtle details which point to a certain 'optimism' within the intolerant context of *convivencia*. In *Cantiga* 109, for example, a Jew rather naively asks some devils why they never seek to harm his people and is told that this is because Jews belong to the Devil, the latter only being interested in seeking out those who bear the sign of baptism. Clearly this story fits the 'Jew as Devil's disciple' theme. But at the same time it is made clear that the Jew is an unwitting accomplice of the Devil. He does not know the true state of affairs, and in fact when he hears the devils' reply, he is frightened by the revelation and flees. Similarly in *Cantiga* 6 when the Jew kills the boy who sings in praise of the Virgin Mary, it is made clear that this murder is the work of one man and not of the Jews as a group, other Jews in fact joining the Christian in praising the young singer. Indeed, while there are stories in which *individual* Jews kill children, there is no suggestion or hint to point to the later belief that Jews killed children in order to use their blood or flesh in any demonic act against Christianity or in any horrific ritual of their own religion. Similarly, although the *Cantigas* include stories about host desecration, the 'desecrators' in these stories are Christians and not once is this accusation made against a Jew.

Compared to subsequent centuries, therefore, the thirteenth-century *Cantigas* provide a less hostile image of the Jews, and 'the optimistic view' is based on the assumption that once the Jews have seen the light, they will realize the error of their ways. The Jews in other words are seen as potential Christians who are to be won over by persuasion or by miracles and, 'optimistically', this is what will happen by peaceful means. In fact, as far as stories about Jews are concerned, the largest number of these in the *Cantigas* are conversion stories. In *Cantiga* 85, for example, a Jew converts after the Virgin has shown him the pleasures of Heaven and the pains of Hell, and in *Cantiga* 89 a Jewish woman is converted after the Virgin, responding to her entreaties, intervenes in a difficult childbirth and delivers a healthy baby. Such stories make the point abundantly clear. The Jew who remains a Jew is doomed to the pains of Hell; the Jew who becomes a Christian is saved. Hopefully, 'optimistically', this will happen.

To what extent did the attitudes revealed by these stories in the *Cantigas* reflect reality? If we turn to the great law code of Alfonso X of Castile, the *Siete Partidas*, we find the same rather ambivalent attitude. The king orders that all allegations or rumours about mock-crucifixions carried out by Jews should be referred to him for examination. The implication here is one of uncertainty. Rumours should not be accepted as fact; Christians should not take the law into their own hands; the king must investigate. In another law Jews are admonished to live peacefully among the Christians, 'observing their Law, and not denigrating anything about the Faith of our Lord Jesus Christ, observed by the Christians.' Above all, the optimistic view of Jews as potential Christians is emphasized by the law declaring that conversion is to be achieved by peaceful means and not force:

> Force and violence should not in any way be used on any Jew in order to convert him to Christianity. On the contrary Christians should convert them to the faith of our Lord Jesus Christ by good example, quotations from the Holy Scriptures and friendly persuasion. For Christ does not want or love any service which is done on his behalf by force.

Moreover the king then goes on to forbid Christians from reproaching converts with their Jewish origin; the latter, indeed, are to be allowed to retain all the property which they had owned as Jews, and, as Christians, they should be allowed access to all offices open to Christians. Above all, and in sharp contrast to subsequent centuries, the implicit assumption behind these laws is that conversion, which will be effected by peaceful persuasion, will be genuine and not insincere.[25]

The rise of anti-semitism

This optimistic view of the Jew, soon to become a Christian through friendly persuasion, was reflected in social reality. Allegations of ritual murder, for example, became quite common elsewhere in Western Europe after the case of William of Norwich in 1144, but the first such charge in Spain, made in Saragossa, dates from as late as 1250. And in the relatively free exchanges of arguments between Christians and Jews, as in the disputation by 'friendly persuasion' between Pablo Christiani, a convert, and the great Nahmanides, held in the presence of James I of Aragon in Barcelona, the Christian assumption was that rational arguments would win over the Jews. But Rabbi Nahmanides was given freedom of speech by James I, and the friars who staged the disputation failed miserably in the presentation of their case.[26]

Here indeed was the nub of the matter. Peaceful conversion could not be achieved except in isolated cases because, if freedom of speech was allowed, the Christian arguments, as far as Jews were concerned, were particularly unconvincing. The main point at issue, of course, was whether a certain Jesus of Nazareth, who had been brought up as a Jew, was the Messiah (let alone whether he was in some way the son of God, and miraculously conceived by a virgin, and miraculously resurrected three days after his death). As far as the Christians were concerned, the proof of all this lay in the New Testament, a collection of writings composed soon after Christ's death but not accepted by Jews. However the Old Testament, which recorded the history of the people of Israel as God's chosen people, was accepted by both Christians and Jews alike, and it foretold or prophesized matters concerning the Messiah. The question now was: did the New Testament logically fulfil the contents of the Old Testament? The Christians, faced with this problem, increasingly resorted to allegory in order to prove their case as best as they could. But by doing so they ran directly counter to Jewish insistence on the *peshat*, that is the literal interpretation of the Old Testament. In contrast, Christian attempts at literal interpretations of Talmudic *aggadah* (non-legal sections of the Talmud) were rejected by Jews who insisted on allegorical interpretations of the same texts. In all these dialogues between the deaf and the deafer the Jews were clear about one point. The Messiah was a Davidic king, the New David, a man and not God, a prince who would deliver them at the climax of human history. He might appear at any time and in any place. Many linked his appearance with Constantinople, but round about 1391 he was believed to have appeared in such places as Burgos, Palencia, and Cisneros.[27] A man, not God; the deliverer of the Jews: in what way did Jesus Christ fit the bill? The context within which the Christians attempted peaceful conversion failed because, quite simply, the Jews regarded Christian arguments as being illogical, not to say absurd.

The Jew as potential convert was not totally evil. But what about the Jew who refused to see the light and who deliberately persisted in his errors after friendly persuasion had shown that he was wrong? The unwitting accomplice of the Devil was spiritually 'blind'; the witting accomplice of the Devil was aware of his intentions and actions. And so there began conversion under pressure, a change that was to a large degree prompted by the fanatical zeal of some members of the mendicant orders, as well as the belief that all infidels would be converted before the end of the world (always fast approaching in medieval times). Already in the 1240s Jews (and Muslims) were compelled to attend the sermons preached by friars, and subsequently successive campaigns of 'Christianization' by force occurred.

But there was another subtle change in Christian attitudes which profoundly affected the Jews. Relying on Aristotelian, Stoic and Roman Law concepts, the great scholastic philosopher and Dominican St Thomas Aquinas (1225–74) elaborated ideas about man and natural law: quite apart from what religious law might say, natural law shows man that good is to be preferred and evil avoided; that man by nature is inclined to do good; and that, consequently, man is naturally inclined to know the truth about God. Man, therefore, is naturally and by reason inclined to be good. But the question then arose: can the precepts and inclinations of the natural law be destroyed in man? To this Aquinas answered that natural law, in the abstract, cannot be blotted out from mens' hearts; it is always there. But in practice it can be blotted out by evil persuasions, vicious customs and corrupt habits – to such an extent, indeed, that even unnatural vices might not be thought of as sinful. It followed from this that homosexuals, lepers, and Jews were unnatural; the Jew was not simply religiously wrong, he was by nature corrupted because he had blotted out the natural law from his heart. Indeed the 'clustering' of these metaphors of corruption was such that they could 'contaminate' each other by analogy. Thus, for example, the presence of homosexuals and Jews within the fabric of Christian society could be likened to the foulness of leprosy, and the laws could envisage that convicted homosexuals and Jews, like traitors, should not be hanged normally but upside down by the feet. True, it is difficult to document such cases, although a certain Solomon of Barcelona, condemned in 1391 in Paris, was informed by the judges that, being a Jew, he would be hanged upside down (he converted and was hanged normally). Yet there can be little doubt that the way in which Christians perceived Jews was changing radically for the worse, and was indeed acquiring nightmarish characteristics. In the south of France in 1321, for example, a satanic plot to overthrow Christendom was discovered. Lepers from several different countries had assembled in order to plan a mass poisoning of wells, springs and rivers. The poison in question, which included a pulverized host, and various bits and pieces of snakes, toads, bats, as well as human excrement, had been given to the lepers by the Jews, who in turn had been helped by the Sultan of Babylonia and the King of Granada. The conspiracy was found to have ramifications in Aragon where Jews were discovered to have helped poison the water of Teruel.[28]

During the fourteenth century the Jews of Spain were to be subjected to horrific attacks. But before discussing the reasons and consequences of this persecution, it is worth pausing to consider one prominent Jewish courtier and the magnificent synagogue which he built in Toledo. Samuel Halevi acted as chief treasurer to King Peter I of Castile, Peter the Cruel. Using other Jewish officials, Samuel served his king well, accumulating revenues, checking the activities of tax farmers, confiscating the lands of rebel nobles, and on one occasion leading a diplomatic embassy to Portugal. He also acquired considerable wealth for himself, and in 1357 invested some of it in building the famous synagogue in Toledo, which still survives and is usually known by its Christian name, the *Tránsito*.[29]

Shaped like a high rectangular hall, Samuel Halevi's synagogue is notable for its richly ornamented plasterwork. Of course such ornamentation had to be non-representational, and so full use was made of intricate arabesques which combine Muslim and Gothic influences. But, in addition, the Hebrew alphabet was used as a means of both decoration and communication. For example on the eastern and most important wall, an engraved inscription to the left of the Ark contains six lines of Hebrew surmounted by the arms of Castile and León. These lines invite the 'reader' to contemplate what Samuel has built, as well as the wooden *almamar* for the reading of the Law, the lamps, and the windows. A matching engraved inscription to the right of the Ark, also crowned with the arms of Castile and León, is fulsome in its praise of Samuel Halevi and his royal patron. Samuel, for example, is as a prince, magnate, and leader of his people; he enters into the presence of kings, standing firm and defending or promoting the interests of his fellow-Jews. Elsewhere in the synagogue, including even the women's gallery in the south-east corner, biblical quotations in Hebrew profusely decorate the surfaces; at times entire psalms are cited. Samuel had created an astonishingly beautiful temple, and in the process provided epitaphs for himself and his king. Yet, not long after, Peter I had Samuel Halevi and some other Jews arrested and viciously tortured; Samuel died in prison in Seville in 1361. It was alleged that in Toledo he had amassed a fortune of 160,000 *doblas*, 4000 marks of silver, and jewels and precious cloths. Was this allegation true or false? It would not be long before allegations would surface that King Peter I himself was the son of a Jew named Pedro Gil!

By the mid-fourteenth century the fortunes of the Spanish Jews had already taken a turn for the worse. In religious terms this was most apparent in the accusation of host desecration and in the blood libel, both of which often led to anti-Jewish violence. In Mallorca, for example, it was rumoured that in 1309 a Christian boy had been ritually murdered and the Jews there were subjected to an enormous financial penalty; in Seville the Jews were attacked in 1354 because of alleged host desecration. Other similar examples could be cited, but it is more important to stress the general significance of such cases. Accusations of this type were obviously part of a demonization process. According to the blood libel, ever since the crucifixion the Jews had thirsted, especially at Easter time, for the pure and innocent blood of Christian children. Such cases could not therefore be isolated ones; they were the demonic counterpart of the cyclical Christian calendar. Accusations of host desecration appeared only after the Christian doctrine of transubstantiation had been formulated by the Fourth Lateran Council of 1215. Jews allegedly bribed Christians to supply them with a consecrated host which they then tortured. In doing so, of course, they would in theory be torturing the body of Jesus. Allegations of host desecration, therefore, served two purposes. In the first place they validated the doctrine of transubstantiation because in most such cases the typical result would be that the tortured host bled. Secondly, the question that posed itself was this: why should Jews, who were not Christians, even bother to desecrate a host? And the answer to this was that the Jews knew very well that the consecrated host *was* the body of Christ, that Christ was the Messiah, and that, far from being unaware of the truth, they knew what the truth was and deliberately wished to torture Christ again. Blood libel and host desecration allegations could also be extremely significant precisely because of their sporadic and isolated nature. It was typical of such allegations that the Jews were supposed to have acted with extreme secrecy, their crimes only being discovered by mere chance or accident. How many such other crimes, therefore, had not been discovered? It only needed one allegation of this sort to disseminate anti-Jewish feeling far and wide. This was a point which the Jews themselves understood only too well. Very shortly after the attack on the Jews of Seville in 1354, for example, officials in far away Mallorca were preparing for 'copy-cat' repetitions of similar incidents once the news from Seville should reach the ears of the populace.[30]

In all this matters were certainly not helped by the fact that the Jews also became the victims of what may be termed 'official propaganda'. Accused of all manner of enormities, Peter I of Castile had to fight a civil war against a coalition of nobles led by his bastard half-brother, Henry of Trastámara. To make matters worse, French and English armies intervened on opposing sides, and Castile was plunged into an anarchy from which it only partially emerged when Henry finally defeated and murdered Peter at Montiel in 1369, becoming Henry II (1369–79). Many factors explained Henry's ultimate victory in the civil war, but one of the most important of them was undoubtedly his skilful use of anti-semitic propaganda. While in exile, Henry had busied himself in spreading throughout western Europe the black legend of Peter 'the Cruel', an illegitimate monster who had committed countless murders and who not only protected the Jews and Moors but enriched and empowered them at the expense of Christians. By the time he invaded Castile in early 1366 his campaign had taken on the air of a crusade aimed at freeing the kingdom from a tyrant and from the infidel, particularly the Jews.

It was inevitable that the Jews would suffer during the civil war, either by being forced to pay large sums of money or by being physically attacked. In 1366 the Jewish communities of Burgos and Toledo were each forced to 'contribute' one million *maravedís* to the Trastámaran cause. The next year similar sums were once again extorted from the Jews of Burgos, Palencia, and Toledo. In the case of Toledo in 1367, for example, Henry of Trastámara ordered the officials of the city 'to sell by public auction . . . all the Jews and Jewesses of the Jewish community of Toledo and all their landed and moveable possessions' until the sum he had demanded had been raised. To facilitate matters, his treasurer was empowered to torture any Jews who offered resistance. Henry of Trastámara claimed to be king of Castile, and in a sense his actions could be seen as 'official'. But the violence could easily spread and get out of hand. Mercenaries practically wiped out the Jewish community of Briviesca, the English ran amok in Villadiego, and the Christians of Segovia, Avila, and Valladolid attacked their Jewish citizens.[31]

The civil war over, Henry II reverted to traditional royal policy. Joseph Picho, for example, ran the royal finances, Joseph ibn Wakar looked after the king's health, and the king himself, mindful of the economic and cultural contribution of the Jews, attempted to prevent the worst excesses.

But it was too late. In particular the king failed to cope properly with a fanatic who had begun to cause trouble in Seville and its archdiocese, Ferrant Martínes, archdeacon of Ecija. Evidently Ferrant Martínes had started to cause trouble towards the middle of the 1370s, preaching rabble-rousing sermons, threatening to excommunicate town councils that allowed Jews to reside in their midst, and using every pretext to interfere with all legal proceedings involving Jews. On 25 August 1378 the king sternly ordered Ferrant Martínes to desist from his anti-Jewish activities forthwith. The archdeacon, however, appears to have paid little attention to these royal orders and Henry II's successor, John I of Castile (1379–90), had to send similar royal commands to Ferrant Martínes on 3 March 1382 and 25 August 1383. From these documents it is clear that by this stage the archdeacon was indulging in the most cynical anti-semitic propaganda possible, publicly preaching, for example, that the king and queen secretly wanted Christians to kill Jews and that, if they did so they would be forgiven in both legal and religious terms. The royal action quietened matters for a time, although in February 1388 the Jewish community of Seville once again complained about the demagoguery of Ferrant Martínes. Up to this point the royal and ecclesiastical authorities had managed to contain the problem. But then, in 1390, both King John I and the archbishop of Seville died – the new king, Henry III (1390–1406) was a minor; worse still, in the absence of an archbishop, Ferrant Martínes became the administrator of the archdiocese of Seville. An explosive power vacuum existed, and the archdeacon made sure that it did explode.

The horror began in Seville on 6 June 1391, with Jews being massacred and synagogues converted into churches. But the conflagration then spread very rapidly – to the other towns of the archdiocese, then to Córdoba, to Toledo (by 18 June), to Valencia (by 9 July) by way of Orihuela and Játiva, to Barcelona (by 5 August), to Logroño (12 August), to Lérida (by 13 August). Hardly a Jewish community in Spain was spared massacres and looting. This was the great pogrom of 1391. It is impossible to quantify the number of deaths to which it gave rise or the destruction it involved. Yet certain general features are very clear.[32]

The size and wealth of the most important Jewish communities of Spain suffered drastically as a result of the 1391 pogrom. The great centres of Spanish Jewry in the thirteenth and fourteenth centuries had been located in the large towns like Seville, Barcelona, Toledo, Burgos, and Valladolid. Fifteenth-century tax assessments, however, show that these Jewish communities declined sharply in terms of numbers and wealth. But the assessments also show that Jewish communities in small towns, and even villages, grew in importance. The obvious explanation, therefore, is that persecution had the effect of either expelling Jewish families from the large urban centres into the smaller towns and villages, or that, faced with massacre, terrified Jews accepted conversion. In Seville the Jewish quarter virtually disappeared; in Toledo and Burgos the Jewish communities suffered catastrophically; in Segovia the Jewish population in 1460 was only half the size it had been in 1390.[33]

The massacres of 1391 should have brought the history of the Jews in Spain almost to an end – but they did not. In Seville, for example, Jews as such virtually ceased to exist. But there was a corresponding increase in the number of New Christians or conversos; in the second half of the fifteenth century their numbers ran into tens of thousands. Were these 'converts' genuine Christians or crypto-Jews? The Christians had created a 'final solution' which would raise new, and more serious, problems for them. The officials of the Spanish Inquisition, once it was set up, would rightly suspect that many of these New Christians secretly held to what they believed was the only true faith: Judaism.

Chapter Two

Towards Expulsion: 1391-1492

ELEAZAR GUTWIRTH

The age of decline?

Ten years before the pogroms that spread throughout Spain, in the summer of 1381, a Jewish couple laid the foundation stone inaugurating one of the six tower gates of the city walls of Aguilar de Campoó near Palencia, in Castile. The commemorative inscription, still on the gate of the town in our century, was written in *aljamía* (Spanish in Hebrew characters) and read: 'First day of June of the era of a thousand four hundred and nineteen years. Don Saq ben Maleke... son of don Selomo ben Maleke... and dona Bellida his wife began to erect this tower... may they reach gladness and joy...'. The inscription surrounds a relief of the couple and is topped by the symbolic eagle of Aguilar.

About ten years before the expulsion of the Jews in 1492 Joseph ibn Hayyim, a painter in La Coruña, Galicia, was illuminating one of the most lavishly and expertly illuminated of all medieval Hebrew manuscripts, the so-called first Kennicott Bible. What used to be thought a regional and archaic style seems now to be indebted to contemporary influences, particularly of the engravings of German playing cards whose presence in Spain has been seen as attesting to their use there. The taste for the engravings on these cards was shared by other Jews throughout Europe as shown by ornaments in Hebrew manuscripts and bookbindings.

The two facts may seem random but they are certainly not trivial. They suggest the concrete forms of interaction of fifteenth-century Hispano-Jews with their milieu. The first is an emblem, and a celebration, of civic pride and confidence in the future of a town by those who as Jews, as a couple, and as burghers participate in that town's expansion. The combination of Hebrew letters and the vernacular typify a cultural trait which extends to various other spheres. The second recalls the private sphere, usually neglected in historical accounts of pre-expulsion Spanish Jewry. It also signals the complexities of a society which was by no means homogeneous in its cultural and social identity: like Spanish society as a whole, Spanish Jewry was subject to a multitude of influences, regional variations and social differences. And yet historians have painted unshaded pictures of a decline that is thought to extend from the summer of the pogroms to that of the expulsion. For an anonymous chronicler of the late fifteenth century the 1391 pogroms were the first part of a divinely decreed catastrophe (*gzerah*), and the expulsions were the second part of that decree. Later historians enlisted metaphors of light and darkness to express a basically similar periodization. According to one nineteenth-century historian, after 1391 '[the] spirit [of the Jews] became permanently darkened'. The organic world served as metaphor for literary decline: 'The literature of the Spanish Jews, however, was powerless to recover itself. In the midst of the dead calm [of the reign of Juan II] it seemed to wither like autumn leaves'; or again, there is the description of how poetry 'which has blossomed so fairly on Spanish soil, faded and drooped'.

Even if historians of our own century eschew such obvious rhetoric, the basic tenets remain. The most widespread texts still see the century as one of destruction, conversions and expulsions. It is therefore not surprising that there have been those who have perceived the main question concerning fifteenth-century Spanish Jewry as 'why were the Jews not expelled as early as 1391?'. The composite picture produced by many writings about the period seems, at times, to compound demographic, political and social decline with cultural isolation, stagnation and 'obscurantism'. Nevertheless, paradoxical as it may seem, the period which begins with pogroms and ends with expulsions need not be seen as one of unmitigated decline. An examination of both, the persecutions on the one hand, and the religious, cultural, political and economic patterns on the other, may reveal what rich, complex and perhaps contradictory trends were at work in fifteenth-century Hispano-Jewish history.[1]

The pogroms

The quest for 'unitarian' explanations – social or religious – has been one of the dominant features of the historiography on the pogroms of 1391. To the modern eye, internal Hebrew sources are apparently surprising, in some respects, in their response to the events. One contemporary in 1403 sees the massacres as divine punishment for neglect of Bible study. Another, in 1416, sees them as a retribution for the social and economic injustice perpetrated by a small group of Jews who 'had been given the keys of the treasury'. About a century later, a chronicler would write that the Jews had cohabited with Christian women and it was their bastard offspring who had been prominent in the attacks against the communities. A chronicler of the events, writing in the autumn immediately following the attacks of the summer of 1391, implies by the allusive texture of his account that the pogroms belong within a continuum of Jewish suffering whereby every local community (whether in Castile, Andalusia or Aragon) is another Jerusalem, destroyed by the Divine Will in retribution for the sins of God's people.

Evidently, modern historians cannot simply paraphrase medieval explanations which often reflect the writer's own obsessions or the constraints of the genre within which he is writing. Nevertheless these reactions are important indices of mentality. Despite antecedents, such as the attacks on Jewish communities during the civil war in Castile (1366–68) and the Black Death in the crown of Aragon (1348), they all seem to agree in seeing 1391 as a major turning point. Emblematic of this attitude is the attempt to turn a date into a motto. In the Hebrew calendar, where letters act as numerals, QN' ('zealous', which = 5151 [i.e. 1391]), became 'the year of the zealous God'. Christian chroniclers had other, probably more short-sighted perspectives on the events: for the aristocratic chancellor of Castile, López de Ayala, this was one more example of the dangers of rousing the greedy rabble; for an anonymous Mallorcan, the killings of the Jews seem to be on a par with the killing of the island's governor's horse. The chronicler of don Pero Niño – a minor Castilian courtier – devotes only a few lines to the events in a long chapter on 'how don Pero Niño killed a great boar'.[2]

Despite the influence of Ferrant Martínes (chapter 1, p.49f.) in rousing the masses in Seville, the focus on one figure cannot successfully account for the intensity, virulence and geographic extension of the pogroms. In an age of highly personalized monarchical authority the frequent minority and regency situations of the Trastámara dynasty had a profound impact on the politics of Jewish status. In 1391 the problems caused by the minority of the king, Enrique III, 'the Ailing', a mere lad of twelve, are highly relevant to the pogroms in Castile. They helped to create an atmosphere of civil unrest. In Seville itself riots occurred some months before the pogroms. The social explanation is particularly persuasive for the crown of Aragon: the inflation of 1340 to 1380, and the crisis and bankruptcies of the main bankers of Barcelona had implications for a Jewish population, some of whose members were *corredores* (licensed middlemen) and many of whom lent small amounts of money to the burghers and to the peasantry of the hinterland, especially in Mallorca and Barcelona. Wolff's theory that the pogroms belong with the 'social revolutions of the late Middle Ages' such as the English Peasants' Revolt is enhanced, for Barcelona, by the fact that after the Jewish population had disappeared either by death or conversion the riots continued unabated and were directed against members of the city council.

And yet, even in the crown of Aragon it would be misleading to see the attacks in purely social terms. A typical document of the collaboration of all classes in the anti-Jewish activities might be the testimony before a Christian notary of Joseph Abraham, a Jew of Valencia:

At noon of the ninth of July past, the plaintiff being in his house they closed the gates of the *judería* with great noise and shouts from the Jews and he shut his door. Before the hour of three, the people of the town assaulted the wall by the Old Valladar and even though he had his gate secured by great and strong nails, they forced it down with a battering ram and his house was assaulted by twenty men armed with swords, sticks and knives, some with blackened faces and hoods. They immediately broke and splintered boxes, desks, wardrobe. They even took the little mattresses off the beds without leaving a nail on the wall... all assessed at three thousand gold florins. They also stabbed his brother Nahor in the neck while he was trying to repell their attack.... Because the plaintiff complained about the damage... the head of the criminals hit him, wounding his arm and also behind his ear.... Asked whether he knew... the perpetrators of the assault and those who raped the women, he said that by certain words and a golden earring which one of those with a blackened face wore *he suspects a man of estate* but he cannot be sure.

On the fifth of August the Valencian town councillors wrote to the king to explain why 'no real punishment has been carried out' subsequent to the pogroms.

It seems to us that this does not happen because... some magnates, because they themselves or their relatives are guilty... impede that those who are most guilty should be denounced by threatening the claimants who have been damaged... because the guilty are of all conditions: men of the country and the town, of the Order of Montesa and of the mendicant orders, gentlemen... they also induce the people to show displeasure towards us giving them to understand that we do this to damage the lower orders...[3]

Polemics

Whether the robbings and killings of 1391 were a result of religious fervour or not, it was, nevertheless, religion which demarcated the boundaries of the conflict between Jews and Christians. Polemics, whether oral or written, might be seen as a metaphysical, theological extension of the violence. In his *Scrutinium Scripturarum*, Pablo de Santa Maria created a vision of contemporary Jewish history whose main protagonists were Jewish 'courtiers'. According to Pablo, these embodied for the Jews the fulfilment of the prophecy that 'the staff [i.e. rulers] shall not depart from Judah'. For him, 1358, one of the many putative dates of redemption, was transformed into the beginning of the political downfall of Hispanic Jewry personified in the fall from favour of Samuel Halevi, Peter the

Cruel's courtier. The attacks of 1391 were understood by Pablo as the result of the actions of 'the mob inflamed by the blood of the Messiah'. This work, and the *Fortalitium Fidei* (discussed in chapter 4, p. 96f.) have been seen as products of the atmosphere which led to the expulsion, the latter even as a blueprint for it.

The Tortosa Disputation has captured the attention of scholars who seem to see it as the major event of religious polemic in fifteenth-century Spain, particularly because of its putative effect: the conversion of large numbers of Aragonese Jews. In this context it would be useful to note the converts' own perception of the circumstances of their conversion. And here very little evidence has been adduced to show that converts viewed their conversion from Judaism as a result of the Tortosa Disputation. Much more common was the memory of conversion as a result, not of the arguments of Jerónimo de Santa Fe, chief spokesman for the Christian side at Tortosa, but of the appearance of Vicente Ferrer and his flagellants in the towns during the period 1411–16. Thus in the 1480s a Castilian Jewess, Clara, was said to have converted 'in friar Vicente's time'. Diego Arias, formerly a Jew, when asked at the synagogue by his neighbour whether he had difficulty in singing the liturgy replied: 'I had a good start. If it had not been for the coming of friar Vicente's commotion (*rebuelta*)...'. Nor are such examples restricted to Castile. Jacobo and María de Gracia from Montalbán in the crown of Aragon converted 'at the time of Vicente Ferrer'. A member of the old and famous Jewish Aragonese de la Cavalleria family recorded in the pages of a manuscript that his family had converted, not at the time of the Tortosa Disputation, but 'in the time of friar Vicente'.

Nevertheless, it would be an error of perspective to see these polemic texts, written in Latin and hence accessible to a small fraction of the laity, as the most significant aspect of the Jewish Christian polemic in fifteenth-century Spain. Although they have attracted a great deal of attention, the research of recent years has considerably increased our awareness of the many other similar texts written in late medieval Spain. Indeed it sometimes seemed as though Spain lagged behind European scholasticism precisely because its intellectual energies were directed towards such polemical activities. To privilege one group of Latin polemics over another would require a more convincing explanation than is available in the literature at present. Similarly, the fifteenth century in Spain saw the appearance of works in the vernacular which appealed to the rising lay literate public and can be documented as forming part of fifteenth-century libraries. One such work is the *Memorial* of Maestre Juan el Viejo, a work which, whatever its theological merits, did have a wide diffusion in manuscript. In it, even those Christian laymen without access to Latin, who formed the public of the various translations into the romance of Latin works in fifteenth-century Spain, could find a store of arguments against Judaism.

Characteristic of these was the tendency to use Jewish post-biblical and post-talmudic texts (Saadyah, Ibn Gavirol, Ibn Ezra) in an attempt to show the truth of Christianity.

But polemics were a much more extensive phenomenon than these technical treatises would suggest. They were topics for poetic development in Hebrew as is clear from the work of such Hebrew poets as Solomon Bonafed. They also formed part of courtly entertainment, as we can see from the works of courtly poets included in the *Cancionero de Baena*. There are incidental references in the works of Ibn Musa or Arama to such debates. Above all, when we speak about polemics in the fifteenth century, unlike in previous centuries, we need not restrict ourselves to the hypothetical assumption that Latin technical texts faithfully and accurately reflect the reality outside the text. Indeed, the preservation of Inquisition files means that we have documents in the original romance of the polemical conversations held by Jews and Christians outside any formal framework. For example, around 1470 the Calatayud Jew, Judah Benardut was told:

> Benardut why do you not become a Christian? You are dejected, you are subjected, you are humiliated by any child. This is insufferable. This one throws stones at you. The other calls you a Jewish dog. If you turned Christian you would be honoured, you could be obeyed, you could get offices and a thousand other honours.

To this the Jew replied:

> I, . . . do not wish to become a Christian, neither for those honours nor in order to escape insults. I hold fast to my religion and I believe that I will be saved in it, and the more humiliations I have to endure to sustain my religion the more shall my soul be saved.

The many spontaneous conversations of this type reported in Inquisition files may lack theological precision, but they probably reflect much more accurately the actual realities of Judeo-Christian polemics in fifteenth-century Spain than any Latin text.[4]

The written Jewish response to these attacks constitutes one of the literary genres which has been recognized, despite the theories of decline, as a significant contribution of the fifteenth century to Hispano-Jewish religious history. Hasdai Crescas' *The Refutation of the Principles of Christianity* reflects the continuing of an internal Jewish tradition of mastery of Aristotelean and other Greek philosophical ideas transmitted through the medium of translations into Hebrew.

Perhaps more startling and original in its emphases is the work of Profayt Duran, *The Shame of the Gentiles*. This is so not because of the theological arguments which he had used also in his *Be Not Like Thy Forefathers*. What does seem strangely familiar to the modern observer is his use of what might be called 'protocritical' methods in his reading of the New Testament. He tries to identify literary strata in the New Testament, tries to reconstruct a Jewish historical background for it, uses arguments of anachronism, attempts philological analysis and proposes emendations. Various other works in this genre testify to its vitality but it might be noted that there were 'subproducts' of such activity as well. An example might be the translations and studies of late scholastic works (e.g. by Versorius) with the justification that such an acquaintance with logic might prove fruitful in debate.[5]

Learned and popular culture

As an alternative to the image of an ailing Hebrew literature and culture one may propose another of a flourishing popular Jewish culture, sometimes in the vernacular. In this context, 'popular culture' is undoubtedly a problematic concept. Thus, magic and 'superstition' have been generally viewed as 'popular' and opposed to an elitist, theosophic, Kabbalah. Nevertheless, throughout the fifteenth century, some of the leading exponents of learned culture amongst the Jews of Spain occupy themselves with the problem of magic and related areas and try to explain and perhaps legitimize them through rationalizing explanations. For example, Efodi writes:

> Those who are perfect in this science (or wisdom) know how to change the nature of existing things and to do signs and miracles by means of the names of the creator and holy angels ... and this knowledge has spread amongst them and they call this knowledge *Simus Tehilim* and the choice of the famous name of 72 letters.

Abraham Shalom, the famous Catalonian physician and translator of Albert the Great, refers to the possibility of thaumaturgical feats being performed by means of amulets and names. He credits and rationalizes such beliefs by reference to current theories about the properties of plants and stones. Most of his references to kabbalistic works occur in this connection.

Nor were these mere theoretical speculations. Although most Hebrew amulets surviving in private and public collections today date from the nineteenth and twentieth centuries and medieval Hispano-Jewish amulets are very rare indeed, a recent study describes a Hebrew amulet from Spain, of the fifteenth century, which displays those features of amulet composition known from later counterparts. Jews provided Christians, often conversos, with Hebrew amulets or explained their meaning to them. The wearers of the amulets cannot by any means be described as part of 'the populace': they include high dignitaries of the state or relatives of such church dignitaries as an abbot. Around 1400 Isaac Eli, an Aragonese Jew, wrote a small treatise on witches in which he describes in detail the beliefs as to their nocturnal practices, their abilities to move objects or find them. Although in one case he attributes these beliefs to the *hamon*, the masses, the most notable tendency throughout the treatise is to try to explain them by means of concepts taken from the conventional philosophy of the day.[6]

The use of the vernacular and oral literature may perhaps be included in this category of popular culture. Statements made with increasing assurance by linguists, folklorists and students of oral literature point to this period for the origins of Sephardi folk literature. For a long time historians have been wary of accepting such assurances, possibly because most of the material has been collected in the late nineteenth and twentieth centuries. Nevertheless, recent finds, mostly amongst the Judeo-Spanish materials of the Cairo Genizah, have enabled scholars to antedate the evidence by at least three centuries. Liturgical texts, translations, popular medicine, songs related to the corpus of Judeo-Spanish ballads, *endechas* (mourning songs), proverbial idioms in private letters, have increased the confidence of the historian in accepting the earlier dating of linguists and folklorists for a number of phenomena appertaining to the domain of popular culture.

The omission of Christian elements in such songs was not always consistent or necessary. Similarly, the rubrics or tune markers of liturgical poems, where the first line of a current Spanish song follows, are to be found in fifteenth-century Hebrew poems. That some of them are dirges lamenting Christian persecutions is culturally significant: even when the theme was allusive of persecution, the melody, expected to be recognized by cantor and congregation alike, was not outside Spanish culture.[7] These complex cultural ambiguities extend to various other realms. Onomastic usage is another example of the continuity of attachment to the romance, though Arabic forms exist as well. Toponymics especially are shared by Jew and Christian but there is also a tendency towards using names of animals (e.g. Gato or Gategno, but also Trucha) or nicknames such as 'Correnviernes' (he who runs on Fridays). Particularly noteworthy is the continuity of women's romance names taken from a relatively restricted semantic field (Sol, Oro, Dona, Orosol). The proverbs which paremiologists believe entered Hispano-Jewish usage at this period also have Christian parallels.

Similarly important in understanding the fifteenth-century cultural horizons of Spanish Jewry is the Jewish *nachleben* of works written in other periods. It was in the fifteenth century that Jews copied, read and at times memorized such Jewish vernacular literature as the *Poema de*

Yoçef or the *Proverbios Morales* of the fourteenth-century Rabbi Sem Tov of Carrion. A recently discovered manuscript probably of the same century shows that Jews were interested in Christian paremiology, copying and transcribing it into Hebrew characters. The *Proverbios* of Rabbi Sem Tov were quoted in the sermons of the Zamoran Rabbi Abraham Saba. It has been argued that the teacher of the Toledan Yeshivah, or religious academy, before the expulsion, Rabbi Isaac Caro, used such vernacular proverbs in his sermons. A striking example of the predilection for the romance vernacular is the attachment to the romance translations of the Bible. Women and 'ignorant' men insisted on having the Book of Esther read to them in the vernacular during the Purim festivities. Rabbinical attempts to stop the custom in Saragossa in the 1380s seem to have been fruitless. There seems to be evidence of the continuity of this tradition in the second half of the fifteenth century in Segovia. The idea of a purely textual transmission of biblical translations by an 'elite' of learned 'biblicists' cannot be supported by the evidence. Jews of varying social provenance were able to translate extemporaneously biblical and liturgical passages into the vernacular when required to do so before the tribunals of the Inquisition.[8]

These features of Hispano-Jewish 'popular' literature and culture do not support the notion of isolationism which is part of the usual image of a declining Hispanic Jewry, whether in Graetz's formulation (the rise of orthodoxy and a consequent obscurantism) or in more recent variations.

And yet it could be argued that the fifteenth century was one of the periods of the most visible and documentable mutual influence or contact between Jews and Christians in the Spanish kingdoms at other levels as well. It is true that some of the examples of putative Jewish influence are not entirely convincing: the suicide of the young heroine of the *Celestina*, the long dramatic novel by Fernando de Rojas, written around 1500, would be as abhorrent to the Jews as to the Christians. One of the earliest examples of dramatic writing in medieval Castile is the *Diálogo del Amor y un Viejo* of Rodrigo Cota. One of the major features of the work has been attributed to the influence on a writer of Jewish origin of 'biblical dramaticism'. Nevertheless there are more convincing examples. For example, verse written by Christians in this period, in Castilian, may be said to have the highest incidence of Hebrew words and references to Jewish customs. Of course, such references are within a satiric context. But it is hardly likely that they would have been learnt for the purposes of writing a particular poem. Rather they should be understood as revealing the high awareness of Jewish customs amongst the Christians. More relevant than the fact that the writers are frequently conversos is the point that they expected their Old Christian audiences to understand their allusions to concepts such as the rabbi, the Torah, sabbath, mamzer, etc.

More direct evidence would be the case of such prose writers as the Bachiller ('Bachelor of Arts') Alfonso de la Torre who composed his *Visión delectable de la Filosofia y las artes liberales* for the Prince of Viana around 1438. The allegory of the liberal arts may be inspired by Allain of Lille but Maimonides is also an important source. Enrique de Villena alludes in his works to Israeli, R. Asher, Crescas and *Sefer Raziel*. Even if his references are highly dubious it is significant that a Castilian noble, educated in Aragon and related to the royal family, took a certain and evident pride in accumulating quotations from Jewish sources in a epoch which has been seen as one of isolationism.

Fifteenth-century Castilian Christians could read the *Guide for the Perplexed* or the *Cuzari* in translations into their own vernacular. The same could not be said for most other Europeans of the period. A Córdoban expressed in verse this feeling of a Hispanic culture which did not absolutely exclude the Jewish element by lauding Córdoba for its Seneca, its Averroes and its Maimonides. One could not imagine easily a fifteenth-century poet in Troyes taking pride in Rashi. Recent research has shown that an influential civil servant of Juan II of Castile and an important Castilian prose writer, Fernan Díaz de Toledo, was the patron of a translation into Hebrew of Maimonides' *Treatise on Asthma*. It has been argued that unless proof to the contrary is found, it should be assumed that he was able to read the translation which he commissioned.[9]

Jewish affinities with surrounding culture have also been pointed out. Some of the research has been concerned with thematic affinities in poetry. Hebrew poets develop such motifs of European poetry as 'the world upside down', 'town versus country'. In other genres we may point to the threefold division of society or the contempt for those engaged in manual labour as being found in Hebrew writings of this period. The attitude to Christian scholars of fifteenth-century Hispano-Jewish writers is by no means unanimously negative. In the introduction to his *Ma'ase 'Efod* (1403) Profayt Duran tries to convince his contemporaries of the importance of Bible study. To this effect he cites a story which he found in 'one of the Roman scholars'. It has been recently recognized that this is in fact an elaboration of Jerome's letter to Eustochium.[10] The Chief Rabbi of Castile around 1400, don Meir Alguadex, translated the *Nichomachean Ethics* into Hebrew. He justifies his reliance on a Latin translation (or paraphrase) by the fact that 'for the Christian writers moral philosophy is a splendid science...'. Eli Habilio, a scholar from Monzón, in the crown of Aragon, heaps extravagant praises on Thomas Aquinas and on Jean Versorius, the influential writer on scholastics from Paris.[11]

Although normally, popular and elitist culture are seen in isolation from the mentality of the rulers, in Spain at this period the cultural interaction which we have shown in other areas can be found in that of the court as well. And here pageantry can serve as an emblem of such cross-currents. During the coronation of Ferdinand I of Aragon, as the Paris manuscript of the chronicle of Juan II tells us, the Jews of Saragossa 'were dressed as Christians, dancing with silver ribbons, their jugglers (*juglares*) going before them... making merry till they entered the palace of the King'. When the Castilian courtier Pero Niño visited Muslim Málaga, before 1448, members of his crew 'went into the town... and visited the *judería*'. Scholars have debated the meaning of the passage written by the (converso) Toledan chronicler, the Bachiller de Palma, concerning the visit of the Catholic Monarchs to Toledo in January 1477 when 'the Queen, our lady, dressed exceedingly richly, wore a necklace of precious stones... especially one which was said, in the letters in it, to have belonged to King Solomon'. Whether or not the inscription on the stone was in Hebrew there are other examples of the attitudes of Ferdinand and Isabella. When they entered Saragossa in 1481, the chronicler Bernáldez tells us that:

> the Jews and their chapter [i.e. the *aljama* authorities] presented them [i.e. the Catholic Monarchs] with [a gift] based on the number twelve in a very singular order. This was as follows: twelve calves, twelve sheep, all adorned. They were followed by the most singular silverware borne by twelve Jews carrying plates. One of them carried on his plate a rich cup full of 'castellano' coins [of gold] and another one carried a silver jug on a plate.[12]

Such interest in symbolic acts, ornaments and pageantry cannot be dismissed as superficial. It was paralleled in a number of important fields. The Jewish familiars at the court of the Aragonese monarchs at the beginning of the century (financiers, astrologers, lion-keepers, physicians) have their counterpart in those of the Castilian court. Every fifteenth-century Castilian king had a Jewish physician. Isabella was delivered at birth by Maestre Semaya and her own expense accounts show the presence at court of the physician Abraham. At the urban level, Jewish tax collectors and physicians are extremely common throughout the century. If we are to take the period on its own terms we must pay similar attention to possibly less rational aspects. In the late fifteenth century a sermon of the Zamoran Rabbi, Abraham Saba would tell how

> in Aragon, during a drought they sent all the Jews from the town and they closed the gates till they [the Jews] would bring rain and don Hasdai Crescas, may his memory be blessed, preached a sermon. And he began by saying 'for the water is ours' [echoing the fight over water rights in Genesis 26:20] and the Lord remembered His people and gave them water.

That the story, embellished or not, is not a unique occurrence might be deduced from a later document which records a conversation *c.*1478–80, in Calatayud, where Joseph Sarfati, officer of the *aljama*, answered in the affirmative to the question 'will you [Jews] take out the Torah so that it rains?'. Similar evidence for taking out the Torah to cause rain comes from Daroca.[13]

At the more mundane level the use of Christian notaries by the Jews increases at this period. Hence the many wills and other legal documents extended to Jews which have been preserved in fifteenth-century notarial records, particularly in Aragon. Similar increases may be noted in the communal documents composed in *aljamía*. According to a fifteenth-century *responsum* local communities recorded legal acts in a *regist[r]o*.

Self-government

Historians who have taken for granted the unmitigated decline of Hispanic Jewry in the fifteenth century were faced with the problem of explaining how the most ambitious and extensive internal legislation which has reached us from medieval Spain is the product of precisely this period: the *taqqanot* or bye-laws of Valladolid (1432).[14]

To begin with there was the problem of the language: why was there so much Spanish and so little Hebrew in the text? Nevertheless rather than seeing the language of the text as a mark of the decline of Hebrew knowledge it may be understood as a product of the ethnic identity that was being crystallized after the pogroms of 1391. The *taqqanot* are the final product of the work of a *junta* or assembly of the Jews of Castile, which gathered at Valladolid in March 1432. Recent research has tried to modify the understanding of the *junta* as an *ad hoc*, isolated event whose only standards of evaluation come from the rabbinical assemblies of the Rhineland. Rather, it has attempted to reveal the strong connections with Castilian political and parliamentary history. The assembly was a logistic and administrative achievement. The fact that it could take place should be understood against both the immediate political conjuncture and the inner tradition of Jewish self-government.

The central figure of the 1432 assembly is the Rav de la Corte Abraham Bienveniste. Research on the image of the Jews in Castilian chronicles shows how closely connected he was with Juan de Furtado in the minds of his Castilian contemporaries. Juan de Furtado belonged by family and other ties to the circle of Alvaro de Luna whose victory at Higueruela three years earlier had raised his prestige and status by the time of the Valladolid *junta*. Abraham Bienveniste had been responsible for much-needed loans some years earlier. The time was propitious for a far-reaching initiative within Jewish self-government. Such an initiative could base itself on a number of legitimizing traditions: that of the previous *juntas* was one of those mentioned in the text of the *taqqanot*. Attention to the procedural aspect of the assembly may dispel notions of an *ad hoc*, extemporized event. And here it is necessary to point to the issues at the meeting of the Cortes in nearby Zamora some months earlier where the procedural problem of letters of presentation of the delegates was discussed. At Valladolid the *junta* demanded and examined such letters from the Jewish delegates. The formulation of the *taqqanot* suggests a differentiation between various types of members of the *junta*: the delegates from local communities, the rabbis and scholars, and finally the Jews 'who are about the court', with Abraham Bienveniste presiding. Such stratification is strongly reminiscent of that operating at the Cortes themselves, though it does not contradict the Hispano-Jewish ideology on the threefold division of society which was being articulated with increased frequency in the fifteenth century. The formulation of the *taqqanot* with their paragraphs of explanation and justification headed by the word '*porquanto*' and the paragraphs of legislation which begin with the word '*otrosi*' similarly parallel the formulations of the Cortes notebooks. The *soferim* or notaries of the assembly are another centralized institution which legitimizes and is responsible for aspects of the work of the *junta*.

The actual content of the legislation could be seen as secondary to the fact that the assembly took place at all. After the preamble which, more than a rhetorical piece is a carefully conceived argument for legitimizing the work of the *junta* with its appeals to Jewish tradition, the authority of the king represented by Abraham Bienveniste and the will of the communities, there follow five sections or 'gates'. The fact that the first one is concerned with education, a subject which was less likely to arouse opposition, is not only consistent with communal ideology but with the inner politics of such committee work as well. In line with the claims of pedagogues throughout the ages, the statutes paint a grim picture of the educational prospects. In response to this they devised an energetic and thoroughly thought-out system to be funded mainly on indirect taxation of conspicuous consumption of wine and meat at festivities – weddings, circumcisions and even funerals. Similarly the text reveals the different educational expectations of rural and urban Jewish communities.

The second chapter concerns the election of judges and other officers. This may be another example of the centralizing tendencies which characterized the political thought of Castilian Jewish leaders as they did that of the circle of Alvaro de Luna, precursor in some ways of the centralizing policies of the end of the century. The statutes envisage local communities dominated by small power groups. Phrases such as 'and in the places where there are no judges' or 'let them choose the judges without tricks ['*alilah w-mirmah*] and without regard for partisanship in interest groups' or 'the said officers should not coopt their offices without communal licence' may at first sight seem to show the shortcomings of the appointment of officers. But in fact the statutes tend towards enhancing the central power of the Rav de la Corte: they legislate that if communities fail to agree on the election of 'judges . . . *veedores*, treasurers, those who take care of public needs and other communal officers . . . they must let the Rav de la Corte know so that he should appoint them and the community is obliged to follow his orders about this'. Centralization depends on the tensions and disagreements at local, communal level.

As was the case in other medieval corporations – towns, monasteries, universities, military and religious orders – internal discipline was paramount to the survival of the corporation. The crown, highly interested in the smooth running of the tax collecting machinery, had long since granted *privilegia* (particular laws rather than the modern 'privileges') legitimizing the punishment of members who broke internal discipline. It is probable that the highest incidence of such attempts against internal discipline concerned taxation. The highest punishment for those who had repeatedly threatened internal discipline was death, although in previous centuries documented punishments had included the cutting out of the tongue.

The fourth chapter concerns one of the most important and problematic issues of communal life: taxes. The main problem here was the influence of powerful non-Jewish nobles who granted exemptions to their Jewish favourites. Although the chapter mentions exemptions granted by the king, most of the problematic exemptions seem from the text to be granted by the nobility, creating within the Jewish community a class of exempt Jews who increased the taxation burden on the rest of the community. The centralizing tendency is expressed here by complaints against Jews who move to seigneurial lands and those who obtain privileges from the nobility. Royal privileges such as those to the family of the former Rav de la Corte or to Abraham Bienveniste himself, are defended.

Finally the last section consists of sumptuary laws which, although legitimized by the allegation that clothing causes 'the envy and hatred of the Gentiles', give the impression of a standard of living far removed from that of impoverished communities. The most detailed legislation is against women although here, as in the complaints at the Cortes against Jewish clothing, men are included as well. The women's clothing mentioned may be useful as documenting the female Jewish version of the much discussed Castilian conspicuous consumption of the period: dresses with long trains, embroidered in gold, or made of *azeituni* – the costly cloth imported from Ceitun in China – fine gauze, silk, or camel hair. Linings were embroidered in gold or made of *azeituni*. Bandeaux were made of pearl or mother-of-pearl and worn around the head. The high-necked *mantones* – large shawls – or undergarments and stockings made of vermillion cloth are also mentioned. Fifteenth-century Hispanic texts in general singled out for mention the long dress with extremely wide sleeves, the *alicandora*. It had aroused the indignation of the Franciscan moralist Eiximenes when worn by widows and its alluring oriental associations are implied in a poem by Villasandino. The width of the sleeves of the *alicandoras* worn by Castilian Jewesses is restricted by the statutes of 1432. But men also wore silk, gold-embroidered or silken cuffs and linings. Other, non-Jewish texts, are more explicit as to the luxury of Jewish male attire: swords, gold and silver spurs and jewelry. But there is no doubt that legislation, both internal and external, responds not to merely economic considerations but to a complex semiotics of fashion whose 'grammar' – social, sexual, seasonal and regional – one can only begin to fathom in the current state of research. Thus unmarried young women are exempt from the Valladolid regulations and so are all Jews and Jewesses who take part in the frequent *alegrías*. These were joyful pageants and celebrations on occasions such as that of the arrival of the monarchs in town, a monarch's wedding, a victory over the Moors. Similarly complaints against Jews who wear silk or carry swords are paralleled by those against the *pecheros* (taxpayers) who don similar attire. The same fabrics would hardly excite any comment when worn by non-taxpayers, i.e. *hidalgos*, members of the nobility.

Commerce

Economic decline has been assumed in a number of areas. The main focus of attention used to be the upper socio-economic echelons which in practice meant collectors of income, mostly tax collectors but also *mayordomos* (stewards) for the nobility. At other levels, that of the artisans, it has been usual to use legislation as evidence. The statutes of Valladolid (1412) do indeed try to enact economic discrimination against the Jews. These were followed by those of Ferdinand I of Aragon and by the Bull of Benedict XIII in 1415. There have been affirmations to the effect that the economic horizon of Hispanic Jews was very limited and that they only thought in terms of attending to the shop or, at best in terms of interurban commerce; their economic experience was limited to Spain and had shrunk even further in the fifteenth century. Such affirmations are made with an eye on the great Sephardi financiers of the sixteenth century. A comparison with previous centuries, especially with the thirteenth century in Aragon, leads to postulating a 'difficult period' which begins around the mid-fourteenth century and seems to extend to the expulsion. The main support for this last argument comes from the study of the commercial relations between Catalonia and the Maghreb as reflected in archival documentation. The Jewish role in maritime commerce with the eastern Mediterranean seems to have become less frequently reflected in the documents even earlier, around the beginning of the fourteenth century.

It may be doubted, however, whether we really are in possession of the total evidence concerning the economic activities of fifteenth-century

Hispanic Jewry and whether this does indeed amount to such a simple uninterrupted decline. One of the main arguments has been the putative density of the upper socio-economic echelons amongst the converts to Christianity. This tends to equate Jewish economic well-being with that of the moneyed minority. There is no doubt that some very well known wealthy families, especially in Aragon, did have some members who converted (de la Cavalleria, Golluf). But in the absence of any reliable statistical source one may pay attention to other facts as well. In a list of the converted Jews buried in the cemetery of Jerez de la Frontera, most of the occupations listed after their names are those of artisans. The list of converts elaborated for Seville on the basis of late fifteenth-century Inquisition documents shows mostly individuals of the middling and lower economic groups.

The discrimination envisioned by the legislation of the second decade fell out of practice within a short space of time. Baer had been explicitly cautious when stating that *c.*1444 'Jews controlled about two thirds of the indirect taxes and customs within the country, on the frontier and at the ports' in Castile.[15] He pointed to the need for 'diligently scrutinizing these documents'.[16] Scholars who have followed this advice have lowered the figure. The documents are not yet published but their value as representative of the whole fifteenth century is debatable. It may indeed be argued that we have more names of Jewish tax collectors for the fifteenth than for previous centuries. Since Jewish tax collecting functioned through companies or networks of sublessees we cannot be entirely sure whether all the sublessees are mentioned in the documentation.

Given the ambiguity of such statistics based on partial archival documentation, one may pay attention to other, possibly unexpected sources. One such comes from Algiers rather than Spain. It is the collection of *responsa* on juridical themes of Simeon b. Zemah Duran, the Mallorcan rabbi who escaped in 1391. The *c.* 800 items of the collection are mostly sent as answers to questions emanating from the north of Africa but some come from the crown of Aragon, Mallorca or even Castile (Soria, Ocaña). There are *responsa* dealing with aspects of commerce during the period 1391–1444. Some of these concern intercontinental trade between the Hispanic kingdoms and North Africa. One case concerns the trade relations between 'Reuven' (the names are of course fictitious) in Mallorca and 'Simon', his partner in Algiers. The capital was invested by them and two other partners. Simon sells some merchandise to a non-Jew in Algiers and returns to Mallorca, leaves the sale documents with 'Levi' and goes on to Valencia. Levi leaves the documents in Mallorca with a young assistant. Reuven orders the assistant to collect the debts and give the money to 'Juda'. What is significant here rather than the halakhic entanglements of the question is the image provided: that of a consortium of Jews in Mallorca who trade with Algiers and make credit transfers.

Since the *responsum* mentions Moses Gabay we can date it to between 1391 and 1427, the date of the latter's death. Another question comes from Mostaganem and concerns a Jew who gives merchandise valued at 'one hundred golden pieces' to an agent. The agent is meant to receive 'six golden pieces' as annual salary. The agent is meant to sell the merchandise in Spain. Because in this case he was unable to travel, he had to sell the merchandise in North Africa at a loss.

The family was a main basis for trade. An example might be the case of a document cited in a *responsum*:

I Reuven certify that I have received all that was owed to me by Simon my brother and that all our debts are cancelled, both those which concern the merchandise which he used to send me to Mostaganem as well as that which I used to send him from Mallorca and this document is extended as proof of this...

Responding to a consultation concerning the payment of a *ketubbah* [matrimonial contract] written in Mallorca, Barfat makes explicit allusion to the export of gold from North Africa ['this land'] to Spain ['the Christian country']. He compares 'reales' with 'dinars', alludes to the work of engraving and generally shows an awareness of numismatics which would be hard to imagine in a Jewry which was really isolated financially and commercially from its Iberian neighbours across the strait.

Specialized types of merchandise imported from Spain and mentioned in the *responsa* include a substance for washing hair, imported from Valencia and used by women. A 10% duty was imposed on books imported by such refugees as Amram Efrati. Wheat, ostrich feathers, and the ubiquitous raisins are other items of intercontinental commerce mentioned in the *responsa*. But wine was probably one of the most important items of Jewish export to North Africa. Within Spain the documents about Jews owning vineyards are extremely numerous, to such an extent that they left traces in Hebrew literature. Profayt Duran, in 1403, deplores the fact that the artisans of his day gather in the taverns to play chess rather than read the Psalms. Solomon da Piera wrote verses to lament the bad vintage of 1417. The Bishop of Burgos, Pablo de Santa Maria – known before his conversion as Solomon Halevi – as a Jew had written a humorous Purim letter bemoaning his sobriety and the lack of kosher wine at court. These writings have little in common with the old conventional wine poetry of the Arab period. The wine bought from Mallorca gives rise to a number of questions sent from North Africa and from the Hispanic kingdoms to Barfat. A long question from Mallorca describes the case of a Jew who used to buy wine in quantity from a Christian neighbour. She used to deposit the keys to the wine cellars with the Jew as demanded by halakhic ruling. There is mention of a royal agent who orders the drafting of a report on the 'kashrut' of the wine. Converso neighbours also give their opinion. This is hardly a matter of wine elaborated and bought for purely domestic consumption. Various *responsa* from North Africa refer to Jews who sell wine to their gentile neighbours. One refers to a Jewish tavern keeper in Miliana and his Hispano-Jewish wife, Mona.[17]

The wealthy Jews: Abraham Seneor

It would be difficult to argue for a decline or lack of the type of wealthy Jew who attracted the attention of historians of other centuries. Indeed it may be argued that we may find such types with increasing frequency and with better documentation in the fifteenth century. There are those in possibly unexpected occupations such as cattle owners.

Income collectors are, however, much more numerous and they could include *mayordomos* for nobility and church dignitaries such as Isaac Abravanel. But there can be little doubt that the best documented and most influential of these was Abraham Seneor.[18] Indeed if a random document of royal tax collection at the municipal archives of Chinchón bears the signature Abraham, it is not because this was a rare name which needed no additives but because in tax collecting circles in the Castile of the 1470s it was known that there was only one Abraham who, unlike his Jewish and Christian colleagues and subordinates, was sufficiently well known and important to be able to sign by his first name. The chronicler Bernáldez, curate of Los Palacios, closely associated with the monarchs' court and a keen observer of social differences, departs from the conventions of chroniclers when describing Jews when he writes about Seneor and gives us an estimate of his fortune: a million *maravedís*. Reading a recent attempt to trace his career based on surviving documentation, one cannot but associate him with the typical image of the Renaissance courtier. Machiavelli's well-known references to Ferdinand (with whose court Seneor was ultimately in close contact) as the model prince make such an association less implausible than might appear at first sight. True, there is little evidence to support such an association in a cultural sense, although a Hebrew chronicler did attribute to him a treatise on friendship and amongst his family we find some well-known intellectuals (Luis and Antonio Coronel) and, amongst his close connections, individuals who patronized the arts (Diego Arias was visited by painters in search of buyers and Juan Arias is responsible for an example of Renaissance architecture in Turegano).

But in another sense Seneor's instinct for political survival, his foresight in choosing the right alignments and maintaining them, as well as his practical, daily efforts on behalf of the implementation of increasingly centralized policies of collecting revenue are too consistent to be dismissed as mere inertia or good fortune. Indeed when no less than a disciple of George of Trebizond – Alonso de Palencia – referred to him as 'a faithful observer of the laws of friendship' he was leaving an important testimony as to his image in the circles of the Segovian 'civil service'. Certainly, one should always beware of Palencia's malicious irony and particularly so in reading the *Décadas*. Palencia was touching on one of the central puzzles in Seneor's career: his smooth transfer of loyalties between warring factions. It was in the service of Enrique IV and his treasurer, Diego Arias, that he seems to have risen to the higher ranks of the tax collecting hierarchy. Even in 1468 Enrique still refers to his 'efficiency, loyalty, the many and good services which you [i.e. Abraham Seneor] have done and do every day' and rewards them. When in the violent factionalism of Segovia in 1473 he decided to support the small party of Isabella and sway Cabrera to it, he was making a momentous but as yet uncertain decision. We need not accept the popular legend (elaborated by the somewhat unreliable Cretan, Elijah Capsali) of his being a matchmaker between Ferdinand and Isabella to understand why about twenty years later Isabella still remembered the faithful and many services Abraham Seneor had rendered at the time of her coronation in 1475. This change of alignment may well underlie the hitherto unexplained formulation of Palencia.

Seneor's daily activities, as documented in many central and local archives, are far removed from the spheres which interested those who wrote about him in the fifteenth and sixteenth century. Obtaining, sometimes in auction (*puxa*) the rights to collect taxes, establishing partnerships to do so, following up arrears throughout years, collecting debts, advancing or paying sums obtained through collection at critical junctures, sometimes during wars (especially with Granada) as well as taking care of the treasury of the Santa Hermandad (the newly created centralized militia) are some of the areas covered by the documentation on Seneor during the reign of the Catholic Monarchs. If the text-book description 'minister of finance' is both fanciful and anachronistic, it is true that his documented activities go far beyond those of previous Jews in the service of the crown: the extension of his activities which encompassed even Llerena and Jerez, the strategic importance of timely payments and provisions to frontier castles at a time of war and of course his office as treasurer of the Santa Hermandad are difficult to understand within the context of the putative 'decline' of the Jewish 'courtiers'.

His financial and political ascent was paralleled within the Jewish community. From the appointment as *alguacil* (bailiff) of the Segovian *aljama* in 1468 to the mention of him as Chief Rabbi over the whole of Spain, a gradual but extremely successful increase in the extension of his powers within the structures and hierarchies of Jewish self-government may be discerned. Historians who thought in terms of the 'puppet' rabbis-by-appointment of say, Czarist Russia, have had difficulties in coming to terms with offices such as those held by Abraham Seneor. There is however no evidence to support the tendency towards minimizing the role of these institutions. The alternative, as far as the documents show, was not the rule by a saintly *saddiq* but the encroachment on Jewish autonomy by municipal and other non-Jewish jurisdiction on the one hand, or the rise of factionalism and interest groups on the other.

A letter written *c.* 1487 by the Jews of Castile to those of Rome and Lombardy is held to refer to Seneor in the words

> blessed be the Lord who in his great mercy and goodness has not averted and shall not avert the staff from Judah that is our Exilarch who holds in his hand the seal from the King over the Jewish community to uproot and to fine, not in order to trangress the words of the Torah but in order to erect a fence around it.

This description possibly emanates from circles close to Seneor and certainly from a tax collecting milieu, but it was not especially sycophantic in comparison with other examples from the Hispano-Jewish tradition of elegies to leaders in which it belongs. The 'courtier's' success as a product of Divine Providence's 'special relation' with his people is an old and frequent topic of Hispano-Jewish thought, as is the exegesis of the Genesis verse applied to Jewish self-government. The use of the old Babylonian title to describe the Castilian 'Rabbi Mayor' is consistent with an ideology which legitimized institutions by mentioning antecedents. Most significant is the phrase that Seneor was empowered 'to uproot and to fine', where the quotation from Ezra 7:26 is no mere embellishment but the legal basis, in Talmudic law, of the Jewish court's power to 'fetter, arrest and prosecute' (cf. T.B. M.Q. 16a).

That is not to say that there was no opposition to him. A careful reading of the documents may reveal the attempts by Vidal Astori (the Jewish Aragonese courtier of King Ferdinand who is remembered by historians of Hispanic art for his work as a silversmith) to rival Seneor's powers within the Jewish communities around 1476. Another case would be that of the affair of Juan de Talavera in 1485, the converso from Segovia who brought a law suit before the royal council to obtain an appointment within the Jewish communal bureaucracy. It has been recently maintained that this is to be understood not as a case of a conflict between Jews and apostates but as a reflection of Segovian Jewish social and family factionalism in which Juan de Talavera was only one of a whole group of Jews opposed to Seneor and his circle. Other cases would include Trujillo. But what is significant about these examples is that they bear no resemblance to later negative assessments of Seneor. For when in 1492 his conversion was staged as a great propaganda event at the Hieronymite monastery of Guadalupe, this one act overshadowed, for later writers, the daily and more mundane aspects of his previous career. Seneor became a symbol of the Jews who converted, and descriptions of him lost the awkward and untidy individuality which may be regained through a reading of contemporary sources.

The expulsion

All these examples present a picture that is in many ways at odds with the traditional one. According to the received view, as we noted at the beginning of this chapter, the years between 1391 and 1492 saw a steady decline in the situation of the Jews, a mounting persecution of which the expulsion was the logical climax. The records that have been described here, on the contrary, show some of the complexities of the period. Why, then, the expulsion?

The text of the edict gave a religious reason: to preserve the Christianity of the conversos. The Catholic Monarchs have been seen as exemplary in their religious fervour. It is necessary, however, to read critically a document which is, after all, an official state pronouncement, not a personal confession.

The previous expulsions (from Andalusia, or the partial ones from the towns) are certainly important precedents. And, similarly, the history of anti-Jewish discrimination in the fifteenth century (segregation into separate quarters, the badge etc., culminating in the legislation of 1480, discussed on p. 77f.) is undoubtedly part of the background. It is also true that the particular formulations used in the edict can largely be attributed to Tomas de Torquemada, the representative of the Inquisition at the royal council. But is this enough completely to 'explain' the moving factors behind the decision?

Various recent theories have tried to account for the expulsion. One sees it as part of the general struggle between crown and nobility in Europe (England, France) where the crown had acceded to demands of the third estate (wishing to eliminate competition) in order to find an ally. Another puts forward the view that the conversos, who dominated the town councils, and whose anti-Jewish tendencies are visible in some of the treatises they wrote, were the prime movers in the drive to expel their former coreligionists and potential witnesses for the Inquisition. A third identifies the expulsion as a use of religious antagonisms to 'mobilize' the emergent nation into unity and encourage submission to the ever increasing power of the crown.

But although the subject of the edict itself is religion, most of the documents following upon it are concerned with the appropriation of Jewish capital and property. Readers of the Hebrew accounts of the expulsion would be wrong in undervaluing them as mere examples of the 'martyrological' genre or as exponents of 'lachrymose history'. The ever increasing documentation on the daily workings of the expulsion shows quite clearly that, on the contrary, if there is a tendency in these accounts it follows a different direction: that of selecting only a minimum of the possible examples that could have been adduced. It is not from these chronicles but from archival documentation that we learn details of the physical attacks on Jewish victims of the expulsion in the roads of Spain, such as those on the Jews of Huesca on their way to Navarre at the valley of Ortilla; those perpetrated by Christian thieves on the Jews of Biel in the *desfiladero* of Isuerre; those of Pina at Gelsa as well as the looting of Jews by Christians near Sos or Uncastillo.

Most of those expelled seem to have made their way on foot, leaving the mules for the sick and elderly. Similarly, the use of boats and fluvial routes was restricted to few cases within Spain. The Christian population capitalized on this need and the price of mules rose inordinately at this time: on 22 June, in Magallón, a Jew had to exchange whole houses for a black mule, a silver cup and a piece of cloth. In a number of cases, the expulsion meant that the quarters in which there had been a Jewish presence for centuries became abandoned and hence degraded, creating municipal problems and devaluing the property. Thus, in Teruel, after the expulsion, there followed looting, mainly of the door posts, the windows and the beams of Jewish houses which were used for rebuilding or as firewood. Some of the houses were occupied by beggars. Some municipalities tried to demolish those icons of isolation of the *juderías* – walls and gates. Others erected squares and widened roads. Synagogues were frequently appropriated by the Church: the Synagogue of the Torneros in Saragossa passed into the hands of the monastery of the Beatas of Santa Maria de Jerusalem; the Biqqur Holim Synagogue was bought by the Provincial of the Jesuits. In Albarracín the synagogue became the *Ermita de San Juan* and in Calatayud a synagogue became the Church of Saint Catherine of Siena.

The crown was particularly anxious to establish a prior claim to all other creditors of the Jews, trying to recoup what it claimed was the loss of revenues in taxes or debts on the one hand and prohibiting the sale of communal property to pay for such debts on the other. The result, in some cases, was that single wealthy families had to carry the burden of paying the taxes of the rest of the community. This is particularly noteworthy when we come to assess the Hebrew narratives of the expulsion which pass over these sacrifices of property on the part of the moneyed class and only attribute to them a tendency to convert. Within this context of intense Christian preoccupation with appropriating Jewish estates it is not surprising to learn that in communities such as Saragossa, works of art such as the 'pomegranates' of silver or the embroidered silk and damask covers of the Torah scrolls were not kept but simply melted for the value of the silver (turned into ingots) or golden threads.

The expulsion was, of course, viewed as catastrophic by the Jews, and the full significance behind the rhetoric of Hebrew accounts, poems and incidental references in biographies remains to be revealed. European reactions to the expulsion were varied. Most of them have been loosely described as 'anti-semitic'. Images of disease abound. Jews were compared to a leprosy from which Spain had been cured, or a cancer that had been removed by surgery. There were those, nevertheless, who exhibited some empathy in their accounts – Bernáldez, Pico della Mirandola, Montaigne – but to explore these would take us too far from the theme of this book.

Chapter Three

The Expulsion: Purpose and Consequence

HENRY KAMEN

The decision to expel the Jews

On 31 March 1492, three months after they had accepted the capitulation of the city of Granada, Ferdinand and Isabella of Spain decreed the expulsion of the Jewish population of their united realms. Though the historical event is incontestable, its origins, nature and consequences are all still within the realm of controversy, and in examining it more closely we become aware of the great problems posed by lack of evidence and of adequate historical research. The expulsion has seemed so transcendent an event that commentators both then and now have virtually suspended their judgment before it: Machiavelli regarded it as an act of statesmanship and like other contemporaries praised Ferdinand and Isabella for their purification of the realm;[1] modern scholars are inevitably united in their condemnation, but claim to see in the expulsion dire economic consequences for the country.

The focus on 1492 follows from the symbolic importance of that year in Spain's history: Moorish Granada capitulated to the Christian forces in January, the decree expelling Jews was issued in March; then in October Columbus made his landfall on the outer Antilles. Despite the coincidence in time, and the fact that resolution of the Granada wars enabled the crown to turn its attention to other matters, the Jewish expulsions have little to do with the Moors or with America,[2] and must be looked at rather in two quite different but fundamental contexts: the situation of Jews in western Europe in the 1480s, and the evolution of the Castilian Inquisition.

Well before the Spanish decree, Jews in western Europe were under pressure.[3] International events and opinion thus coincided with the decision that the Spanish rulers were shortly to make.[4] But when the Spanish decree was issued in 1492, neighbouring states were unlikely to be happy about large-scale immigration of Jews, a problem aggravated by further decrees in Portugal and Navarre[5] and later in the Italian states associated with the Spanish crown.

Who was responsible for the decision and the decree? Though experience leads us to assume constant unanimity between the king and the queen on every policy decision, and though we may attribute simply to Isabella's modesty her statement to Isaac Abravanel, the leading rabbi in Castile, that 'the Lord has put this thing into the heart of the king',[6] it is striking that most recorded public statements on the execution of the decree emanate more from the king than the queen. The distinction between the two is assuredly of no importance, except that greater emphasis on the king's role serves the purpose of exploding the traditional image of a fanatical queen leading a more restrained husband.[7]

In realpolitik terms, the decision came from neither of them but, it would seem, from the Inquisition. The terms of a letter from Ferdinand to the count of Aranda, which was sent the same day as the decree, are unequivocal:

> The Holy Office of the Inquisition, seeing how some Christians are endangered by contact and communication with the Jews, has provided that the Jews be expelled from all our realms and territories, and has persuaded us to give our support and agreement to this, which we now do, because of our debts and obligations to the said Holy Office; and we do so despite the great harm to ourselves, seeking and preferring the salvation of souls above our own profit and that of individuals.[8]

The Inquisition, says the king, 'has provided' and 'has persuaded', phrases which confirm Baer's suspicion, written long ago, that the decree 'by its content and style was drawn up in the language of the inquisitors and the jargon of their documents, and undoubtedly came from the workshop of the Inquisition'.[9] The 'Inquisition', however, was at this period a tiny group of men with no firm organization or authority at their disposal, and certainly with no power to impose decisions on anyone; so that its capacity to persuade the crown may be explained by one of two reasons: either the expulsion followed logically from previous policy, or the decision coincided with advice and pressure from other quarters. On either count, we need to go back in time to look at the circumstances that may have contributed to the events of 1492, and among them we need to consider the foundation of the Inquisition.

What had been the policy toward Jews just before the expulsion? Behind the whole issue looms the shadow of the Inquisition, which has dominated the historiography of the theme, and we should begin by considering its part in the story. Founded by papal bull in 1478, at the request of Ferdinand and Isabella, the Inquisition began its activity in 1480 under the leadership of Torquemada as first Inquisitor-General.[10] There is no doubt that the tribunal was in its origins an instrument of anti-semitism: the first calls for it to be created arose out of the prosecution of judaizers in the 1460s, and in its first years it devoted itself almost exclusively to the prosecution of Christians of Jewish origin (conversos), who represented well over ninety per cent of its victims in the final decades of the century. Since its foundation antedated the expulsion by over twelve years, we must treat those years as a time of serious trial not simply for conversos but for Jews as well. What took place was a veritable holocaust by the normal civilized standards of western Europe, unprecedented in the history of Spain or any other country; but it was a holocaust, let us remember, *not of Jews but of baptized Christians*. And it continued in intensity well after the expulsion, up to the early years of the reign of Charles V.[11]

Let us look more closely at the holocaust. It was, strictly speaking, not Spanish but Castilian, and in its early period predominantly Andalusian. Over the greater part of northern Spain no comparable fires were lit, and when they were eventually lit the incendiaries were Castilian inquisitors forced on the other realms despite their bitter opposition. The memorable words of the Catalans in 1484 – 'we are all aghast at the news of the executions and proceedings that they say are taking place in Castile'[12] – testify to their horror at what was happening on the other side of the country. It was in the south of the Peninsula that the confrontation was taking place in the 1480s, especially in the cities of Andalusia. And the conversos were totally isolated. On the one hand, Jewish leaders, while conscious of the implicit threat from the Inquisition, were in no position to show any sympathy with the Christians[13] and were obliged to collaborate by denouncing judaizers to the tribunal;[14] on the other, most Old Christians – those of non-semitic origin – felt no threat at all and did not raise a finger to protest unless they were dragged in involuntarily, as happened in the local case of Córdoba, where the excesses of the inquisitor Lucero forced the king to intervene. The remarkable protest by the queen's converso secretary Hernando de Pulgar is one of the few surviving examples of open criticism.[15]

Because the inquisitors believed that the presence of Jews and of synagogues acted as an incentive to judaizing, a belief for which there was ample justification (since the coexistence of cultures in many towns encouraged converso Christians to follow Jewish customs, on the premise that these did not invalidate Catholic belief), they began pressure to separate the two religious communities without actually calling for the suppression of Judaism. Two policies were pursued: firm separation of the religions by putting into effect the old decrees for confining Jews to ghettos; and the expulsion of Jews from select areas, specifically the region of Seville, where the first measures took place.

Separation, whether voluntary or obligatory, had long been part of the medieval Jewish way of life, but was seldom rigidly practised. In the city of Soria, for instance, the last separation order had been in 1412, but it was never implemented. In 1477, for reasons that are unclear, the crown ordered separation in the city, but this too was never put into effect.[16] Only in 1480, on the petition of the towns in the Castilian Cortes that met at Toledo, did the crown agree on a general decree that Jews should be restricted to ghettos, and walls built where necessary; a period of two years was allowed for the measure to be implemented. Like much previous legislation, this remained all too frequently a dead letter:[17] in Soria for instance as late as 1489 richer Jews were in undisputed residence outside the *aljama*, their houses backing directly on to the cathedral. Many municipalities used the 1480 decree to take harsh measures against their Jewish population, but the crown vigorously resisted what it considered illegal moves, since the Jews were directly subject to its jurisdiction and discrimination against them could hurt the crown's fiscal interests. Despite the constant pro-Jewish legislation by the government in these years, there is no doubt that it stood firmly by a policy of thorough separate development. In a supplementary order of 1480 the king explained that, for example, 'no Christian may eat or drink with a Jew nor invite them nor live with them nor bathe with them'; Jews could not act as sponsors at weddings or other Christian ceremonies; and so on. The prohibitions are of course evidence that the two cultures still frequently socialized, but also indicate (if ever observed) a harshening of the public mood. The policy of expulsion was begun at the end of 1482, when a partial expulsion of the Jews of Andalusia was ordered. Such measures implied nothing more than moving to a different part of the country. In January 1483 the Inquisition ordered the expulsion of Jews from the dioceses of Seville, Córdoba and Cadiz. The crown delayed implementation and they were not actually driven out from Seville until summer 1484; if, indeed, they were driven out at all, for a contemporary source reports that only the poorer Jews left and all the rest remained.[18] In 1486 a royal order was issued for the expulsion of Jews from the Aragonese dioceses of Saragossa, Albarracin and Teruel; the order was later suspended, and the Jewish population appears to have been still in place in 1492. From about 1480, therefore, a limited policy of separation was attempted, and it was pursued for over ten years, a long enough period for the authorities to decide whether it had been a success. The expulsion decree of 1492 had ample precedents, and apparently involved little change of policy, the one new factor being the demand for forced conversion.

It seems unnecessary, in short, to look for pressure on the crown by specific groups such as the towns.[19] It is purely speculative to speak of such pressure, for which in any case no documented evidence exists; moreover, no material interests could have been served by it.

The Inquisition, of course, in the light of the failure over ten years of a policy of separation and expulsions, had opted for expulsion; but

Ferdinand was always in control of the inquisitors, never they of him, and it is likely that the crown had made up its own mind, did not need the advice of the Inquisition, and cited it only as a justification. What would have been the motives of the crown? And what was the role of the Inquisition in all this?

Historians have, until recently, suggested that the 1492 decree was related to the foundation of the Inquisition, because both allegedly arose from three main motives: the crown wanted power, it wanted to impose religious unity on Spain, and it wanted to rob the Jews. Let us consider these three questions, taking our cue from a recent useful essay by Benzion Netanyahu.[20] Juan Antonio Llorente was possibly the first scholar to argue, from credible evidence, that Ferdinand of Aragon 'considered the Inquisition a useful tribunal for his political ideas' and that it gave him 'an opportunity to confiscate immense riches'. Ranke in 1827 went further and stressed that the Inquisition supplied the king with a tool for absolute authority over both Church and state. This interesting interpretation was taken up by Catholic scholars, who could thereby lay all the blame for the tribunal on the secular power. Hefele in 1844, in a work that was eagerly seized upon by conservative Catholics in Spain, followed Ranke in asserting that 'the Inquisition was the most effective instrument in completing the absolute power of the monarch'.[21]

In fact no evidence has ever emerged to substantiate the view of an absolutist monarchy exploiting the Jews through the Inquisition. Though Ferdinand certainly did use the Inquisition as a convenient tool to interfere in the crown of Aragon (just as Philip II was to do exactly one century later), it is impossible to demonstrate that any 'absolute' power was gained by the crown; and certainly, in the case of the Jews, no such move was necessary, since the crown in most of Spain already had full and direct control over the Jewish communities, whose representatives had the custom of meeting the crown regularly, and who paid virtually all their taxes to the crown alone.[22] In these circumstances the crown emerged as the foremost defender of the Jews. As part of his argument in 1844, Hefele claimed that the primary cause for the establishment of the Inquisition was the threat from the judaizers or secret Jews, who 'threatened to uproot the Spanish nationality and the Christian faith' and 'to Judaize the whole of Spain'. Four years later, in 1848, in a work written from a wholly different (liberal) perspective, Amador de los Ríos in one of the most influential studies on the question, fused together the political and religious motives as a single fundamental policy of the crown: 'the idea of the political unity of Spain, and, enveloped within it, the idea of the religious unity of the country. To create the first, the second was a necessary condition'.[23] Regardless of the fact that this thesis of unity rested on no visible fact, document or statement, Amador credited Ferdinand with a policy of political and religious unity directed towards the achievement of civil peace, and, in contrast to Hefele, blamed the Church for excesses committed along the way.[24] The prevalence of such views, unsupported by historical evidence, owed more to the political climate of the nineteenth century than to research: had religious unity been their main intention, the king and queen who in March 1492 decreed the conversion of the Jews would hardly have agreed, three months before, to the permanent guarantee of the Islamic faith, believed in by five times as many Spaniards as adhered to the faith of Israel.

The argument that the Inquisition and the expulsion formed part of a plan to rob the wealth of the Jews can be found in Llorente, who suggests that the Inquisition 'gave Ferdinand an opportunity to confiscate immense riches'. More recent scholarship has continued to follow this line.[25] The continual insistence on wealth and riches, and on a plot to rob the Jews, represents an undesirable distortion of the context within which the expulsion was decreed. The decision of 1492 can be properly understood only in the light of the twelve years since the foundation of the Inquisition, and for that our focus must shift once again to the Christian conversos rather than to the Jews. The entire period 1480–92 was quite simply a time of conflict and fear, in which a few (like Pulgar) stood their ground and attacked the whole rationale of the Inquisition, in a controversy that reminds us yet again that Spain was a society in which disagreement was both possible and permitted.

However, here a significant difference in the position of conversos and Jews must be emphasized. Jews were underprivileged and mostly of modest means. By contrast, conversos were Christians and many were neither underprivileged nor of modest means, and right from the beginning there were accusations, which common sense leads us to accept, that the Inquisition was picking its victims from the richer conversos in order to obtain income. There is no doubt at all of the tenor of the many early denunciations of the Inquisition's activities: 'what was noticeable', commented a chronicler of Seville, 'was the great number of prosecutions against moneyed men'; and in 1483 in Ciudad Real a woman claimed that 'this Inquisition is as much for grabbing property as for exalting the faith'.[26] The money, however, was Christian money, and the property was Christian property; by no stretch of the imagination can the quantity of wealth seized in those early years be described as Jewish. It should be recalled that the Holy Office did not have (until the mid-sixteenth century) any secure source of income, and had to subsist entirely out of confiscations, a system that many people tried unsuccessfully to reform. In these circumstances plots by converso leaders, and involuntary emigration of many, were logical consequences of the crisis in the 1480s. The years 1480–92 were far more damaging to the economy than the expulsion of 1492. Emigration from Andalusia took on grave proportions and when, according to Pulgar,

> the queen was informed that commerce was declining . . . setting little importance on the decline of her revenue, and prizing highly the purity of her lands, she said the essential thing was to cleanse the country of that sin of heresy.[27]

The shock waves went through the whole Peninsula. In Catalonia the Consellers of Barcelona complained of the large number of conversos who were leaving even before the Holy Office had arrived, and claimed in 1486 that their city would be 'totally depopulated and ruined if the Inquisition were introduced'.[28] Though they undoubtedly exaggerated there is little doubt that economic dislocation occurred, especially in the larger towns where conversos had played a part in the financial structure. None of this should lead us to overestimate the cash benefits to the Inquisition, which certainly did not become rich nor even consolidated itself (when some tribunals had done their work, they were abolished or transferred to another town). The number of conversos brought to trial may be higher than was once believed,[29] but the figures do not affect the accepted conclusion that these bloody years constitute one of the most appalling chapters in the history of Western civilization.

The Inquisition, then, was certainly not invented to 'rob the Jews'. Those who suffered, both rich and poor, judaizers or not, were Christians. If anything, some Jews seem to have flourished in these years, which coincided with the wars of Granada, when both Abraham Seneor and Isaac Abravanel (who entered the court administration in 1484) made profits in the royal service. What cannot be denied is that the Holy Office owed its birth to anti-semitism, and that many conversos were in the popular mind looked upon as Jews; in Netanyahu's words, 'the Spanish kings felt the rising tide of anti-semitism, and rather than resist it they decided to ride it'. But while thousands of converso Christians died in the fires of the Inquisition, Jews remained immune; and it is interesting to note that it was not until as late as 1491 that the inflammatory story of the murdered child of La Guardia surfaced (see chapter 4, p. 113f.).

The motive: exile or conversion?

The decree as issued in March 1492 had a curious feature which few historians have seen fit to comment upon.[30] At this stage we should cite the crucial parts of the decree, since they also clarify some of our argument:

> Because of the communication of Jews with Christians, in the Cortes we held in the city of Toledo in 1480 we ordered the separation of Jews in all the cities and towns of our realms, giving them separate places wherein to live, hoping that with this separation the situation would improve. We also ordered an Inquisition to be set up in these realms, which has been in operation now for twelve years and many guilty have been punished by it. But we are informed by the inquisitors

and many other people, religious, churchmen, and laymen, of the great harm suffered by Christians from the contact, intercourse and communication which they have with the Jews, who always attempt in various ways to seduce faithful Christians from our Holy Catholic Faith... And since we felt that the effective remedy for all these ills was to separate Jews completely from Christians and expel them from all our realms, we ordered them to leave the cities, towns and villages of Andalusia where it was felt they were the most harmful, believing that this would be enough for the others in the other cities of our realms to cease their activities... But since we are informed that neither that nor the justice done on some guilty Jews are enough for a full remedy... we with the advice of some prelates and great gentlemen of our realms, and of other men of learning and conscience in our Council, decree that all Jews male and female depart our kingdoms and never return... and that all have until the end of July this year to leave all our realms, with their children and servants and relatives both old and young, and not dare to return... And if they do not observe this and are found guilty of remaining in these realms or returning to them, they will incur the death penalty and confiscation of all their goods... And let nobody in our realms dare to receive, shelter or defend publicly or secretly any Jew after the end of July, on pain of loss of all goods, property or income...[31]

From the wording of the decree it is easy to conclude that this was a total expulsion, giving no alternative, and that death and confiscation were the lot of those who came back. Yet there can be absolutely no doubt that *the decree had conversion, not expulsion, as its motive*, even though not a single word in it offers the alternative. On this point both king and Inquisition appear to have coincided, and it is a fundamental conclusion which requires emphasis, in order to shift our attention from the highly misleading word 'expulsion'. Indeed, it is possible to maintain that during these years, in *every* case for which we have evidence, and above all for Spain, the motive of legislation was not expulsion but compulsory conversion.[32]

The Inquisition desired nothing more complicated than the elimination of a choice for the conversos, many of whom felt more at home among their Jewish brethren, and more tranquil in the synagogue than in the church. As long as Jews and synagogues existed, they would go on judaizing, and the task of the Inquisition, to purify the land of heresy, would never be done. The objective could be achieved by forced conversion (as in 1391); expulsion was unnecessary, and had been resorted to before only as a local measure. The decree, as issued, was implicitly one of conversion, despite its wording. We know this because 1) a space of three months was given, apparently for settling of affairs but presumably also for conversion; 2) an immediate campaign of conversion was commenced, which would have made no sense had merely expulsion been the intention; 3) the king himself took steps to urge persons and communities to convert, and the Seneors in their own defence claimed later that they too had converted in order to ease the lot of their brethren. The contemporary chronicler Andrés Bernáldez was quite clear about the intention of the edict:

> it was ordered that the holy Gospel and Catholic faith and Christian doctrine should be preached to all the Jews of Spain; and those who wished to convert and be baptized should remain in the realms as subjects, with all their goods; while those who did not wish to convert should leave the realm within six months and not return under pain of death.[33]

By the same token, since conversion was the purpose we cannot describe the decree as 'anti-semitic' in the ethnic sense; the king and queen were not ridding the country of Jews, and indeed by welcoming Jews into the Church and assisting at the baptism of Seneor before the high altar at Guadalupe prior to welcoming him into the royal Council they were giving former Jews a firmer place in Christian society. Many Spaniards had long criticized the pro-semitic stance of the monarchs, and the decree did not change that picture: the king who before 1492 had Jewish physicians and financiers in his entourage continued after 1492 to have (converted) Jews as counsellors, and in 1508 publicly reiterated his confidence in the conversos in his administration. Though anti-semitism was an enduring force in peninsular society, the decree was concerned not to get rid of Jews but to force them into the Church.

With conversion as the main goal, it is very likely that the expulsion was nothing less than a mistake. By allowing the long space of three months, the crown had mistakenly allowed the Jews time to think and rally, and it was in this spirit of sacrifice that many went into exile. The mistake of allowing so long a breathing-space was not repeated. When Isabella by her decree of 12 February 1502 offered the Mudejars of Castile and Granada the choice between conversion and expulsion – a choice, of course, arising out of quite different circumstances – the time allowed (ten weeks) was not much shorter but the conditions stipulated[34] were so stringent that no real choice could be exercised: virtually all converted. By 1525, when Charles V was obliged to take measures relative to the Mudejars of Aragon, even the possibility of choice had vanished: only conversion was decreed.[35]

Though a long historiography has branded the Catholic Monarchs, then, for their brutal 'expulsion', it seems clear that expulsion was not the primary objective. On this point it should be made clear that much opinion opposed expulsion; that a high proportion of Jews themselves preferred conversion to expulsion; and that in any case expulsion was not logistically easy to implement. Each of these questions merits consideration.

Powerful opinion then and later expressed itself against both expulsion and forced conversion. Ferdinand's subsequent biographer, the Aragonese historian and inquisitor Jerónimo de Zurita, reports that

> many were of the opinion that the king was making a mistake to throw out of his realms people who were so industrious and hard-working, and so outstanding both in number and esteem as well as in dedication to making money. They also said that more hope could be entertained of their conversion by leaving them in the country than by throwing them out.[36]

Though we do not know the identity of these 'many' there can be no doubt that their view was both recognized and respected, sufficiently so to appear not only in Zurita's official history but also in that of the eminent scholar and Jesuit Juan de Mariana, who reported that the decree 'provoked many to criticize this decision of the king'.[37] Indeed, many Spanish theologians then and later made no bones about their opposition. The inquisitor Luis de Páramo, in the standard history of the Spanish Inquisition published in 1598, reports that

> there were learned men who did not feel that this edict was sufficiently justified, and among their reasons the first was that unbelievers should not be compelled into the faith ... The scandal is even greater if adults are compelled by violence.[38]

To the argument that many rulers of medieval Spain had converted the Jews by force, and that this justified the decision of 1492, Páramo states explicitly that 'this zeal of the kings is not supported by theology', and cites the leading sixteenth-century theologian Domingo de Soto in evidence. Much other similar testimony can be produced to demonstrate that educated opinion was not uniformly favourable to the events of 1492. The validity of forced conversion was also debated when the Portuguese crown issued its expulsion decree on Christmas Eve 1496, which allowed a comparably long period, up to October 1497, for the decision to be made; like its Spanish counterpart, the Portuguese decree was aimed explicitly at conversion, as policy in subsequent months showed. In February 1497 several members of the Portuguese Council of State opposed the decree as invalid, and one, the bishop of Silves, stated that 'the Jews cannot legally be forced to embrace Christianity, a religion which requires liberty and not violence'.[39] As with every other government decision in the history of early modern Spain, including the later expulsion of the moriscos, there was controversy and difference of opinion about policy.

Contemporary Jewish commentators were explicit in roundly condemning the large number of conversions that took place. Those who converted were no doubt confident that this time of trial would pass, as all others in the history of Israel had done. Oddly enough, most scholars have chosen to ignore the reality of conversion. Statements by contemporaries such as Rabbi Ardutiel that 'most of the Jews and their great men converted'; and by Rabbi Ya'abes that 'the majority of the [learned elite] converted'; and by Rabbi Capsali that 'thousands and thousands of Jews apostasized';[40] have usually been relegated to footnotes or dismissed as hysterical exaggerations. Yet, as modern scholars are beginning to realize, the scale of conversions was impressive. From some towns, such as Lérida, the entire community seems to have left. But in others (such as Palencia) the entire community is reported to have converted, and in others only some departed;[41] while a high proportion of refugees also returned after 1492 (the laws guaranteed return of property to those who returned before 1497, hardly a measure consonant with 'expulsion'). In the Aragonese town of Borja the rabbi converted, and a royal decree of 1493 recognized that thanks to him 'many Jewish men and women converted to our faith', and rewarded him suitably with a cash gift; among the converts was 'Fortun Pérez, who used to be one of the most important and rich Jews in the *aljama*'.[42] Taking into account those who converted and those who returned later, it is reasonable to suggest that possibly a half of Spain's Jews converted, many of them doing so years after the expulsion, when they could persuade the other members of the family to adopt the same path; in short, the scale of conversion bites deeply into the highly unrealistic figures for the expulsion suggested by both contemporary and modern sources.[43]

Logistics and consequences

The logistics also made it unlikely that a true expulsion could have been carried out. The morisco expulsions of 1609–14, when some quarter of a million people were expelled, were made possible because the entire resources of the state (militia and navy) were put into service; the moriscos could not have gone anywhere had government-chartered ships not taken them. In 1492, by contrast, nothing comparable happened. In those parts of Spain under seigneurial jurisdiction crown control over the operation was patchy, and Jews seem to have reached agreements with their seigneurs about procedure. The royal commissioner in the bishoprics of León and Astorga cited examples of this, but wrote to the king that he could not check personally for fear of his own security, since 'in these bishoprics the whole country is seigneurial, and I don't dare to go into seigneurial land nor into the mountains'.[44] We know that in Valencia the Jews had to charter their own vessels,[45] and that some Jews from Aragon bought passages to France.[46] For the bulk of expatriates, the only realistic route was overland to Portugal. Bernáldez tells us that ships went to Africa, a statement supported by much other evidence, but until supporting documentation is found we remain in ignorance about the scale and mechanics of this operation. What seems certain is that the oft-repeated image of Spanish Jewry fleeing to Turkey[47] cannot be substantiated from the documentation, and appears not to be supported by the population figures for the eastern Mediterranean.

The details of the expulsion have ironically attracted little interest among historians since it always seemed to represent the closing of a book rather than merely of another chapter in it.[48] The lack of interest has helped to nurture many of the misconceptions that have passed into official historiography.

In contrast to the inefficiency of all previous legislation on the Jews, the decree of March 1492 appears to have been complied with quite remarkably. Civic authorities everywhere were authorized to draw up inventories of the assets of their Jewish population, and to await the appointment of royal commissioners who would make the relevant decisions. The inventories, which despite their deficiencies remain our most precious source for any survey of the true position of Jews in 1492, did not imply seizure or embargo but were meant to avoid legal disputes by establishing ownership. All Jews who converted retained their property. Those who wished to leave had a right to sell, but it may easily be imagined that this was difficult to implement in practice, mainly because of frauds perpetrated against the vendors (principally by the royal commissioners, as the king himself later complained), but also because of the difficulty of realizing debts and similar assets at short notice.

What numbers were expelled? All available estimates for the Jewish population of Spain, even those given by contemporaries, err on the side of gross exaggeration, and modern historians have been reduced to relying exclusively on tax censuses, which happen to be unavailable for the non-Castilian realms. Even if the overall population were reliably known, there still remains the unresolved issue of how many Jews left the country. I have suggested elsewhere that out of a possible Jewish population of 70,000 in Castile and 10,000 in Aragon the likely total to have left permanently over the period 1492–99 was about 40,000 souls,[49] or half the total. The figure applies only to Jews. A handful of conversos may have accompanied them, but it would have been the wrong time for them to leave, since the legal guarantees offered by the crown affected only Jews.[50] The conversos had had their own emigration a decade before, provoked by the establishment of the Inquisition in the 1480s, when contemporaries spoke of five thousand families fleeing Andalusia, and of a Barcelona threatened with depopulation,[51] sufficient testimony to a time of crisis that swept Castile and Aragon. The crisis, however, affected Christians and not Jews, and must not be confused with the expulsions of 1492. Nor was the crisis simply one of persecution. Within their own communities the conversos and Jews were faced by agonizing pressures, and Haim Beinart has graphically illustrated the misery of the semitic communities in Ciudad Real, above all when in 1483–85 an ex-rabbi,

Fernán Falcón, became the chief witness employed by the Inquisition against conversos accused of judaizing.[52]

The decisiveness of the expulsion decree, which abolished on Spanish soil the legal existence of the faith of Israel, has frequently led to the mistaken impression that the rulers of Spain were dedicated to exterminating Judaism not only throughout their dominions but everywhere else. We know that the Portuguese conversion was decreed as a result of the marriage treaty with Spain, and the Navarrese decree of 1498, affecting the *aljama* of Tudela, was also due to Spanish pressure. But there is no basis whatsoever for asserting that 'the Catholic Kings tried to get [Jews] expelled from all Christian realms'.[53] In 1493 the king was, quite logically, annoyed that many Jews expelled from his realms the year before were being received with open arms by the pope, and he accordingly protested through his ambassador;[54] but this did not represent pressure for expulsion of Italian Jews. Similarly, his concern over Jews who reached England was limited to one case with financial implications; and the raising of the issue with the English king six years later in 1498 was due to the obvious anti-semitic views of the Spanish envoy, the prior of Santa Cruz.[55] It was logical for the king and queen to attempt to extend the Spanish decree to all the other realms associated with Spain, and it was therefore issued in Sicily, which Ferdinand ruled directly.[56] But there the attempt to extend the expulsions ended. As the monarchy grew in subsequent years, new realms came under Spanish control, but always on terms that retained their constitutional autonomy, with the result that it was almost impossible to impose Spanish practice outside Spain. Since the Spanish monarchy was not an empire but a confederation of realms in which each nation had its own laws, Jews were able to live freely in almost every non-Spanish territory subject to the crown of Spain, an ironic situation which the crown appeared to be in no hurry to change. Jews could therefore be found in the early sixteenth century practising their religion legally in Orán, Naples, Milan,[57] the Netherlands... an image quite different from the one often entertained. Although the expulsion was certain to deliver a death-blow to Jewish culture in Spain, the crown was not, at this stage in history, aiming to eliminate aspects of culture that did not concern religion. To a physician returning from Portugal, for example, the government conceded a licence 'that he may have in his house any books whatsoever on all the sciences, whether in Hebrew or in Arabic, provided they are not the Talmud or other books on the Mosaic law'.[58]

The economic aspects of 1492 are probably the most misunderstood of all. In his classic study of 1918 R.B. Merriman claimed that 'the economic consequences were disastrous',[59] without going on to discuss the matter. Distinguished scholars like Vicens Vives have maintained that the expulsions 'eliminated the only groups capable of giving an impulse to capitalism, snuffed out the prosperity of many towns and realized an enormous quantity of wealth'.[60] It has been claimed that 'the effect was to weaken the economic foundations of the Spanish Monarchy . . . The expulsion deprived industry of skilled workers and much-needed capital'.[61] Though these categoric statements appear in works written many years ago they are still cited and for that reason are particularly unfortunate, since no town has yet been identified where prosperity was snuffed out, no enormous wealth has been documented, the skilled workers have never been discovered, and the Jewish capital invested in industry still remains to be found. It is in theory possible that all such statements may one day be vindicated by research, but a number of considerations make the possibility unlikely.

All the contemporary complaints of economic dislocation in Spain precede 1492 and refer exclusively to the persecution and emigration of Christian conversos;[62] Jews do not feature. There is an obvious reason for this. Conversos, whether of recent or distant Jewish ancestry, were Christians and as such enjoyed all civic rights and the right to participate in economic affairs. They therefore played a significant role in the political and economic life of Spain,[63] and the inquisitorial campaign against them in the 1480s was bound, as we have discussed above, to have an impact on sectors of economic life.

By contrast, there is not a single protest over the economic consequences of the Jewish expulsions. The Jews were a disadvantaged minority, with many firmly established rights – notably the right to own land (a right denied them in eastern Europe) – which were always subject to restriction in some parts of Spain, and which in the 1480s were sharply cut back with the policy of ghettos. The restrictions made it difficult for Jews to develop their incomes, buy property freely, trade on equal terms with Christians, or hold any public office: some Jews did all these things, but they were both an exception and a tiny minority. All the contemporary Spanish criticisms of the expulsion, cited above, restrict themselves to saying that the Jews were hard-working and made money; there is no claim, nor could have been, that they were wealthy or contributors to industry. When an Aragonese writer in 1620 looked back at the events of 1492 he categorized the expulsion as 'an astonishing decision', because the Jews 'were highly esteemed, being more industrious than the moriscos'.[64] Whatever the merits of this comparison (which was made with the recent morisco expulsions of 1614 in mind), there appears to be no doubt that the Jews, like many other cultural minorities in modern times, did not allow themselves to be crushed by their secondary status in society, and dedicated themselves to survival. Even then, they were always dependent on Christians. It is significant that so-called 'rich' Jews such as Seneor were in reality managers of other people's money; no matter how much cash they might accumulate personally, or how impressive their houses, they could never invest in large-scale trade or extensive property or social status. Jews in fifteenth-century Spain were neither a capitalist class nor a middle class. Essentially the Jewish economy of medieval Spain was a stagnant one, interlinked with the Christian economy through the mechanism of loans and debts but otherwise used largely in the service of the Jewish community and incapable of any development because of the social restrictions. When Jews accumulated wealth they did it not in investments but in cash, jewelry and rural credits, which significantly was the form taken by the assets of the community in Saragossa in 1492.[65]

To these general observations there are important exceptions. Although in much of Spain and particularly in Andalusia the Jews seem to have remained an urbanized minority, in the north after the urban fury of 1391 they had drifted into the countryside, and there, in a more tolerant environment, had become an industrious rural grouping. In the area of Toledo, by the late fifteenth century a high proportion of Jews were peasants working their own smallholdings.[66] In some parts of the north where the seigneurs were tolerant Jews could become relatively prosperous landholders: in Buitrago the community at the moment of expulsion owned 165 fields of flax, 102 meadows and 18 market gardens, and even had a representative on the town council.[67] The economic state of Jews thus depended completely on local circumstances, and there were several exceptions to the rule of their general distress. By the same token, one cannot look at the very few exceptions and present them as typical: towns such as Avila in Castile, Morvedre in Valencia, and Cagliari in Sardinia, did not suffer from the 1391 riots and managed to retain large and active Jewish populations; but Christian society kept their activity within strict limits.

The importance of the Jews in the Spanish economy has certainly been exaggerated.[68] Their economic role prior to 1492 varied according to social environment. In Andalusia, where Muslims and later Christians had restricted Jews to an urban existence, the Jews managed to make a living from urban professions, giving us the highly unfavourable picture presented by Bernáldez and other contemporaries, of a minority who by choice refused to work the soil and preferred to work in service and retail trades where they could rob Christians more freely. In a different urban context, that of Saragossa, Serrano y Sanz has also concluded that Jews were almost exclusively in retail and finance.[69] In Saragossa, the financial interests of Jews and Christians were interlinked (Jews and Christians had, for instance, joint guilds of traders),[70] and as a result there were numerous complaints by the city over the taxes which they lost in 1492 from the Jewish community, and over the inability to realize debts from Jews; whereupon the king, in an act that was no doubt repeated through most of Spain, gave the public areas (that is, the streets and squares) of the walled-off Jewish quarter to the city.[71] The complaints by the city should not lead us to assume that the Jews were a well-off community;

on the contrary, in 1492 the ghetto in Saragossa was, if we may believe a contemporary witness, 'in extreme need, and lacking cash or goods with which to pay the taxes'.[72]

The expulsions therefore gave people an opportunity to rob Jews of their many personal possessions, but the public economy was apparently unaffected, and nowhere throughout Spain was any voice raised to complain of the unfavourable economic consequences. This conclusion, again, must vary according to context. If all the Jews of a large *aljama* emigrated, there must have been at least short-term dislocation. It is possible that in Zamora, where Jews in 1492 were as much as fifteen per cent of the population, the repercussions were significant;[73] but since we have no evidence of the number who left the supposition remains no more than a possibility.

The king led the way in protesting over looting and robbery perpetrated on emigrants, for the royal treasury was, as Ferdinand admitted, the chief sufferer from the decree: his letter to the nobility speaks of 'the great harm to ourselves' that the expulsion might cause. Indeed, the decree issued by the king on 26 September denouncing the frauds and outrages and abuses committed in Aragon by the royal commissioners sent to supervise the disposal of Jewish goods, and about the 'daily complaints and clamours' reaching him,[74] is testimony to the collapse of control over the operation. A stream of such decrees from the royal chancellery was issued throughout the year and in all parts of Spain. Nowhere is there any proof that the crown profited substantially from the expulsions, and the idea of great wealth raked in is pure fiction. It is important, moreover, to make a distinction between public and private assets. Jewish public assets everywhere (of limited extent, and taking the form principally of real estate within the *aljamas*, furnishings of the synagogues, and *censos* or credits belonging to the community) were embargoed by crown commissioners, but in most cases a portion seems to have been handed over to the local municipality to compensate for loss of revenue, so that the crown received only a part, compensation to itself for its own loss of revenues. The question of private assets is more complicated, and may be impossible to resolve even when the requisite research has been done, since it may never be clear what proportion of Jews converted and thus retained their property, or returned and thus received back what had been taken from them. It seems certain that those who returned were given back their property in its entirety.[75] Even where we have details of embargoed goods it is not possible to state the destination of the moneys involved; certainly, private claimants had as much of a right as public, so that the income did not necessarily go to the crown.

A case-study of the role of Jews may be seen in Sardinia, where the island economy inevitably invited participation in sea-going trade.[76] Ruled over directly by Ferdinand the Catholic, and linked administratively with the crown of Aragon, Sardinia in the 1480s had two small Jewish communities, one in Cagliari of about seventy households, and a smaller one in Alghero (Alguer). The Jews suffered no major pressures until the 1480s, and in the prevailing climate of tolerance several, particularly in Alghero, chose to convert when offered the choice in 1492. The preferred professions of the Jews were in money and in small trade, and some participated in sea-going trade thanks to the possibility of using contacts with fellow Jews in Marseille and Trapani. Individual Jews were known to be physicians, administrators and tax collectors. Given the positive but modest role of the community in the economic life of the island, and the fact that some were already conversos and thus able to rise socially, it would appear that emigration in 1492 (the numbers involved are not known) had no perceptible impact.

Conclusion

We may summarize our conclusions as follows. The 'expulsion' decree of March 1492 was, like the subsequent decree of 1502 directed against the Muslims of Castile, not a decree of expulsion: it aimed not to expel but to convert. Both decrees were part of a consistent policy of religious persecution, but did not form part of a programme for religious unification, since the Islamic faith continued to be legally recognized for another quarter of a century in Spain, in the crown of Aragon. The decree of expulsion was opposed by many advisers of the crown, who considered it unjust in principle, just as they considered previous such decrees to have been unjust. The measure formed part of a general drive against Jews in western Europe in the last decades of the fifteenth century and was not peculiar to Spain alone; but there were differences of policy between states, many of which (like the papacy) were happy to allow entry to a limited number of refugees. There were contradictions in the policy of Spain itself, which prohibited Judaism within realms directly subject to the crown (Castile, Aragon and the Balearics, Sicily and Sardinia), but permitted its existence outside (as in Orán), and tolerated its exercise in all the other states of the monarchy (at this period, Naples) where local laws gave Jews the right to exist. Possibly not more than 40,000 to 50,000 Jews were finally expelled from Spain, since many converted or returned to the country after leaving it. The refugees went to neighbouring Christian territories (Portugal, Italy) and to north Africa; there is no evidence of substantial emigration at this date to the eastern Mediterranean, though many undoubtedly went there in the course of the sixteenth century.

The expulsion/conversion decree was largely inspired by the Inquisition, but it had the active support of the king, and there is no firm evidence of other interests being involved. The motive was simply to deprive the converso judaizers of an active religious choice, and the decision was taken only as a last resort, after the failure of a policy, pursued intermittently over ten years, of separation of Jews by confining them to ghettos or by expelling them from select areas. The campaign of fear mounted against converso Christians in the 1480s was concentrated in the south of Spain, but the Inquisition subsequently took it to the north. Persecution of conversos certainly – if we credit the many complaints made – had a dislocating effect on sections of the economy, but the Jewish expulsions had no perceptible economic repercussions, and their fiscal impact was cushioned by the seizure of Jewish property assets in the form of houses or credits.

Time and again in later years the measure of 1492 was seen as a mistake, partly because it seemed to have been unjust, but for the most part because it seemed to initiate a chain of unwise government policies. In the crisis years of the 1620s many felt that the expulsions, when 'there left these realms over 420,000 Jews, some say over 600,000',[77] needed to be undone; and the blurred images of vast emigration and of vast Jewish wealth came together to offer a faint, some would have said desperate, hope of a cure to the ills of the monarchy. It was precisely in these years that members of the Inquisition drew up a report on the Jews, suggesting that 'the remedy is to take steps so that those who have remained in these realms should not leave, and those who have left should return, bringing their money with them, and that all should accept the Catholic faith'.[78] That final clause, which may possibly have been slipped in for appearance's sake, was unfortunately the sticking point on which the children of Israel had, a century and a half before, gone out into the dispersion.

Chapter Four

The Conversos and Their Fate

HAIM BEINART

The 1391 pogroms against the Jews swept through Spain like wildfire. They were followed by conversions to Christianity which lasted for about two decades into the fifteenth century.[1] In 1492 came the expulsion and more conversions, followed by further such conversions in 1497 in Portugal, where many had fled. According to traditional estimates a third of the Jewish population in the Iberian Peninsula converted, while another third died a martyr's death for their faith. Only a third saved itself.

A new kind of population – the conversos – thus came into being, a population which had ceased to be Jewish by faith and in theory should have been assimilated into the Spanish (or Portuguese) Old Christian population. But they had been converted by force or out of despair and they remained an 'in-between' or 'intermediate' society. Abandoning their past life and faith, they had to assimilate overnight into the surrounding Christian society. Their communal institutions had to be dissolved, their ancient religious life abandoned and forgotten. From a Christian point of view there was no way of return. However, the mass conversions did not open Christian society's gates to the converted; they were left to their fate. Neither Christian society in Spain nor the Church created means for their assimilation, doing nothing to teach them its tenets or to accept them as equals in its fold. From a Jewish point of view the act of conversion could be discounted on the principle expressed in the Talmud (Tractate Sanhedrin 44:a): 'A Jew even though he has sinned remains a Jew', which guided not only the generations which in a moment of weakness had converted, but subsequent generations as well. Penitent conversos were accepted back into the fold and allowed to take part in Jewish rites as long as Jews remained in Spain. Conditions changed after their expulsion in 1492, when a Sephardi Diaspora came into being within the existing Jewish one.

In order to survey the converso problem and its development down the centuries, we may divide it into three parts. The first goes from the mass conversion of 1391 to the expulsion from Spain in 1492, taking in also the violent and forced conversion in Portugal of the Jewish refugees from Spain, and that of Portuguese Jewry in 1497. The second period for both Spain and Portugal would end in 1580 when Portugal came under the Spanish crown during the reign of Philip II. During that period the Portuguese National Inquisition was founded. The third period lasted from 1580 to well into the eighteenth century. This is the period of important converso emigrations within the Peninsula and outside it. The Portuguese Inquisition underwent a reform in 1769 and was finally abolished in 1821. The Spanish one was dissolved by Napoleon in 1809, reinstated by Ferdinand VII and finally abolished in 1834.

First period: from the pogroms of 1391 to the expulsion of 1492 and the forced conversion of 1497

At first, the conversos continued to live in their old living quarters, the former *juderías*, often side by side with their former brethren who remained faithful to their religion. These *juderías* were renamed *barrios nuevos* (new quarters or neighbourhoods), a nickname applied to the Jewish Quarters for centuries to come. In time, various government and Church circles realized that the two groups must be separated. The prime mover behind this idea was the Dominican preacher Vicente Ferrer, who propagated it in 1393.[2] The government accepted his ideas and advice, and thus it became an issue in the Valladolid statutes of 1412.[3] However, the separation of living quarters was the only measure taken. In other spheres of life, the conversos were left to fend for themselves, since neither Church nor Christian society had made up their minds about what must be done. Only when Castile and Aragon united under Ferdinand and Isabella (1474) were official steps taken to solve the converso-Jewish problem, as will be seen below.

Two generations were to pass before Old Christian society became aware of the problems the mass conversion had caused. In the early forties of the fifteenth century, the chronicler Diego de Valera mentioned the problem in his work *Espejo de la nobleza y tratado de fidalguia*,[4] but only in 1449 did it become an issue with serious repercussions. On 27 January 1449 Pedro Sarmiento, a personal aide to King John II of Castile and Chief Justice of Appeals in Toledo, seized power in that town. Riots against the conversos broke out, started by a war tax collection against Aragon farmed by converso tax collectors. The riots spread to neighbouring Ciudad Real, an expression of the hatred nurtured by Old Christians against the 'newcomers'. When the riots were quelled, fourteen conversos were put on trial for having usurped public offices which were barred to 'Jews and those who were considered descendants of Jews' ([*a*]*ut iudaei aut hii qui ex iudei*[*s*] *sunt*). According to the ruling of the Fourth Synod of Toledo held in 633 under King Sisenand,[5] and the privilege attributed to and granted by King Alfonso to the town of Toledo, 'no converso of Jewish descent will hold any public office or be a beneficiary in Toledo and its limits, since they are not faithful to their religion and many other reasons mentioned in the privilege'.[6] Those arrested held posts as notaries and *alcaldes* (local judges) in the town, and this was seen as an infringement of the laws of the town and its privileges, and an unlawful penetration into Christian society. They were also accused of having kept the Jewish commandments (Mitswoth) and of leading a Jewish way of life. The sentence passed by the court became known as the Sentencia-Estatuto (Sentence-Law), forbidding any converso to hold an office in Toledo. However, it provoked a controversy, some Church personalities advocating the conversos' absorption into the ranks of Christian society. The Sentencia-Estatuto, in this view, was an affront to their genuine efforts to become true Christians and Spaniards. The dispute clearly reflects the social rift that existed in converso-Christian relations.

From these writings we learn what charges were levelled against the conversos.[7] Of prime importance was the book written by Alonso de Cartagena, Bishop of Burgos, *Defensorium unitatis Christianae*.[8] He was the son of Pablo de Santa Maria, the former Rabbi of Burgos, baptized as an infant by his father, thus a first generation converso. Another author in favour of the conversos was Cardinal Juan de Torquemada, a close adviser to Pope Nicholas V (1447–55) and uncle of Tomas de Torquemada, the future Inquisitor-General of the Spanish National Inquisition. His treatise was named *Tractatus contra madianitas et Ismaelitas*,[9] a title which in itself suggests his attitude. He compared those who persecute the conversos to the Midianites and Ismaelites who pursued the stragglers of Israel during their wanderings in the desert. The conversos are to be identified with the Israelites. Two other memoranda should be noted. One was by Fernán Díaz de Toledo, an adviser (*relator*) to King John II and henchman of Alvaro de Luna, the Condestable of Castile (executed in 1453),[10] the other by the Bishop of Cuenca, Don Lope de Barrientos, the only Old Christian to appear on behalf of the conversos.[11]

Alonso de Cartagena's work contains a practical approach to a solution. For him the Sentencia-Estatuto was a direct offence against Christianity. No doubt he is to some extent his own advocate. The whole issue centred around defining who are 'those who descend from the Jews'. Cartagena rejected the ruling of the Visigothic Synod of 633 as well as the privilege of King Alfonso, and declared that only those conversos who fall back and lapse into their old Jewish ways and practices should rightly be called: 'hii qui ex iudaeis sunt'. According to the Sentencia-Estatuto, he himself was disqualified from being a bishop, and the same would have applied to his father, notorious for his attitude and deeds against his former brethren. (His was not the only case; many other conversos had become priests or found their way into monastic orders.) He presented himself as an example of a converso who should be permitted to hold any office in State and society with jurisdiction over Old Christians.[12] He went further and suggested ways by which a merger between Old Christians and conversos should be carried out, each converso adopting the role of his counterpart in Christian society. Thus rabbis should become priests, merchants merchants, artisans artisans, etc. He stressed that by conversion their ancient Jewish character, as it had been when they were still in their land, was resurrected and they inherited the courage and military skills which they possessed before Christ. Only those who continued in their blindness, i.e. those who continued in their Jewish way of life, should be prevented from holding any offices, titles and benefices.

Juan de Torquemada was deeply offended by the Toledan decrees of Sarmiento. For him they had no legal basis. It was he who influenced Pope Nicholas to promulgate the Bulla '*humani generis enemicus*' against Sarmiento and his followers. The appeal of the Bishop of Cuenca, Don Lope de Barrientos, was in a similar vein. He questioned why those who saw the light in Christianity should be wronged instead of benefiting.[13] He believed in the assimilation of the generations to come.

These apologetic writings bear witness to the gravity of the problem of the converts' absorption into Old Christian society. Socially speaking, it found other forms of expression. One satirist invented a 'privilege' granted by King John II to a Christian nobleman to act and behave like a converso.[14] The king allows the nobleman to cheat and act under false pretences. He can be a priest in order to learn in the confessional the secrets of Christians of good families; lend money on usurious interest; act as a physician and give his patients bad medicine; keep Jewish precepts and customs; act as an adviser to Christians and give them bad advice . . . in short learn Christian secrets in order to destroy Christianity from within. The contents of the 'privilege' must have been known in court circles. This kind of writing does not stand alone. A fictitious 'correspondence' between someone called Chamoro, head of the Jewish community in Toledo, and Yussuf, his counterpart in Constantinople, was widely circulated. Chamoro asks Yussuf's advice about what should be done in these evil days, and Yussuf gives him similar advice: to become lawyers in order to penetrate into Christian society and destroy it from within. The date of this 'correspondence' can be determined as just after the fall of Constantinople to the Turks in 1453, thus purporting to constitute evidence of an international Jewish plot.

This was not the only way to create a negative image of the conversos. A genre of poetry and couplets widespread in court and society and practised by poets in the court of Alfonso V (1416–58) King of Aragon, King John II (1406–54) and Henry IV (1454–74), described the double dealings of the conversos. An anthology of such poetry was compiled by

Juan Alfonso de Baena, a notary in the court of King John II,[15] and by Juan Fernández de Ixar.[16] The chief poet represented in this anthology was Juan Alvarez de Villasandino, himself of converso descent, as indeed was Juan Alfonso de Baena too. Derision and mockery of conversos and their ancestry, their daily behaviour, their living according to Jewish norms, their yearning for Jewish Sabbath dishes, their opportunism, etc., were the most common subjects.

Converso poets wrote verse expressing their own problems and dilemmas. Two deserve a special mention: Rodrigo de Cota and Anton de Montoro, both of whom suffered from the poisoned pens of various Christian writers.[17] Rodrigo de Cota (born between 1430 and 1440 and died after 1505) was a descendant of a renowned converso family from Toledo and related to Diego Arias d'Avila, the treasurer of King Henry IV. A satirical poem on his wedding, in which Jews and conversos took part, ridiculed him and his bride. She was to give birth to a son as big as Goliath the Philistine who would inherit his parents' trade and become a tax collector. Anton de Montoro (1404–*c.*1474) tried very hard to be a true Christian during his lifetime but was always reminded of his ancestry. He appealed to Queen Isabella on behalf of his converso brethren when they were cruelly attacked in 1473 during anti-converso riots in Córdoba, and he bemoaned the fate that befell the conversos of Carmona in 1474. He was satirically advised to compose poetry about how the Adafina (the Jewish Sabbath dish among Spanish Jewry) is prepared and cooked; on no other subject was a Jew (or converso) capable of writing; how could they express high and lofty ideas like love? In his old age, he complained to the Queen that after seventy years as a Christian he was incapable of erasing the Jewish image which had stuck to him.

These kind of writings, poetry, false privileges, forged letters, rumours, etc., all created an image of the converso as a person unworthy to be called Christian. No effort to bring him into the Christian fold would ever be successful. He would always remain a Jew. Hatred of Jews was thus transformed into hatred of conversos.

Of special influence in those days and for a long time was a book written by a Franciscan monk of the Observantine rule, Alonso de Espina, under the title *Fortalitium Fidei* ('The Fortress of Faith'). It was written in 'defence of the Holy faith, for the consolation of believers'.[18] The author stressed how acute the converso-Jewish problem had become, emphasizing the urgent need for a solution. The book, probably written in the late fifties of the fifteenth century, reflects the converso situation of those times, and offered itself as a manual for all those who were to become involved in the search for a solution to what he considered as a malady in Christian life.

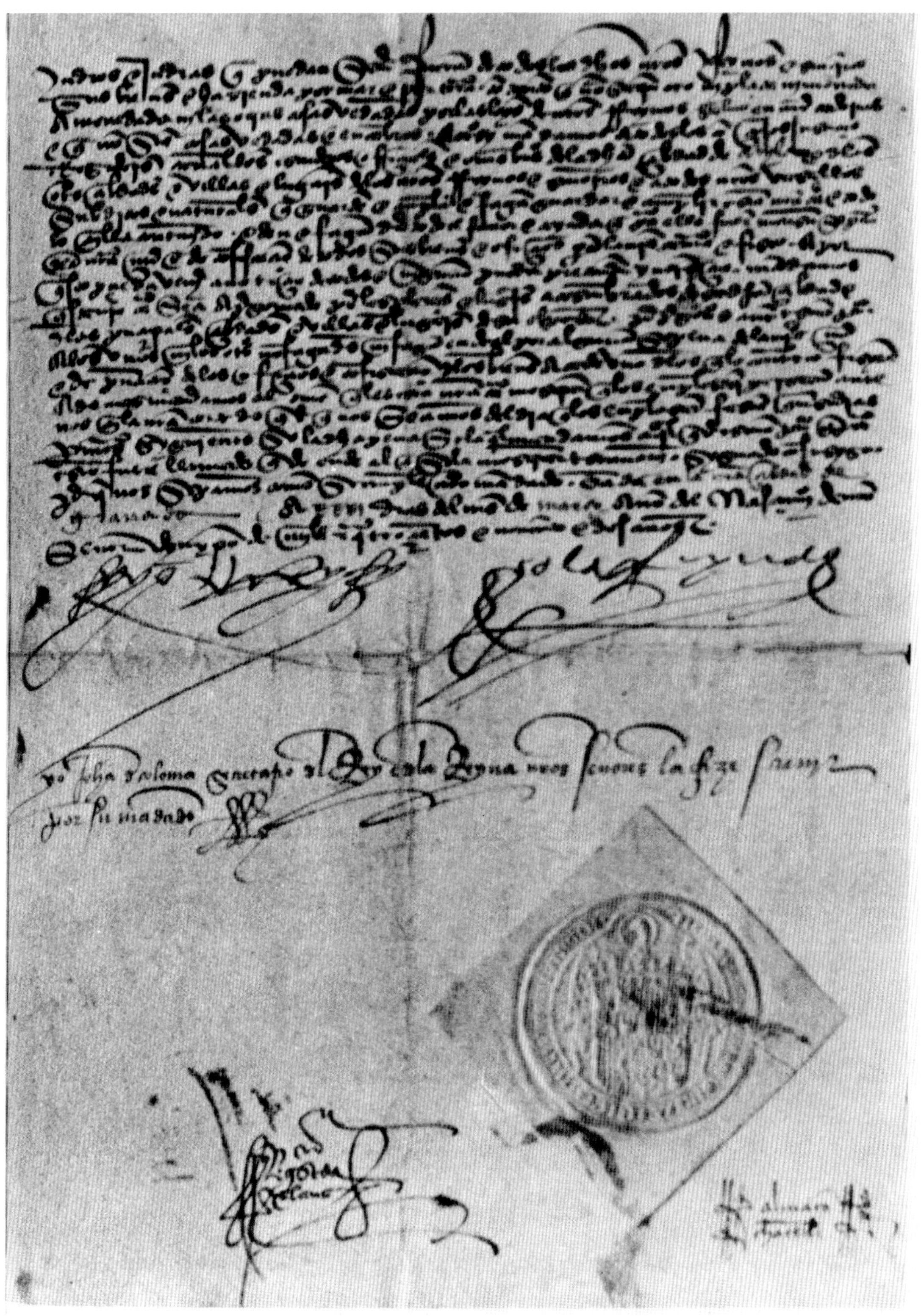

The expulsion order was signed by Ferdinand and Isabella on 31 March 1492 at Granada, shortly after the Catholic Monarchs had entered the city in triumph.

Christians justified their persecution of Jews by circulating and believing stories to their discredit. Their wilful misunderstanding of prophecies announcing Christ was explained as the work of devils. Here (left) hideous demons stop a Jew's ears against the truth and blindfold his eyes. Below: Jews are represented as trying to destroy the eucharistic host by hammering it, slicing it with a sword and boiling it over a fire.

Jews were obliged to wear a badge (right); even distinguished scholars like Rabbi Moses Arragel (see p. 25) are portrayed wearing it.

In formal disputations between Jews and Christians (left), the Jews always lost, further proof of their perversity. Below: a Christian, after a quarrel with a Jew, prayed that the Jew's son should be born with his head turned the wrong way. The baby is taken away from the father, who repents and is baptized (from the Cantigas de Santa María*).*

Overleaf: an auto de fe *at Madrid, 1680. The king and queen sit on a dais at the back. Those condemned, clad in white with tall hats, are most likely to be lapsed conversos.*

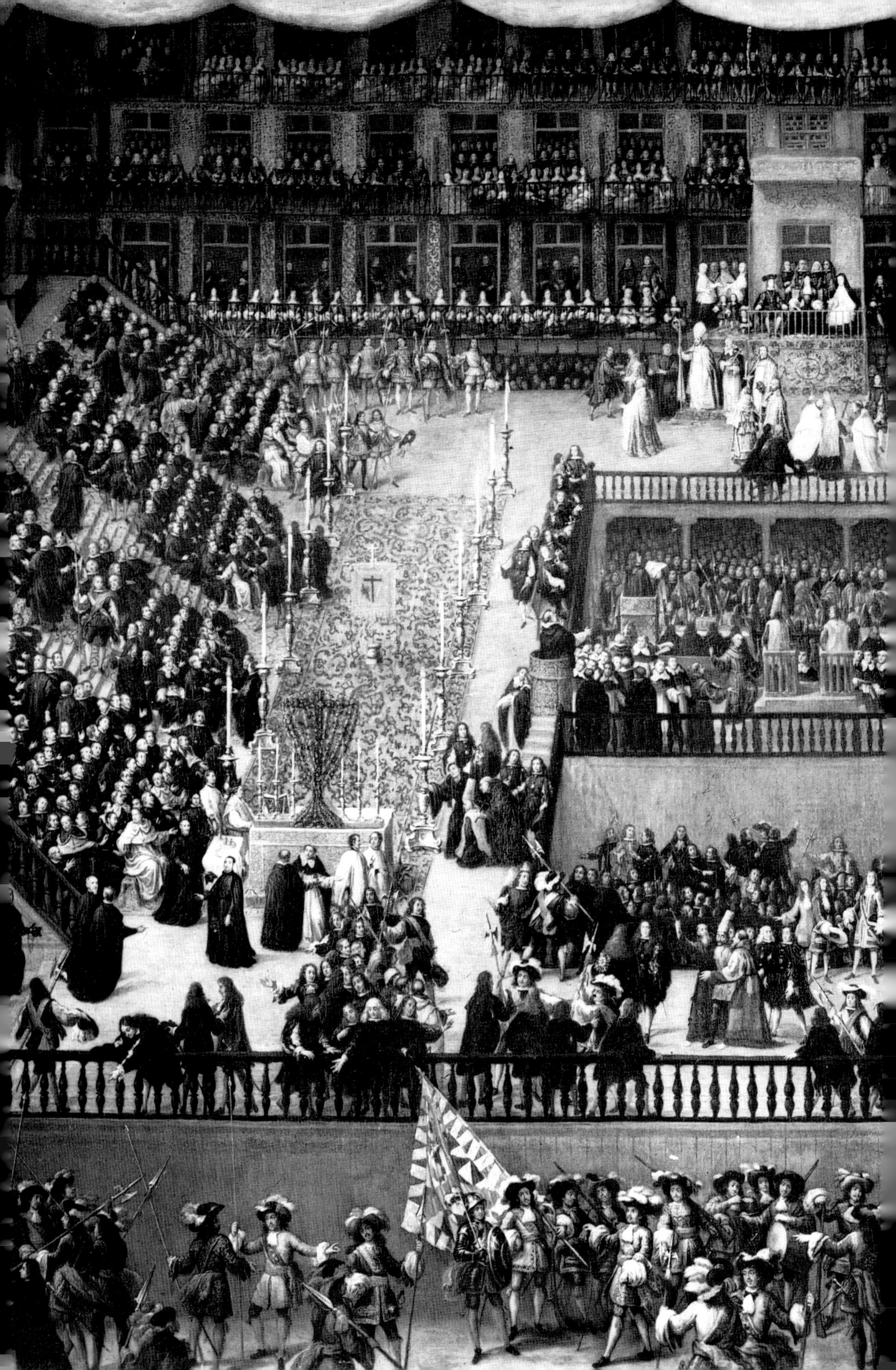

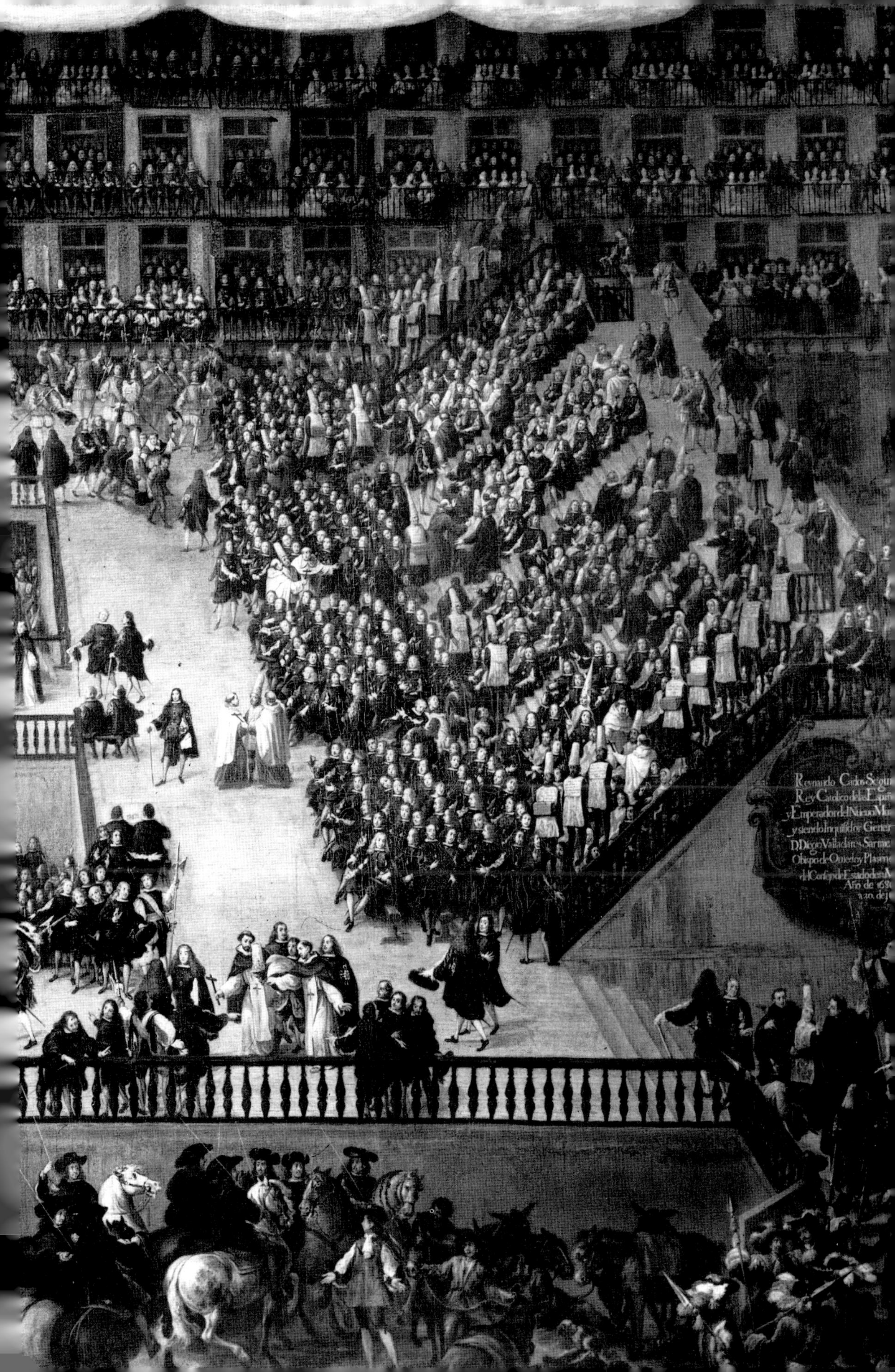
Reynando Carlos
Rey Catolico de las
y Emperador del Nuevo
y siendo Inquisidor
D. Diego Valladares
Obispo de Oviedo y
del Consejo de Estado de su
Año de
a 30. de

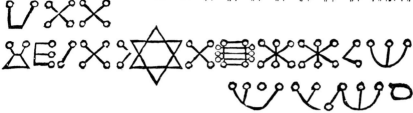

ספר רזיאל

קמיע אחרת לחן ולחסד כתוב על קלף צבי כשר בשמן דחנינה וח סר יהוה בעולם יהי חסדן יהוה על
פב"פ לכשם שהיה עם יוסף הצדיק שנאמר ויהי ה' את יוסף ויט אליו חסד ויתן ארח חנו בעיני כל רואיו
בשם מיכא"ל גבריא"ל רפא"ל אוריא"ל כבשיא"ל יה יה יה יה יה יה יה יה אהיה אהה אהה
אהה אהה יהו יהו יהו יהו יהו יהו יהו יהו יה

קמיע אחרת שלא ישלוט באדם שום כלי זין כתוב בקלף של צבי כשר ותלי בצוארך שמות הקדושים האלו ·
עתריאל ואיאל הורריאל המדריאל שובריאל שובראל עורריאל שוריאל
מיכאל גבריאל הגריאל הגדה אל שובריאל צבחר אתניק צורטק אנקתם פסתם
פספסים דיונסים ליש ועת כקו יתי יהוה אבג יתץ קרע שטן נגד יכש בטר צתג חקב
טנע יגל פזק שקוצית קבצקאל אהמנוניאל ומסתיה הירשתיאל עאנה פיה אלעה
אבג יתץ אלעה עה עה
עזור לפלוני בן פלונית

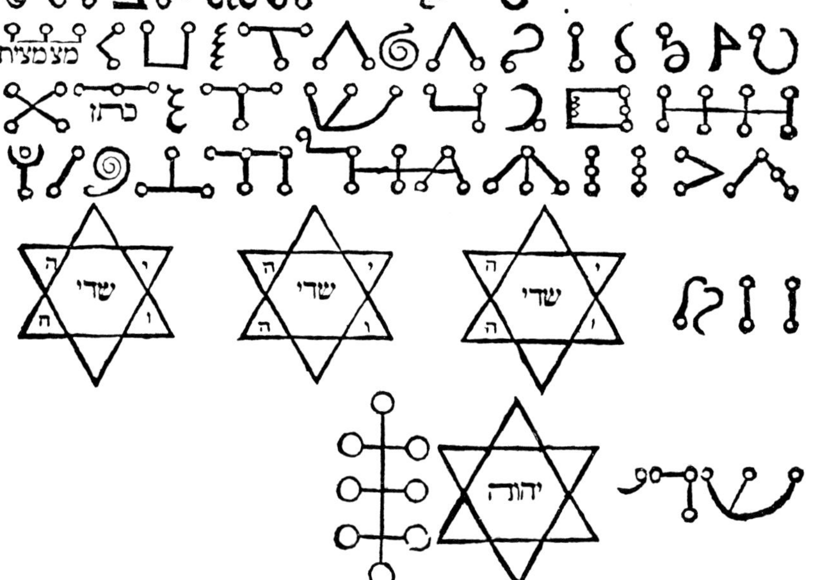

Kabbalah, a body of Jewish mystical lore, flourished particularly after the expulsion. Formerly this was explained by the need to make spiritual sense of the disaster; now it seems more likely to be the effect of cultural cross-fertilization. Above: 'angelic writing' from the Book of Raziel, with Hebrew equivalents, printed in the Netherlands in the 17th century. Right: signature of Shlomo Molkho, a kabbalistic visionary, martyred in 1532.

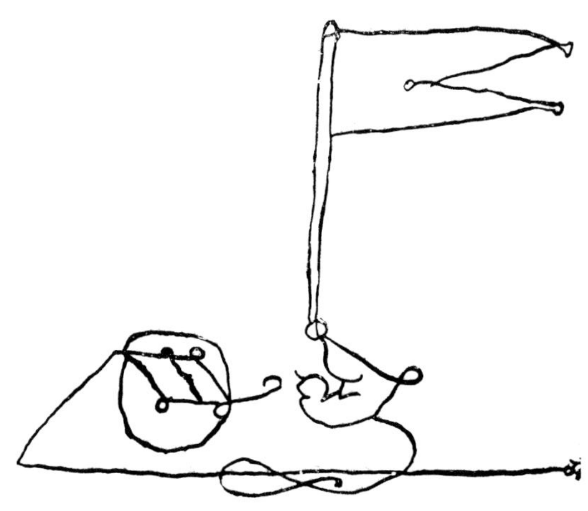

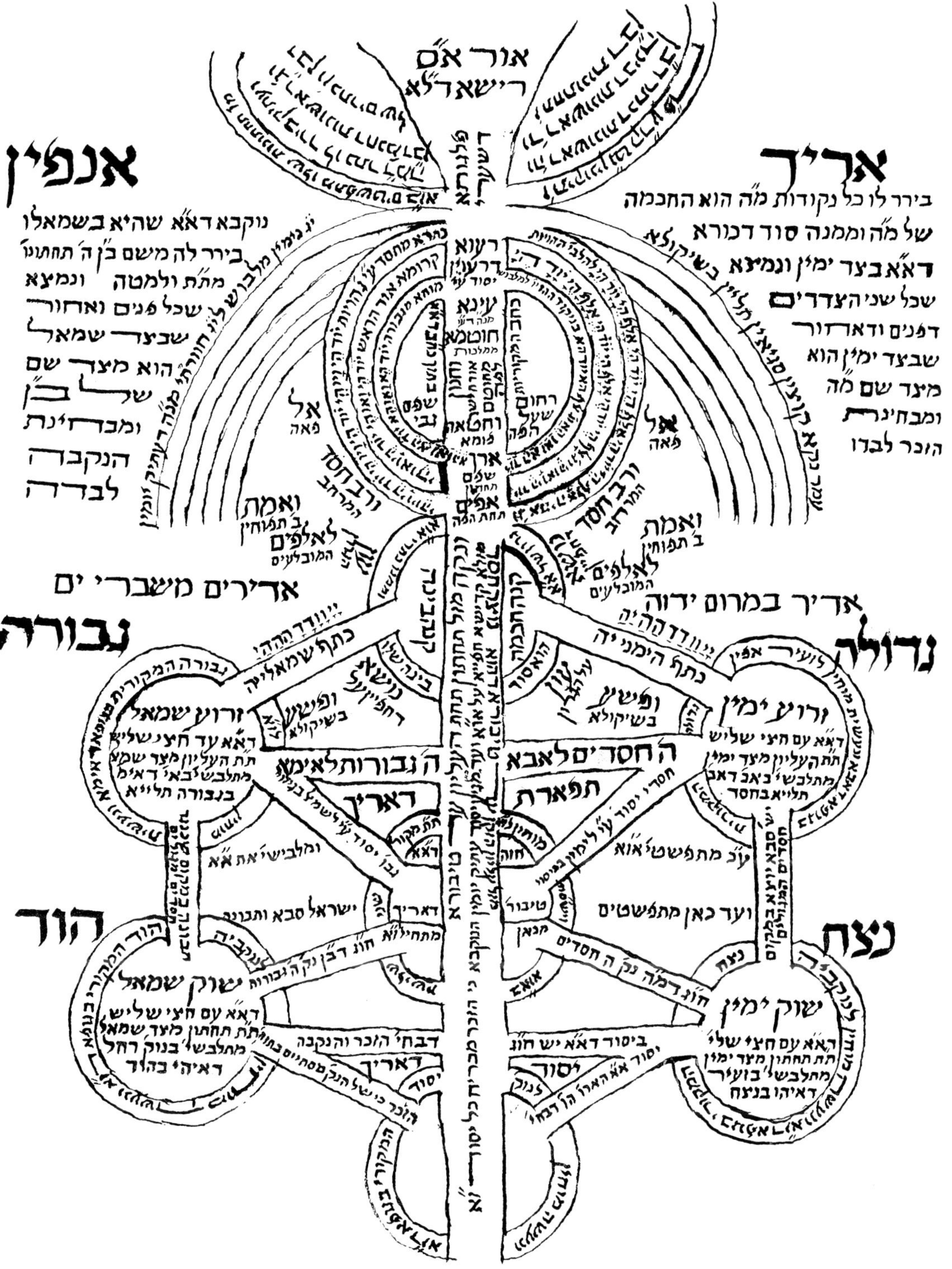

Diagram equating the Sefirot-system with the trunk and limbs of Adam Kadmon*, the celestial archetype of the First Man.*

Goya saw these victims of the Inquisition in Saragossa in 1808. Both are women, about to be burnt for heresy and witchcraft and wearing the paper tunic and hat given to those who had been condemned. Five years later, the Inquisition was abolished, only to be revived in 1823.

The author insists on drastic measures being taken against Jews and conversos alike. He describes all the transgressions of the conversos and their lapses from Christianity, passages which read as if they had been copied from the files of the Inquisition more than twenty years after his book was written. Conversos, the author maintains, adhere to the faith of their ancestors, a thorn in the flesh of Christendom. He describes in detail the precepts of Judaism which they keep, the trickery they use to arrange circumcision for their newborn sons, the way they intermarry in order to avoid being assimilated into Christian society, often with relatives of degrees forbidden by the Church.[19] He attacks educated conversos for their philosophical views, for their search for fraudulent Gospels, for their rejection of the immortality of the soul, quoting a maxim prevalent among them: *En este mundo non me veras malpasar, e en el otro non me veras penar* ('In this world you will not see me suffer, and in the next you will not see me being punished').[20] The observance of the tenets of the Jewish creed and precepts, such as donations of oil to the synagogues; observance of Jewish burial practices; observance of the Sabbath; education of their children in Jewish ways, as well as their transgressions against Christianity, all these are described in his book. The eventual solution is two-fold: the foundation of a Spanish National Inquisition; and the expulsion of the Jews. In the meantime Christians should not live in Jewish neighbourhoods, since through their bad influence the Jews lead good Christians to lapse into Jewish ways. This view is in line with that of Vicente Ferrer, and was to become an issue in the Cortes of Toledo in 1480.

As to the Jews, their problem was to be solved by their total expulsion along the lines of the expulsion of the Jews from England in 1290 and from France in 1306. If England and France could exist without Jews, so could Spain. The religious problem of the conversos would thus be solved, the Inquisition being the remedy for those who judaized.

The foundation of the Spanish National Inquisition and the expulsion of the Jews

The first steps to solve the converso problem were taken by Ferdinand and Isabella in 1477. Shortly after they ascended the throne in 1474, a group of Castilian noblemen and members of military orders rebelled in support of Juana, only daughter of Henry IV, who married her uncle, King Alfonso V of Portugal. Had their rebellion succeeded, Castile and Portugal would have been united under one sceptre already in the seventies of the fifteenth century, instead of Castile becoming united with Aragon. Many conversos of the La Mancha region were involved in this uprising. Only after great efforts was the rebellion quelled. The decisive victory was won at Toro (1475) with the help of the Santa Hermandad.[21]

In order to pacify the country, Ferdinand and Isabella set out to visit various important centres of the kingdom. While they were in Seville in 1477, a certain monk, Alonso de Hojeda, appealed to the crown, describing the state of religion in Andalusia, and requesting that steps be taken to remedy the situation by instituting an Inquisition. An envoy was immediately sent to Rome to receive the blessing of Pope Sixtus IV (1471–84) for the foundation of the Spanish National Inquisition as a national body. Papal permission was granted in 1478, on condition that war was declared against Granada to wipe out of Christian Europe all trace of a Muslim foothold. Two more years elapsed before the appointment of the inquisitors. The Spanish National Inquisition with power of jurisdiction over all Spain came into being in Seville. In 1480 Miguel de Murrillo and Juan de San Martín were given full power, and on 1 January 1481 they issued their first order, against those giving shelter to runaway conversos.

The Spanish National Inquisition, like its forerunner the Papal Inquisition founded by Pope Gregory IX in the thirties of the thirteenth century, was a Church institution whose purpose was to solve a socio-religious problem within the framework of the State.[22] It thus became a tool in the hands of those appointed by the crown. The immediate reason for its foundation was the judaizing of conversos, its objective being to extirpate what was considered by Church and State as a heresy and to put a stop to the conversos' relapse and return to the faith and ways of life of their forefathers. It was vested with power to use drastic measures when investigating, judging and sentencing the culprits. Only the carrying out of the sentences was given to the 'secular arm' of the government, the corregidor of the town.[23] The Church was the only institution with sufficient manpower to organize and carry out this state venture. The Dominican order was charged with the task not only because of its religious mission but also for its zeal and devotion to its aims. Tomas de Torquemada was the ideal person to head this body. It soon became a special council, the *Consejo de la Suprema y General Inquisición*, or in short: *Suprema*. Church and State were united in stating that a person unfaithful to God was a traitor to both; he was to be prosecuted by a special court and punished by the State and Church alike, and his property confiscated for the State's treasury. Confiscation was carried out after trial and condemnation. Inquisition procedure enabled the accused to defend himself, but he did not know who were the witnesses who testified against him. The court accepted any testimony even if based on rumours and hearsay, or given by children against their parents or husband and wife against each other. In theory the accused could be released, sentenced to repent and abjure *de vehementi* or *de levi* and take part in the *auto de fe* procession, imprisoned for any term or for life, ordered to wear the so-called garb of shame, the *sanbenito*, all his life, have his trial suspended while he did penance by pilgrimage to a shrine, reciting certain prayers, etc. or be sentenced to death. The accused was *a priori* guilty and had to prove his innocence, a principle not in compliance with the maxim of Roman Law: *Nemo malus nisi provetur*. To cope with all this became a daily problem for the conversos.[24] In time the Inquisition expanded, becoming a moral police and watchdog of religion as well. A whole nation was placed under the iron grip of an institution that was feared and abhorred. In the end, it failed in its aims after having caused infinite suffering and sorrow. The Inquisition and the State could only explain this failure by blaming Spanish Jewry. In reality it was due to the use of force and physical coercion, which could never achieve more than nominal submission, and to the fact that their attempt to use brainwashing to prove the superiority of Christianity over Judaism was simply not sufficiently effective.

Among the measures taken to solve the converso problem another one should be mentioned. The Cortes convened in Toledo in 1480 ordered the Jews to move out of their *juderías* and settle in other parts of the towns or villages allocated by the municipalities or village councils. They were also forbidden to work in their shops if they were in town centres. Special commissars (*visitadores*) were appointed to supervise the transfer. The Jews were given two years to vacate their living quarters, sell their houses, and buy or construct new ones. The measure was aimed primarily at physical separation, but it was also a means of economic pressure upon those Jews who were weak in heart and incapable of moving to convert. The new locations were small and lay in the worst part of the town. In Avila, for example, the area was situated near the tanneries, in Segovia in the red light district, and Palencia near the town's slaughterhouse. Even so, the separation failed to answer the problem, which was only to be solved with the total expulsion in 1492.[25]

The day-to-day organization of the Spanish National Inquisition was well thought out right from the start. Courts were founded one after the other: Córdoba in 1482, Ciudad Real in 1483,[26] as a forerunner to the main court of Toledo; Saragossa in 1484; the Papal Inquisition of the Kingdom of Aragon was incorporated into the Spanish National Inquisition, and so on.[27]

Nevertheless, as early as 1482 voices were raised publicly against the foundation of the Inquisition.[28] Hernando del Pulgar, then Secretary to Queen Isabella, appealed to the high clergy who headed the Church of Castile requesting their intervention in favour of the conversos. He pleaded for a Christian education for the younger generation of conversos, citing those thousands of boys and girls in Andalusia who never left their homes and thus saw nothing else but their parents' ways. The severe methods of the Inquisition were not achieving their aim. Only through education and the teaching of Catholicism would the conversos become good Christians. Pulgar's hopes lay in the generations to come and their absorption into Christian society. And he was bold enough to suggest that even royalty could err, as in the case of the appointment of Martín de Sepúlveda who was put in charge of the Nodar fortress and then joined the rebel forces who supported the Portuguese – a clear allusion to possible mistakes in appointing inquisitors. He was in favour of an educational system such as that propagated by personalities like Juan de Torquemada, Pablo de Santa María and Alonso de Oropesa, head of the Hieronymite order in Castile.[29] However Pulgar had powerful enemies. His own fidelity to the Christian credo was questioned. He was advised to adhere to the ways of Alonso de Espina.[30] This written polemic ended with Pulgar losing his position as Secretary and being appointed Royal Chronicler. His appeal, a cry for moderation, was the last flicker of light for the conversos. An attempt by the Pope to limit the power of the Inquisition ended in a compromise which added a judge to each court. The Church appointee, to whom the king had to agree, was the '*juez ordinario*' – a fully fledged member of the court. All the inquisitors were members of the Dominican order. Soon exact instructions were given to all courts about how to handle the cases, punishments, etc., which affected the descendants of the condemned conversos.[31]

Converso daily life

Exact figures of those tried by the Inquisition are not available. Shortly after its establishment chronicles tried to evaluate their numbers, stating that up to 1520 some 4000 were burned at the stake in Seville alone and 20,000 reconciled with the Church and accepted back into the fold of the believers. Andrés Bernáldez reckoned about 700 burned in Seville in the years 1481–88 and 5000 reconciled.[32] These figures are probably based on personal impressions. Files were prepared for every accused, but not all have survived. Some of them cover a group of persons accused of the same offence. From the court of Ciudad Real 124 files are extant concerning inhabitants of that town tried in Toledo up to the twenties of the sixteenth century. There was hardly a converso family which did not suffer from the heavy hand of the Inquisition.[33] The conversos represented one third of the population, and the impact of the court was felt everywhere in the town.

In only one place did the conversos take the law into their own hands: Saragossa. On 16 September 1485, while at morning mass Pedro D'Arbues, the appointed inquisitor, was stabbed to death. Not only did this not halt the Inquisition, but on the contrary, it initiated a cruel persecution and many conversos were arrested and sentenced. One of those involved in the plot was a grandson of Jeronimo de Santa Fe (the apostate Yehoshua Halorqui), chief disputant in the Tortosa Disputation (1413–14), which had brought tragedy upon Spanish Jewry. He committed suicide in prison and his remains were burned, the ashes thrown in the river Ebro. Some of the trials went back to events in the past. In Huesca a trial was staged in 1489–90 in which Jews were accused of having twenty years previously accepted back into the fold a converso called Juan de Ciudad, circumcising him with full ceremony. The accusation was based on the fact that to proselytize Christians was a capital crime.

Who were the conversos who were put on trial? We find among them rich people and poor, the educated along with simple people, old and young, men and women, adults and minors. Their only common denominator is their adherence to the faith of their ancestors, and their identification with all that was sacred in Judaism. This united them before the expulsion of the Jews from Spain; after it, their yearning for the past served as the force that bound them. The harsher the persecution, the stauncher they were in their clandestine ways, keeping their Jewishness alive and kindling its fire. In this fight against them, the Inquisition tried first those who were prominent in society then those of lesser standing, then those who could only be tried in absentia, and finally those who were already dead, who were tried posthumously.

The condemned men were burned at the stake as part of the *auto de fe* procession. Those tried in absentia were burned in effigy while the remains of those tried posthumously were exhumed and burned.

The Inquisition defined what it meant by judaizing practices. First and foremost was keeping the precepts personally and joining with Jews in keeping them together. On 10 December 1484 King Ferdinand ordered the rabbis of Aragon to ban all Jews who knew of conversos who kept Mitswoth and did not inform on them to the Inquisition.[34] Jews were forced to inform and testify secretly under a Jewish oath which was to be accepted by the courts. Since the Inquisition had no jurisdiction over Jews they could not be prosecuted as accomplices in judaizing. Rarely did a tried converso guess who had testified against him.[35]

The list of Mitswoth kept by conversos is a long one, whether kept in company with Jews, in groups by themselves or individually. It included daily prayers, gathering for Sabbath prayers and maintaining clandestine meeting places where a converso would act as a reader in the Holy Scriptures or serve as Cantor. Conversos kept Prayer Books, Bibles and Midrashic literature, which they would hide from prying eyes in times of danger, when the *visitador* of the Inquisition made his rounds. They knew the prayers by heart, especially the prayer of Shema Israel, and the Eighteen Benedictions, called 'Amidah'. A favourite prayer was the Prayer of Dreams: *Yo soy tuyo y mis sueños tuyos seran* (I am Thine and my dreams are Thine). Jews would constantly visit converso homes and partake in meals, Grace being said and the table blessed. Such a visit had a double significance. The visitor would instruct those present in Jewish matters, the Jew clearly partaking in kosher food; while the house visited would be enhanced in the eyes of the converso group. From time to time a circumcision ceremony would be carried out by a visiting rabbi or mohel.

Holy days were kept as strictly as possible, especially Yom Kippur by fasting and breaking the fast. A converso monk of the Hieronymite order confessed that he joined the order so that he could keep Mitswoth in seclusion and not be disturbed. On Yom Kippur he would feign illness and stay in bed.[36] Steps were taken to keep the Passover Seder, bake Matsoth (*pan cenceño*), eat Maror (*apio*), buy new dishes, and so on. Sukkoth too was kept. The conversos would leave for the countryside, build huts and stay there during the holy day. So were other holy days celebrated according to their rites and customs. As long as Jews were in Spain they knew the dates. After the expulsion they had their own reckonings, which they passed on to one another. The days of mourning like Tish'a Beav were similarly observed according to Jewish Law and custom.

Conversos would slaughter according to the Jewish rites for their own use; women would slaughter fowls. In keeping this precept they drew suspicion upon themselves by not using the abattoir of the town, as well as by not buying meat from the local butcher. Women would clean the meat and remove the sinew (*sacar la landrecilla*). Burial rites too were kept by burying the deceased in shrouds in virgin soil and keeping the seven days of mourning, abstaining from eating meat and sitting on the floor. On Fridays, before the beginning of the Sabbath, they would put a vessel full of water on the window sill so that the wandering soul could come and cool itself.

Women played a great role in keeping the light of Judaism alive among the conversos. New wicks and fresh oil were put in the lamps and they were cleaned and kept burning till they burned out by themselves. Here the Inquisition sought the intention of the deed, the inner means of keeping this Mitswah. Women would abstain (as did men) from work on the Sabbath, feigning some activity, like holding in their hand a spindle as if they were weaving for the neighbours to see. Women would maintain their personal cleanliness and immerse ritually, change linen and clothing for the Sabbath, and so on. To this should be added the transgression of Christian laws like not going to Mass, not eating pork and so on, all this before the prying eyes of their neighbours.

The conversos had to decide at what age and how their children would be initiated into their secret life and clandestine keeping of Mitswoth. There were methods and ways, but they often provoked an inner crisis in their beliefs and in their relation to their social surroundings. Old Christian society knew how to stigmatize the conversos as a people apart, not worthy to intermarry with them. But the conversos had their own ways of avoiding this. They expressed their rejection of anything

Christianity stood for, denying Christ as an 'invention' of the Church, denying the virginity of Christ's mother, ignoring the Saints, and refusing to make the sign of the Cross, buy holy pictures, and so on.

Although the files of the Inquisition sometimes described an accused as 'rabbi to conversos', none of them actually held this title. But it meant that the person's standing in the community was one of leadership, someone to whom a converso could come for advice and information.[37] A woman could also fulfil this leadership role.[38]

Their inner world was wide in hope and belief. They considered that those who were burned at the stake were martyrs to their God and their faith in Him. For them a special place was reserved in Paradise among the holy who died sanctifying the name of God down the ages.

Converso and anti-Jewish propaganda and its relation to the expulsion

While the campaign against Granada was being planned, further steps were taken in which the Inquisition had its say. In 1482 war against Granada was declared; next year the Inquisition of Andalusia ordered the expulsion of the Jews from the region. One month was given to Jews to leave and disperse throughout Castile.[39] Andalusia was to be the first region without Jews, serving as a testing ground for all Spain. This policy was also implemented in the war with Granada. When the town of Ronda was conquered in 1485 its Jews were taken captive, as were the Jews of Málaga, conquered in 1487. The Jews of Málaga had to redeem themselves by paying 20 million *maravedís*, and till they could collect that sum they were transferred to a special camp in Carmona and their representatives were permitted to collect the funds in Castile, Abraham Senior (or Seneor) and his son-in-law vouching for them. They were released in 1489 and dispersed in Castile.

Ferdinand and Isabella, however, were opposed to local measures being taken against Jews. When in 1486 the town of Valmaseda (in Vizcaya) ordered the Jews to leave, the crown ordered their return.[40] When Tomas de Torquemada ordered the expulsion of the Jews from Saragossa and Albarracín in 1486 Ferdinand intervened and asked for a postponement of six months. This intervention clearly indicates that only in coordination with the crown was such a policy to be carried out.[41] The time was not yet ripe.

Anti-Jewish propaganda continued stressing the close connections between them and the conversos. Two anti-Jewish and anti-converso works were published in 1488. One of them had an introduction by Fernando de Santo Domingo, an inquisitor in Segovia, who was to act as one of the judges in the notorious libel trial of the so-called *El Santo Niño de la Guardia* in 1490–91. The anonymous author of this booklet relates that the inquisitors had ordered Antonio de Avila (also to be connected with the La Guardia trial) and another priest to write it. In his introduction Fernando de Santo Domingo appeals to Tomas de Torquemada to act according to the ways of the mission imposed on the Prophet Jeremiah (1:10): 'See, I have this day set thee over the nations and over the kingdoms, to root out and pull down, to destroy and overthrow, to build and to plant'. The authors raise the question of the Jewish attitude towards the conversos and use for the conversos the term *anuzes* (forced to convert) to mean those who believe in Moses' Law but sometimes are incapable of observing the Mitswoth. The Jews teach them what Jewish Law means. The authors produce a list of the Mitswoth which conversos try to keep, but which, if they cannot keep, they satisfy themselves with the intention, as if they had kept them in their heart. This is one of the early expressions of the idea to 'keep Mitswoth in one's heart', and it became common practice during the sixteenth and seventeenth centuries. The authors justified the measures undertaken by the Inquisition.

The other booklet had a special name: *Libro llamado el Alboraique* (after the name of Mohammed's legendary horse). The conversos are 'Alboraiques', who have a wolf's mouth, human eyes, the ears of a greyhound, the body of an ox, the tail of a snake, and legs hoofed like various animals. Thus symbolically they are credited with possessing the characteristics of these animals: falsehood, cheating, cruelty, laziness, treachery to their religion and desire to spread their venom. The author also presents a list of derogatory terms the conversos use in their daily conversation when referring to what is sacred to Christianity.[42]

Another work which should not be overlooked is a play written by a certain bachiller Trasmiera, inhabitant of Salamanca. It was named *Este es el pleyto de los judíos con el perro de Alua y de burla que les hizo*. The title page also discloses that it was written at the request of a certain gentleman ('*a ruego e pedimiento de un señor*'). The 'hero' is a dog who can differentiate between the smell of a true Christian and that of a Jew, and bites only Jews. The Jews complained to the local judge and presented a series of Jewish witnesses who suffered from the dog's bite. They threaten to appeal to the king if the judge will not do them justice. The dog is tied up in the synagogue so the Jews may savour their victory, but does not stop biting them. Next the Jews demand the burning of the dog, the author using the terminology of the Inquisition. He also mocks the Jewish prayers and describes a circumcision ceremony, but the dog is clever enough to escape and finds refuge in a village, where he becomes the village pet, all the while continuing to smell out the Jews, but does not touch a Christian who disguises himself in Jewish dress (*capa de judería*). When the dog dies a natural death, the villagers mourn him and write out two epitaphs on his tombstone:

Aqui yaze un bravo can	Here lies a brave dog
que nunca comía pan	who never ate bread
salvo hombre o mujer judía	Only a Jew or a Jewess.

and:

Aqui esta un bravo leon	Here lies a brave lion
para judios Pasión	for Jews, a Passion
cuya fama siempre vive	whose fame lives forever.

A satire of this kind was probably performed in the marketplace and held great significance for those present, who would know the people referred to in the play.[43]

But the peak of anti-Jewish and anti-converso propaganda was the staged libel trial of the so-called *Santo Niño de la Guardia*, to which we have already referred, held in Segovia and Avila in the years 1490–91.[44] A group of conversos and Jews, including one called Yuce Franco, were accused of plotting the destruction of Christianity and the Inquisition. It involved black magic worked on the heart of a Christian child from the village of La Guardia, and a host allegedly found in the bag of a wandering converso called Benito García. The body of the child was never found, and the Inquisition did not even bother to search for it. But it was a long and elaborate trial, starting in Astorga, and continuing in Segovia and Avila, where it came under the supervision of Tomas de Torquemada himself. The trial included all the tricks and falsehoods commonly used to demonstrate complicity in plotting the destruction of Christianity. At a certain stage in the questioning of Yuce Franco, the inquisitors even tried to involve Abraham Senior, the Rab de la Corte and chief tax farmer of Castile. But here the investigators realized that they had gone too far and the matter was not pursued. This may have been due to the intervention of the crown which was fully informed of the trial, despite its preoccupation with the last stages of the war with Granada. The trial had no religious basis whatever, but it was important in demonstrating to the world how Jews and conversos were involved in plotting against Christianity. The anti-Christian and anti-Spanish movement among them seemed to have reached its climax. Public opinion was prepared for any moves against Spanish Jewry. A solution had urgently to be found.

By the end of 1491 the war with Granada had come to an end and on 6 January 1492 Ferdinand and Isabella entered the last stronghold of Islam in great pomp and ceremony.[45] Three months later, on 31 March, Ferdinand and Isabella signed the order of expulsion of the Jews from Spain and its possessions, and it was promulgated on 1 May 1492,[46] giving the Jews three months to leave. It stresses in clear terms that the Jews' own guilt was the cause of their expulsion: that is, that their influence on the conversos was preventing the assimilation of the latter into Christian society. Previous attempts to solve the converso problem and local measures which had been taken, including the expulsion of the Jews from Andalusia, had all failed. A total expulsion of the Jews was the only way for the conversos to become true Christians.

The Jews immediately began preparations to leave, as monks and clergy in various towns went from house to house in a final attempt to persuade them to convert. Local authorities assisted in these visits, but few Jews responded. The most prominent convert to Christianity was Abraham Senior. With him converted his son-in-law Rabbi Meir Melamed and part of the family, while other relatives, among them his brother Shlomo Senior, his sister Reina and others left with the expelled. Abraham Senior was baptized on 15 June in Guadalupe, in the favourite pilgrim church of Ferdinand and Isabella. He was given the name of Fernán Nuñez Coronel, his son-in-law that of Fernán Perez Coronel.[47] Both of them were appointed regidors in the city council of Segovia and their descendants fully assimilated into Christian society. Antonio Nuñez Coronel, Senior's grandson, studied theology in Paris and became a Dominican monk. In the twenties of the sixteenth century he was secretary to Alonso Manrique, the Inquisitor-General, and a staunch supporter of Erasmus.[48]

The entire Jewish population left Spain after approximately fifteen hundred years of settlement in the Peninsula. Their departure is an epic saga in itself. Some 200,000 Jews left, of whom 120,000 crossed the border into Portugal. A tax was levied on them as they left Spain and crossed the border, and a special entry payment of eight *cruzados* had to be paid in Portugal. This permitted them a stay of eight months. The border crossings were effected through the towns of Badajoz, Ciudad Rodrigo and Zamora. The rest went by sea to North Africa and eastwards, with Italy and the Ottoman empire as their destinations. Those near the border of Navarre crossed into that state only to be expelled in 1498; others went to the Papal territories in France. 31 July was the last day on which Jews officially left Spanish soil; by the Jewish calendar it was the seventh day of the month of Av 5252.

To connect this with the history of the conversos we must turn to Portugal. Great were the sufferings of those who crossed the Portuguese border; epidemics, deaths and despair were widespread. On 10 November 1492 Ferdinand and Isabella signed an order permitting those who were prepared to convert in Portugal or in a town bordering with Spain and who could produce documentary proof of their conversion to return to their old dwelling places. Their property which they had left behind could be bought back by them at the same price for which they had sold it, plus the value of improvements if there were any or the new owner was to pay to the converted returnee the difference in the property's value.[49] It was an attractive offer, especially for those whose parents had died in Portugal, and many took advantage of this order.

King Manuel, heir to the throne of John II, was betrothed to Isabella, the daughter of Ferdinand and Isabella in 1495. One of the conditions of their marriage was the expulsion of the Jews from Portugal. This union of Spain and Portugal meant that Manuel would become heir to a United Peninsula. On 5 December 1496 an expulsion order, on the same lines as the Spanish one, was issued. This time the Jews were given ten months to leave Portugal.[50] The implementation of this order would have dealt a demographic blow to Portugal, which had a total population of about one million. The order affected some 150,000 inhabitants, among whom were included not only the Jewish refugees from Spain but the autochthonous Jews of Portugal as well. In February 1497 the Jews were ordered to hand over their children up to fourteen years of age for conversion. Soon the age limit was raised to twenty. Many tried to escape, but only a few succeeded because the only possibility was by sea. Children were seized and sent to colonize the island of São Tomé, a Portuguese possession in tropical Africa, where many perished due to the terrible conditions prevailing on the island. On 19 March 1497 a decree was issued ordering all the Jews to gather in a camp in Lisbon where ships were to be made available for their departure. After assembling there they were all taken by force and with great brutality to the baptismal font. Only a handful of renowned rabbis managed to escape this terrible deed, among them R. Abraham Zacut, the famous astronomer and cartographer who had formerly held a chair at the University of Salamanca.[51] On 30 May 1497 King Manuel ordered that the newly baptized were not to be prosecuted for religious transgressions for a period of twenty years. Doctors were permitted to keep their medical books in Hebrew and Arabic. By this order the first cornerstone for the creation of a Portuguese National Inquisition was laid. The whole Peninsula now had to reckon with a converso population, the descendants of Spanish and Portuguese Jews.

Second period: converso life from 1492 and 1497 to 1580 in Spain and Portugal

The expulsion of the Jews from Spain and the calamity which befell the Jews in Portugal left the converso population completely without guidance. Now alone, they had to find ways of maintaining their own identity by commemorating their Jewish past and leading a separate way of life, believing that in time they would return to Judaism. They had to conceal their crypto-Judaism even more closely from the watchful organization of the Inquisition, which was aided by a zealous local population. They had to fight spiritually all that Christian society could offer them and reject all it stood for. Their survival as a people apart was at stake, and in this they found their mission.

At the end of 1499 a 12-year-old converso girl started to prophesy about the coming of the Prophet Elijah, preaching to the conversos and announcing the coming of the Messiah. He was to take the conversos who believed in him to the Promised Land, *la Tierra de Promision*, in her words. Her name was Inés, and she was a daughter of Juan Esteban, a shoemaker and leather tanner and merchant in the village of Herrera del Duque in Extremadura. In her dreams she ascended to Heaven where she met her deceased mother, heard murmuring noises and was told about the glory of the martyred Jews and conversos who dwelt in the presence of the Almighty. An eternity of happiness awaited the conversos, who would be taken to the Promised Land and seven thousand converso brides would find husbands, thus perhaps expressing one of the conversos' concerns about marrying within the Jewish faith. Those who did not believe would remain desolate in one of the seaports. Soon conversos started flocking to her village to see her and hear her prophecies for themselves. Conversos stopped working, dressed in their best clothing in the belief that this was how they would be taken by the Messiah. The movement embraced a great number of towns and villages and more women started to prophesy the coming of the Messiah, saying that Enoch and Elijah had already been seen and that signs had appeared in Heaven to announce the arrival of the Messiah. Conversos would climb to the roof of their houses to look for those signs, believing that it was their own fault if they failed to identify them. The Messiah was to come in March 1500.

One other prophetess deserves special mention: Mari Gómez, who lived in another Extremaduran village, Chillón. In one of her prophecies she mentioned Inés and spoke highly of her. In visions she saw the angels in Heaven and the Prophet Elijah walking hand in hand with the grand-daughter of Jacob. This, it should be stressed, is a Midrash,[52] in which Serach the daughter of Asher and grand-daughter of the Patriarch Jacob is raised to the same category as the Prophet Elijah. According to this Midrash it was Serach who brought the good tidings to Jacob that Joseph was alive in Egypt, and Jacob blessed her saying: 'The lips that told me that Joseph is alive will never taste death'. Thus Serach rose to the category of Elijah, who was taken to Heaven by chariot (2 Kings, 2:11). What is surprising is the knowledge of this Midrash in so remote a village as Chillón. Mari Gómez was the wife of a simple woolcomber. She also prophesized that tables were set in the Promised Land, the bread baked and the Leviathan captured so that the conversos could partake of the banquet which would be held upon the Messiah's arrival. It is also surprising how detailed her knowledge of the Messiah's days was.[53]

The Inquisition acted harshly, extirpating the entire movement to the core. Mari Gómez managed to flee to Portugal, but other adherents were burned. Among them was Inés, who died at the stake in August 1500.[54] However, the Messianic hopes remained alive, to be revived by conversos in later years.

Conversos were forbidden to leave Spain, but in 1503 some of them managed to leave with forged ancestry papers, while others managed to smuggle themselves out. In April 1506 a pogrom broke out against conversos in Lisbon, allegedly after they had been caught celebrating the Passover Seder. Many were killed. After restoring order King Manuel permitted a group of converso survivors to leave the country.[55] Another group managed to leave Spain by purchasing royal permission on 19 June 1512.[56] It was Rodrigo Alvarez de Madrid, an inhabitant of Málaga, who obtained the permit in Burgos, granted by Queen Juana in agreement with her father Ferdinand. Permission was also granted to a group of conversos from Córdoba, Jaén and the Province of León to pay a sum of money to avoid punishment by the Inquisition. They were permitted to go away for a long period and to reside in the Spanish colonies overseas for two years, or to go by land to any other Christian country. This was only the beginning.

Hopes were revived with the arrival of David Hareuveni in Spain and Portugal, sent to Portugal to meet King John III (1521–57) by Pope Clement VII (1523–34). David Hareuveni claimed to be the brother of King Yosef of Khaibar in Arabia. He brought a proposal in his brother's name of an alliance between King Yosef and Christendom against the Turk. At this time Turkey was very favourably disposed towards the Jews and had opened its gates to those expelled from Spain. Uncertain how to react, the Pope gave David Hareuveni a letter to King John of Portugal in the hope that the Portuguese, whose sea voyages embraced East Africa, would be able to judge the seriousness of the proposal. In Spain and Portugal David Hareuveni was followed by crowds of conversos who put their hopes on him. One of his followers was a young converso named Diogo Pires. He circumcised himself, left Portugal and went to Salonica and Safed. Under the name of Shlomo Molkho he then went to Rome as a kabbalist, living among the poor of the city in compliance with the belief that the Messiah would be born in Rome. His prediction of a flood of the city of Rome which came true won him the regard of Pope Clement. Shlomo Molkho was recognized as a saintly person both among the kabbalists in Safed and wherever else he went. He appeared before the Emperor Charles V in Regensburg but he was arrested and brought to Mantua to stand trial before the Inquisition. He died a martyr's death in 1532. Later, David Hareuveni met a similar fate. Arrested and brought to Spain, he was imprisoned by the Inquisition and died in prison in Llerena in 1538.[57]

Early in the twenties of that century efforts were made by King Manuel to establish a National Inquisition in Portugal. Spain was probably exerting pressure in this direction because Portugal had become a land of refuge for conversos fleeing persecution by the Inquisition. King Manuel ordered his ambassador to the Papal Curia, Miguel da Silva, to obtain a

Bull for the establishment of a National Inquisition on the lines of the Spanish one. This was necessary, he argued, because of the influx of refugee conversos who continued their crypto-Jewish way of life. The local authorities were ordered to prepare lists of conversos. However, it was not until the reign of John III (1521–33) that further steps were taken. In 1524 the king ordered Jorge Themudo to institute inquisitorial proceedings. He was assisted by a Castilian converso called Enrique Nuñez, from the Canary Islands. In 1531 another incipient pogrom against conversos was quelled through the influence of the poet Gil Vicente. The king and his wife planned a pilgrimage to Rome for direct talks with Pope Clement, and Bras Neto the Portuguese ambassador, was ordered to arrange the audience. The Pope did not seem to be in any hurry. The days of Sixtus' and Rodrigo Borgia's influence in the Papal Curia were over. However, under pressure from the cardinals, Pope Clement agreed on 17 December 1531 that Diogo da Silva, the father confessor of the king, be appointed Inquisitor-General. But things dragged on and Pope Clement, on second thoughts, considered withdrawing his permission, and on 29 May 1532 he died. His successor Alexander Farnese, elected on 23 October 1533 as Pope Paul III, was more inclined to grant the request since the Portuguese delegates were now being backed by the Emperor Charles V. Converso intermediaries, headed by Duarte de Pas and Diogo Rodrigues Pinto, raised a series of procedural objections, but the Pope was warned that if permission were not granted, King John might well secede from Rome as Henry VIII of England had done. On 23 May 1535 permission was granted and by October the court in Evora had been established. Dom Enrique, the king's brother, was appointed Inquisitor-General.[58] The first converso tried was Ayres Vaz, accused as heretic and astrologer. By 1539 the Portuguese National Inquisition was well established with three courts functioning in Evora, Coimbra and Lisbon, all of them infamous.

A turning point in converso life came with the opening of the French border by King Henri II in August 1550. Conversos were allowed to settle there as merchants, buying property and enjoying all the rights of the French population.[59] The proximity of the territorial border made it possible for conversos fleeing Spain and Portugal to maintain ties with their families who had remained there and to establish business connections supervised from France.

Between April and June 1555 Italy witnessed the burning of 51 conversos in Ancona, which was part of the Papal State. This provoked Doña Gracia Mendes into organizing a boycott of the port. Although her efforts failed, this was the first open reaction to the atrocities. The conversos who found refuge in Venice and its domains in northern Italy were in danger of prosecution, from which many of them suffered. Italy, nevertheless, was in the main a way station and a refuge for them.[60]

During the reign of King Philip II (1556–97) the extent of emigration to Spain by conversos fleeing Portugal grew considerably. Philip's attitude to conversos was extremely negative and he totally distrusted them. He highly favoured the Inquisition's methods and actions, considering himself a defender of Catholicism. He intervened with his cousin the Duke of Savoy, Emmanuel Philibert, putting heavy pressure on him to expel the conversos who settled in his lands. Philip protested against the grant of a special privilege on 4 September 1572, permitting them to settle there and trade with the Levant. The pope, too, became involved in the issue. Finally Emmanuel Philibert ordered a converso expulsion on 27 November 1753. They were granted six months to leave.[61]

Third period: From the union of Spain with Portugal in 1580 until the end of the 17th century

When Spain and Portugal became one kingdom their political bodies still functioned separately and both Inquisitions remained independent, although some collaboration was established. After the defeat of the Spanish Armada in 1588 and the problems it created, Spain suffered another grave crisis, the epidemic of 1598–99. When Philip III (1598–1621) mounted the throne in 1598 the treasury was empty. The Duke of Lerma, his *valido*, or prime minister, came to an agreement with Jorge Rodrigues Solis and Rodrigo d'Andrade, who acted in the name of Portuguese conversos, and after paying 200,000 gold ducats they were permitted to sell their property, to leave the Peninsula, and to return whenever they desired. An amnesty was granted to all conversos who had fled the country and unlawfully sold their property; they were permitted to settle in Portuguese colonies, in India, Brazil, São Tomé, the Cape of Green Hope and elsewhere without leaving a warrant for their return.

By then converso nuclei were to be found in France close to the Spanish border, in St Jean de Luz, Biarritz, Bayonne, Bordeaux and neighbouring Peireorade, La Bastide and even further north in La Rochelle, Rouen and Paris. Officially they were known as Portuguese, but led a Jewish way of life. The permission was an encouragement to a group of conversos headed by Jacob Tirado to leave for the north. They landed in Emden but were advised to continue to Amsterdam, where the first open Jewish community of former conversos was founded between September 1603 and September 1604 under the name of *Beth Ya'acov* (for this and other Jewish congregations in Amsterdam, see chapter 8, p.195f.).

It should not be forgotten that this return to Judaism occurred more than 110 years after the expulsion from Spain, 105 years after the mass conversion in Portugal, and some 210 years after the pogroms and mass conversions of 1391. Thus, after several generations under the Cross, a return to Jewish life became a reality, creating a haven for others to join.

Nevertheless trials of conversos continued in the courts of the Inquisition. On 3 August 1603 Diogo de Asumpcão died a martyr's death in Lisbon. He became an inspiration to Jews and conversos alike, in particular to a converso group at the University of Coimbra, headed by Antonio Homem, himself to be burned at the stake in Coimbra in 1624. In those days another converso, Uriel d'Acosta (born in 1585), managed to leave Portugal. He settled in Hamburg in 1615–16 then moved to Amsterdam. Like some others, he did not find a place for himself in his new surroundings and committed suicide in 1640.

The departure of the conversos from Portugal had repercussions within court circles. The Inquisition advised the annulment of the permission to leave, which in fact happened in 1609, to be confirmed in 1610 and again in 1612. The converso community in Portugal at that time was estimated at 20,000 families.[62] In 1621 a memorandum was presented in the royal council to expel them to Portuguese possessions in Africa (Guinea and Cafraria). They were to be accompanied by priests to educate them in Christian ways, and it was hoped that they would develop these areas for the benefit of the mother country.[63] But converso efforts to leave Portugal continued and on 3 November 1630 a new agreement was reached and a list of ports of embarkation was decided upon: Lisbon, Setubal, Porto, Viana, Faro and Lagosta. Converso ship captains were by then easy to find. They were to play an important role in converso merchant adventures to the New World and the Far East.

In 1624 a contingent of Jews who had formerly been conversos, sailed from Amsterdam to take part in the conquest of the northern provinces of Brazil. One of the ship captains was Esteban de Ares de Fonseca, who returned to Judaism but later repented his deed, returned to Spain and disclosed to the Inquisition the names of those who participated in the expedition.[64] Converso entrepreneurs founded trade missions in the New World, Africa and the Far East, importing and trading spices, sugar, coffee, cocoa beans, slaves, brocades, embroideries and so on. Wherever they went they were followed by the Inquisition which had courts in Mexico City, Lima (Peru), Cartagena de las Indias (Colombia), Brazil, and Goa.

The activity initiated by former conversos in the Low Countries extended to settlement in Hamburg, Altona and Glückstadt, while others were invited and granted a privilege to settle in Zamość (Poland) and even further north. Canariote conversos settled in London, where they were helped by the shipowner Antonio Rodrigues Robles. They settled in England more or less officially in the days of Oliver Cromwell although the petition presented by Menashe ben Israel (formerly Manuel Dias Soeiro; born in Lisbon) had been turned down by Cromwell's Parliament.[65] Among those who settled were Duarte Enriquez Alvarez and the de Francia brothers. They had been tried by the Inquisition in the Canary Islands.

Crypto-Jewish life continued in the Iberian Peninsula. Conversos held various trade monopolies; often an 'Estanquero de tabaco' would also mean a converso. Business enterprises attracted former conversos to return to the Peninsula in an effort to make their fortunes there. Many of them were arrested by the Inquisition and tried. The Inquisition then made great efforts to discover who were their trade associates and '*correspondientes*' as they were called, in order to appropriate their properties.

The Inquisition never ceased its anti-converso and anti-Jewish propaganda and brainwashing. Judaism was considered a 'dead law' (*mortifera ley; ley muerta*). Against this the conversos tried to assert the superiority of Moses' Law in every possible way. In Portugal the conversos were called '*gente de nação*': People of that Nation, a derogatory term although the conversos were proud and honoured to belong to that nation. Preachers would declare in their sermons, especially during *autos de fe* that conversos were nothing but the 'shreds of the synagogue', debased remainders of Judaism.[66] The conversos, they said, continued to reject everything Christianity stood for, hating and resenting everything that Christianity held sacred. A comparison of the expressions used in the fifteenth century with those used later on in the sixteenth and seventeenth centuries shows little change. Education in Jewish ways was harder to achieve in Spain and Portugal, but help came from across the border: books were smuggled in and passed clandestinely among the conversos.[67] Lope de Vera y Alarcón, a youth from an Old Christian family and a candidate for the chair of Hebrew at the University of Salamanca,[68] converted to Judaism and was imprisoned, and while in prison circumcised himself. At his trial he mentioned that he had read the *Itinerary of David Hareuveni* and Leone Ebreo's Spanish translation of his *Dialoghi d'Amore*.[69] More books must have been in circulation.

As keeping the Mitswoth became more difficult, and the idea of observing Mitswoth in the heart became more common, '*Ser observante*' became a lofty aim. Its purpose was identification with the conversos' Jewish ancestry. Queen Esther's deed of not divulging her nationality became a symbol for the conversos,[70] who would fast for three days as she did to commemorate the miraculous deliverance of the Jew from Haman's plot. Former conversos outside the Peninsula who had returned to Judaism and then gone back to Spain and been caught by the Inquisition would sometimes teach other conversos prayers and Mitswoth while in prison. Prison conditions in the seventeenth century were not those of the early days of the Inquisition, and prison guards were bribed to smuggle out information to the families of those on trial, often enabling them to make their escape from Spain.

Trials could drag on for years, the court trying to discover all the family ties of the accused and to trace genealogies as far back as three or four generations. Its files might now contain not only prayers and parts of

Psalms, but also personal supplications, thanksgiving for each day that had passed without being caught by the Inquisition and personal pleas for redemption, asking God for help or for release from a difficult life.[71]

The seventeenth century has its own notable libel trial of a group of conversos who were accused in 1629 of flogging a crucifix and dragging it on the floor on a Friday afternoon or the eve of the Sabbath. It was known as the trial of Cristo de la Paciencia.[72] Forty-four accused, men and women, took part in the *auto de fe* held on 4 July 1632 in Madrid and many of them were burned alive. The accusation itself, of course, was not a seventeenth-century invention.

Notwithstanding this, Jacob Cansino, an agent of the Count-Duke Olivares in Oran, visited Madrid. Although tried by the Inquisition of Murcia in 1628 for possessing tractates of the Talmud in his home in Oran,[73] he negotiated with Olivares in the early thirties about the return of Jews to Spain and their settlement in a ghetto in Madrid near the river Manzanares, where the Jewish community would live as it did in Rome.[74] Nothing came of this, the Inquisition taking strong action against it. Yet in 1638 Cansino printed in Madrid a Spanish translation of Rabbi Moshe Almosnino's book *Extremos y Grandezas de Constantinopla*.

An Inquisition trial which had grave repercussions was that of a group of Mallorcan conversos who tried to escape from the island on an English vessel on 7 March 1688. Their destination was Livorno which in the converso world was considered a second Amsterdam, since once there they could return to the fold of Judaism. They failed in their venture, were caught, tried and burned at the stake.[75]

By the eighteenth century the climax of persecution had passed in the Iberian Peninsula. Conversos continued, however, to seek refuge in Jewish communities in western Europe, the Ottoman empire and the Holy Land. Among those who stayed behind only memories, often remote, of a Jewish ancestry going back to long-forgotten days, remained alive.

As mentioned above, the Inquisition came to an end in Portugal in 1821. In Spain it was abolished by Napoleon in 1809, only to be revived when Ferdinand VII returned and became king. It was finally abolished by Queen Isabella II in 1834.

More than three hundred years of history of a people persecuted for their faith have been summarily related here. Their life embraces sorrow and affliction, hopes for a messianic redemption and steps to take their fate in their own hands, to leave the Iberian Peninsula and find a refuge for themselves and their descendants among their Jewish brethren. Although they lived in fear of being caught for having kept Mitswoth, they believed, that as the saying goes, *Contra la verdad no hay fuerza*: 'There is no power against the truth'.

Chapter Five

Religion, Thought and Attitudes: the Impact of the Expulsion on the Jews

MOSHE IDEL

The expulsion in history: problems of interpretation

It is never easy to define the long-term effects of any event upon the course of cultural history. The special circumstances of the Jews make this problem more difficult than with most other peoples, and if we leave the purely factual realm and enquire about the deeper consequences, it becomes more difficult still, raising as it does the whole nebulous question of the relation between outer events and the inner history of ideas.

The Sephardi communities always remembered the expulsion as crucial both materially and spiritually. The sudden, drastic uprooting of a whole people could not but have a devastating effect, socially, politically and economically. Important centres of learning disintegrated; great spiritual leaders died; and in the new conditions and new environments into which the Jews were thrown, these aspects of their lives – the focus of cultural identity – had to be painfully reconstructed.[1] The experience certainly left an indelible imprint on those who were expelled and on their descendants, expressed more directly in their *belles-lettres*, poems and short biographical or autobiographical writings than in more major speculative works. The Jewish intellectuals, after all, could see things in a larger historical perspective and more easily made themselves at home in their new environment than ordinary people, and were therefore less inclined to indulge in nostalgia, to idealize the past or complain about their fate.

These factors are common to any mass migrations of learned people. Two of those that characterised this one in particular were the atrocities involved in the expulsion and the fact that significant segments of the Jewish population chose to convert and not to leave the Iberian Peninsula. Both must have added to the trauma of those who did leave.

Those written works which attempt to come to terms with the expulsion from a philosophical or religious point of view are extremely diverse. Although most of the refugees underwent roughly similar experiences, their attitudes to them were not necessarily the same. They were differently educated, they belonged to different schools of thought and took life differently. One need not be surprised, either, to find the same fateful events viewed differently in treatises on Talmudic law, in philosophical works, in eschatological and kabbalistic literature (Kabbalah means literally 'reception' and designates the medieval forms of Jewish mysticism) or in poetry. Would it be reasonable to assume, for instance, that the expulsion of the Jews by the Christians from the previously Muslim Granada was conceived in the same way as that of the Jews living in the Christian provinces of Castile, Catalonia and Aragon?

Another complication is the fact that often a feature of Jewish thought and literature that seems at first sight to be a result of the expulsion, proves on closer investigation to be merely a continuation of some earlier development. It so happens that in the decades preceding that event the Jewish community seems to have been rather unproductive, whereas after it we find a period of extraordinary creativity. Consequently it is hard to decide how much older material transmitted orally was being written down for the first time, and how much was actually new. Moreover, some important sources for our understanding of the spiritual life of pre-expulsion Jewry still await detailed examination and may lead to radical revisions of what has been believed hitherto.

On the other hand, even if a certain theme is traditional, the very fact that it is revived at this time must be significant. Is it the result of reverence for the past, or does it carry a new meaning for a new situation?[2] In other words, do changes in Jewish culture after the expulsion reflect revolutionary ideas caused by that event, or are they merely traditional ideas that have found a new application? What is the connection, for example, between the complex system of the Lurianic Kabbalah and the historical conditions that preceded its appearance?

One puzzling feature of the whole subject is the fact that the expulsion, an event of paramount importance in the lives of all those who were expelled, is only rarely mentioned in their literature. Was it unimportant for them, or was it so much a part of their lives that they did not need to allude to it? If a speculative treatise contains no reference, either explicit or implicit, to the expulsion, it seems to me rash to assume that it had a decisive influence on what that treatise contains. Modern historians, however, are reluctant to admit this. The belief that historical events must condition spiritual development is too deeply established to be easily given up.

Last but not least is the question of the effect of the expulsion on non-Sephardi communities. Modern scholars tend to see it as an exceptional event that affected the whole Jewish world.[3] Thus, while the terrible massacres of huge numbers of Askhenazi Jews during the First Crusade remained the concern of that community alone, the Sephardi expulsion is considered to be something different. Reading the literature composed by non-Sephardi authors of the sixteenth century, however, forces one to the conclusion that there was very little interest in the fate of the Sephardim. This does not mean that Italian Jews, for instance, were not ready to assist their Sephardi brethren in time of need: many were helped, especially when the refugees were well-known figures like Isaac Abravanel. But Jewish families in North Africa or Italy, for instance, could not be expected to be traumatized by agonies that they had not experienced. Certainly, the arrival of Sephardim in places where other kinds of Jews were already living was bound to cause problems. The newcomers did not easily assimilate with the older residents. On the contrary, Spanish Jews tended to establish their own synagogues and to maintain their own customs. In some cases, in Rome for example, there were no less than three different synagogues of Sephardi Jews, and only later did they merge because of external *force majeur*.[4] The separatist tendencies of the newcomers are obvious also in North Africa, where the Jews remained even closer to the Sephardi culture than those in Italy. Disputes in matters of Halakhah and customs (*minhag*) had arisen already during the time of the first generation of refugees in Fez, for example. Long after the expulsion, separate Sephardi communities and synagogues were thriving in the East, in several centres in the land of Israel and in Syria.

The idea of a unified Jewish nation at this time is a myth. The expulsion was a tragedy for only one segment of the Jewish people, important as that segment was.

Messianism and eschatology

The aftermath of the expulsion saw a great upsurge of interest in messianic topics among certain of the expelled communities. Modern scholars assume that one was the direct result of the other – a response to their feelings of despair in a hopeless situation. This theory, first formulated by Gershom Scholem[5] and his disciples,[6] has more than any other shaped recent discussions of the subject and therefore deserves detailed examination.

In one of his numerous analyses of messianism and Kabbalah the late Professor Gershom Scholem wrote as follows:

> During one generation, during the forty years after the expulsion from Spain, we find a very deep messianic effervescence and excitement, almost like that in the generations preceding the explosion of Sabbateanism, and this is understandable as an unmediated reaction to the expulsion from Spain. The actual and obvious hope for messianic-political-national redemption is understandable to all . . . From this excitement arose the movements of Shlomo Molkho and [David] ha-Reuveni and some other movements, which are not discussed very much but are

> as interesting as these were. It is easy to understand that the entire religious literature of the first generation after the expulsion is replete with this issue; it is, in its entirety, an actual hope for an immediate redemption.[7]

This far-reaching characterization of the whole religious literature as deeply pervaded by eschatological hope, which came as a reaction to the expulsion, is a consistent theme of Scholem's writings; in his very last summary he asserts that

> with the expulsion, messianism became part of the very core of Kabbalah . . . This combination of mysticism and messianic apocalyptic turned Kabbalah into a historic force of great dynamism.[8]

Nevertheless, a reading of the whole voluminous corpus of literature written by the exiles does not confirm this sweeping and dramatic explanation. There is, certainly, more messianic discussion after the expulsion than before (some of it in still unpublished manuscripts), but on the whole the topic remains marginal. And out of the many thousands of pages written by the kabbalists, it would be difficult to find more than some few hundred devoted especially to this issue.[9] In the vast halakhic literature produced in the Ottoman empire and in the land of Israel, the subject is even further from being central.[10] Sixteenth-century Jewish poetry ignores it, except in some very few and special cases.[11] And with the exception of Isaac Abravanel,[12] Jewish philosophy of this period remained indifferent to eschatology. The exciting messianic document recently published and analyzed by Isaiah Tishby, contains no kabbalistic concepts or terms[13] and few of the documents which explicitly mention the expulsion are fraught with kabbalistic meanings. However, these texts do not form part of larger bodies of literature but reflect the personal views of their authors.

Indeed, the only significant body of literature that may partially substantiate Scholem's contention is Kabbalah itself. As I have already indicated, even in the case of this mystical lore we cannot speak of the dominance of eschatological trends or themes. All the classics of this literature are rather reticent as far as actual and immediate messianic expectations are concerned. The greatest of the kabbalists of the generation of the explusion – Rabbi Meir ibn Gabbai, Rabbi Yehudah Hayyat, Rabbi David ibn Avi Zimra, Rabbi Joseph ibn Zayyah, Rabbi Yehudah Albotini, Rabbi Abraham ben Shlomo Adrutiel and Rabbi Joseph ben Moshe Al-Ashkar – cannot, by any standards, be called messianic. They produced the greatest body of kabbalistic literature and I assume that they also represent the main trend in Sephardi Kabbalah. This is also true of Italian kabbalists writing after the expulsion like Yohanan Alemanno, David Messer Leon or Eliahu Menahem Halfan.

Other kabbalists, it is true, do voice messianic aspirations, but whether they should be automatically related to the expulsion must be questioned. Why, for example, should Rabbi Asher Leimlein of Reutlingen, an Ashkenazi ecstatic kabbalist who entertained messianic hopes and was considered to be a messianic figure at the turn of the fifteenth century, be counted among those who reacted to the expulsion, when he does not even mention it?[14] Those scholars who assert this affinity, like Aeshkoli and Tishby, fail to produce the slightest evidence to prove their claims.[15]

Why, similarly, should David Hareuveni's activity be labelled messianic and not straightforwardly political, as he himself considered it?[16] And why does a rather modest excitement surrounding him, mainly among the conversos in Portugal, constitute a movement?[17] Why, after all, should a Yemenite or Ethiopian Jew, as he probably was, become the representative of the messianic expectations of the Spanish exiles? All these possibilities are, in theory, open and the evidence should be considered impartially. Meanwhile, however, we must suspend judgment. The fact, noted by D. Ruderman, that many of the messianic writings and activities originated in Italy indicates the special nature of the Italian background, where eschatological expectations abounded also among the Christians.[18]

True, among the expelled kabbalists there were a few who did indeed entertain enthusiastic messianic hopes. None of them, it should be emphasized, believed himself to be the Messiah. The most important of them was Rabbi Abraham ben Eliezer ha-Levi, an interesting kabbalist whose writings were rediscovered and explored by Scholem,[19] who presented him as 'typical of a generation of kabbalists in which the apocalyptic abyss yawned'.[20] Ha-Levi, however, was by no means typical. He was one of the great agitators of his generation, who wrote epistles and treatises where actual hopes and messianic computations abound. But it would be very simplistic to believe that all this messianic material emerged under the impact of the expulsion. As he himself acknowledged, his interest in messianic topics went back to his youth in Spain before the expulsion and he mentions an early oneiric consultation related to his desire to know when the Messiah would appear.[21] He was well aware of messianic material stemming from the circle of *Sefer ha-Meshiv* (The Book of the Answering Entity namely God Himself) and was influenced by it.[22] Moreover, the date of the expulsion is not of crucial importance in his messianic computations; he relied more on hopes that the defeats of the Christians in the wars with the Turks were eschatological sign-posts.[23] Thus, even in the case of this 'typical' representative of post-expulsion messianism, the role played by the event of expulsion is marginal.

It should be mentioned that the emigration of the Jews from Christian to Muslim countries was accompanied by ongoing confrontations between these two powers in which the more benevolent Turks were triumphant. Thus the emergence of messianic expectations has to be seen not only as the result of negative factors – repression or despair – but also, and in my view mainly, as what was conceived by the Jews to be a positive historical development: the defeat of Christianity. Hope is as good a catalyst for messianic aspiration as despair.

Scholem assumes that in the first generation after the expulsion there was a certain distance between kabbalistic writings as such and messianic propaganda.[24] How such a statement fits his theories about the infiltration of messianic excitement into all religious literature is unclear. Interesting and influential syntheses of Kabbalah and messianism are well known from the thirteenth century, as the writings of Rabbi Abraham Abulafia[25] and the various layers of the *Zohar* (the mystical commentary on the Bible, composed in Spain between 1275 and 1295, which became the cornerstone of kabbalistic literature) demonstrate.[26] In the generation preceding the expulsion, we find a whole corpus of kabbalistic writings deeply immersed in messianic hopes, expectations and redemptive activities: the writings of the circle of *Sefer ha-Meshiv*.[27] Under its influence, the anonymous *Kaf ha-Qetoret*, and also Abraham ha-Levi,[28] reflect the same combination of interests, as do the extant writings of Rabbi Shlomo Molkho.[29]

Another, and – if proved – perhaps even more important, reverberation of the expulsion is its alleged impact on the kabbalistic thought of Rabbi Isaac ben Solomon Luria Ashkenazi (1534–72), one of the leading kabbalists in Safed. The assumption of Scholem and his school is that Luria, a descendant of an Ashkenazi family, was the person who solved the difficulties of generations of Jews by inventing a new type of Kabbalah.[30] According to his description, the Lurianic Kabbalah was revolutionary and innovative, and expressed a new trend of Kabbalah that was messianic at a deeper level, though not on the surface. This brand of Kabbalah, it is alleged, invested Jewish history, especially the expulsion and the situation of exile, with profound messianic significance. Moreover human action, in this context the performance of the commandments *more kabbalistico*, was considered by Luria and his followers to be fraught with eschatological implications. The assumption of this scholarly theory is that when the specific messianism of the first generations after the expulsion was disappointed, it was translated into a more subtle, inner and long-range type of messianism, which changed the structure of the kabbalistic system of thought.[31] According to Scholem, the central notions of this system, namely *Galut* and *Ge' ulah*, Exile and Redemption, reflect the concerns of the post-expulsion generation.[32]

An outstanding example of such a translation of eschatological concern was attributed to the significance of the Lurianic concept of *Zimzum*, the divine withdrawal or contraction.[33] Again, according to Scholem's view, accepted and disseminated through a long series of scholarly writings, the divine withdrawal or contraction, as the first act which initiates the process of creation, means an 'inner exile' of the innermost stratum of the divinity, the *Ein Sof*, an 'inner exile' of Deity which allegedly reflects, on the metaphysical level, the fate of the people of Israel. However, as Scholem himself admitted in one of his earliest treatments of this topic,[34] this interpretation of the meaning of the *Zimzum* is unsupported by any kabbalistic statement. As Scholem wrote, 'one is tempted to interpret' this term in such a manner, but there is certainly no need to do so, interesting as the suggestion may be. One needs to look very carefully at the thirteenth- and fourteenth-century kabbalistic texts which include the notion of *Zimzum* before attributing to the expulsion a decisive role in shaping kabbalistic theosophy. There, is after all, nothing new in the use of the term *Zimzum* in itself, nor indeed in the concept which looms behind it.[35]

It is surely significant that the most important piece of evidence which could support Scholem's theories – namely a reference to the expulsion – is absent from the whole of the Lurianic Kabbalah.[36] Though messianic elements are indeed present (at least partially because, as already noted by Yehuda Liebes, Luria expanded upon Zoharic messianic topics), we still need detailed analyses in order to substantiate the allegedly strong eschatological underpinning of this kabbalistic system.[37]

Anti-Christian attitudes

Medieval Jews suffered extensively under all the superpowers of the period – Christianity, Islam and the Mongols. In the thirteenth century, however, the Spanish Jews seem to have felt that their plight was more bearable under the Christians than under the Muslims – witness the proverb 'It is better under Edom [Christianity] than under Ishmael [Islam]'.[38] Such security did not last long.

When the Jews were expelled from the Peninsula an intense hostility to Christianity developed. It was nothing new. All the feelings that could not be expressed while they were living among Christians, now – under Muslims – found free utterance. For a hundred years the Jews in Spain had undergone ordeals which included pogroms, forced conversions and expulsions. In 1391, prosperous Jewish communities disappeared, some of their leading figures had to convert, others fled to North Africa. The deterioration of the situation was a fact which contributed to a progressive distancing of the Jewish intelligentsia from their Christian contemporaries and the gradual 'demonization' of Christianity.[39] This process can be clearly demonstrated by a comparison between the anti-Christian expressions used by the anonymous kabbalists who wrote *Sefer ha-Meshiv* or *Sefer ha-Mal'akh ha-Meshiv* (The Book of the Answering Angel) in Spain before the expulsion, and the view of Christianity in the lengthy kabbalistic commentary on the Psalms, *Sefer kaf ha-Qetoret*, written in the Ottoman empire after the expulsion by someone deeply influenced by *Sefer ha-Meshiv*. Though employing several anti-Christian expressions, *Sefer ha-Meshiv* assumes that in the final eschatological battles Christianity will undergo a deep restructuring; its archangel will convert to Judaism and will die, like Messiah ben Joseph, while fighting for the sake of Israel. In *Kaf ha-Qetoret* however, the depth of anti-Christian feeling is undisguised and unconditional.[40]

The dissemination of Kabbalah

Long before the expulsion from Spain, Kabbalah had gradually radiated from this centre to other Jewish communities in Ashkenazi regions – North Africa, the land of Israel, Italy and the Byzantine empire. Here kabbalistic literature developed in different ways, so that in the course of time each region had its own version of Kabbalah. After the fourteenth century, however, most of the classic texts were produced in Spain, where Kabbalah established itself as a significant form of Jewish thought and life among the elite but was not disseminated in larger popular circles. It was the preserve of small educated groups, and part of the curriculum of religious academies, the Yeshivot.[41] But, with the exception of the circle of kabbalists related to *Sefer ha-Meshiv*, the Spanish Kabbalah before the expulsion seems not to have been particularly creative; earlier traditions and texts were transmitted and studied without the feeling that innovation was important or indeed permitted. This conservative attitude is no doubt partly due to the social setting of the Spanish kabbalists who apparently studied in groups led by authoritative leaders.

The dispersion of these groups by the expulsion provoked several types of reaction which, divergent as they may be, worked together towards the dissemination of Kabbalah. The death, conversion to Christianity and dissolution of so many groups of kabbalists must have led scholars to see themselves as the bearers of mystical traditions which might disappear altogether if not committed to writing. This seems to be one of the major reasons for the increase of kabbalistic literature, which was concerned more with the preservation of old ideas than the creation of new ones. Many of the writings in this period are compilations of existing material: e.g. those of Rabbi David ibn Avi Zimra,[42] Rabbi Joseph Al-Ashkar,[43] Yehudah Hayyat's *Minhat Yehudah*, *Sefer Avnei Zikkaron* by Rabbi Abraham Adrutiel[44] and Rabbi Shimeon Lavi's *Ketem Paz*.[45] In some cases I assume that the transition from one place to another necessitated the composition of new writings which would demonstrate the knowledge of the newcomer and its relevance to his new environment.

However, it was the sudden escalation in the status of the *Zohar* which influenced the speculative nature of many of the kabbalistic writings of this generation. The Sephardi kabbalists were clearly under the spell of this book, which had exercised only a modest influence in the fourteenth and fifteenth centuries. A reading of Meir ibn Gabbai, David ibn Avi Zimra, Joseph Al-Ashkar, Shimeon Lavi and Yehudah Hayyat shows that the *Zohar* became the main kabbalistic text. Hayyat states that on the eve of his departure from Spain he had to assemble the different parts of the *Zohar*, which shows that despite the aura of holiness surrounding the book, it was not available in its entirety even to accomplished kabbalists.[46] Evidence from the printing of the *Zohar* corroborates the view that codices of this book were relatively rare. The significance of this fact is that the theurgical-theosophical kind of Kabbalah (theurgy is the assumption of kabbalists that their performance of the commandments with mystical intention has an impact on the divine powers) became dominant among the expelled kabbalists. The printing of the book in 1558 in Italy multiplied copies and contributed considerably to the central role it played from the sixteenth century onwards. The dissemination of this type of Kabbalah, especially in the Ottoman empire and the land of Israel, shaped the later developments of Jewish mysticism.

The expulsion was certainly a tragedy for many of the individual kabbalists. On the other hand, it contributed greatly to the spread of Kabbalah in general and the establishment of the Spanish Kabbalah as the major form of this lore outside Spain.

Spanish Kabbalah at large

The dissemination of Spanish Kabbalah beyond the boundaries of the Iberian Peninsula meant, at the same time, encounters with other types of Kabbalah and other types of culture in general. The arrival of the theurgical-theosophical Kabbalah in Italy, for example, involved a confrontation with the more philosophical, ecstatic, and sometimes, magical understanding of this lore which was already prevalent there.[47] These Italian Jewish kabbalists were in contact with some important figures of the Christian Renaissance.[48] Some of the encounters between Spanish and Italian kabbalists caused tensions, since the Sephardi kabbalists were surprised by the speculative interpretation this lore had undergone in Italy.

The first such encounter took place two or three years before the expulsion, when Rabbi Isaac Mar Hayyim, a Sephardi kabbalist, visited Italy on his way to the land of Israel. He was astonished by the 'rational' interpretation that he met in the circle of Rabbi Isaac of Pisa, probably the Kabbalah of Rabbi Yohanan Alemanno.[49] He condemned this trend, as did his contemporary and fellow refugee, Rabbi Yehudah Hayyat, some four years later.[50] Nevertheless, the Kabbalah of Isaac Mar Hayyim was adopted by an Italian kabbalist, Rabbi David Messer Leon, who interpreted it philosophically – an interesting stroke of irony.[51] The reaction of Hayyat is important for several reasons. He may be considered a true representative of Spanish kabbalists of the time. Deeply steeped in the Zoharic literature and other kabbalistic writings, he fiercely rejected those Spanish and Italian thinkers who did not accept the tenets of the theosophical-theurgical Kabbalah. Among the writings he criticized was also the fourteenth-century commentary of Rabbi Reuven Zarfati on a classic of early Kabbalah, the anonymous *Sefer Ma'arekhet ha-'Elohut*. However, despite the fact that he protested so vehemently against Zarfati's 'faulty' interpretation of the book, Hayyat nevertheless silently incorporated significant passages from the criticized text into his own.[52] In quoting Zarfati, Hayyat was also quoting indirectly the views of Abraham Abulafia, the ecstatic kabbalist whom he strongly opposed in his introduction.[53] This example shows that the expulsion was instrumental in bringing together different types of Kabbalah which would not have met had the Spanish kabbalists remained in their academies in their homeland. Hayyat's Kabbalah is an example of this almost involuntary enrichment.

On the other hand, it is reasonable to assume that a list of 'forbidden' kabbalistic books compiled by Hayyat reflects the library of the above-mentioned Rabbi Yohanan Alemanno, a native of Mantua, where Hayyat composed his book. Hayyat's 'index' was an implicit judgment on the Italian kabbalist. Nevertheless (proof that the influence was mutual), we can discern the impact of Hayyat's book in Alemanno's writings. It seems that the Italian kabbalist was the first author to quote it, while it was still in manuscript.[54] Though Alemanno adapted and modified the Spanish Kabbalah, his encounter with the work of Hayyat added a new dimension to his knowledge of Kabbalah: it brought him closer to the Zoharic literature.

Two other kabbalists, Rabbi Joseph ibn Shraga the Spaniard, and Rabbi Asher Leimlein of Reutlingen, an Ashkenazi author, both living in North Italy at the beginning of the sixteenth century, display an even greater enmity towards each other than the two mentioned above. The controversy between them still awaits a detailed analysis,[55] but it is already clear that one of the reasons for their quarrel was the differences between their kabbalistic backgrounds.[56]

This mutual enrichment through controversy exemplifies the main line Kabbalah took in the sixteenth century as it moved from West to East after the expulsion: encounters, confrontations, frictions, but also syntheses. In the Ottoman empire there was an even more complex encounter between different types of Kabbalah. Abulafia's ecstatic Kabbalah which originated in Spain had already arrived in Byzantium in the thirteenth century. David Messer Leon, coming from Italy with his philosophical version of Kabbalah, brought with him the views of the Sephardi kabbalist Isaac Mar Hayyim. In the former Byzantine region there was a peculiar type of Kabbalah focused on more radical ideas, some of them antinomian, or at least potentially antinomian, such as those expressed in *Sefer ha-Temunah* and *Sefer ha-Qanah veha-Peliah*.[57] From Spain arrived the more moderate form of Kabbalah represented by the writings of Rabbi Meir ben Yehezqel ibn Gabbai, another main representative of Spanish Kabbalah,[58] and one or more kabbalists from the circle of *Sefer ha-Meshiv*.[59] The more visionary form of Kabbalah, as represented by *Sefer Kaf ha-Qetoret*, the later *Sefer Galiya Raza*, Rabbi Joseph Caro and probably others, also enriched the kabbalistic tradition of this centre.[60]

The most influential encounter took place in the two centres of Kabbalah in the land of Israel: Jerusalem and Safed. A descendant of a Portuguese family, Rabbi Yehudah Albotini, was apparently the first Sephardi kabbalist to adopt the ecstatic Kabbalah of Abraham Abulafia and his followers, when he composed one of the most systematic expositions of this type of Kabbalah, *Sefer Sullam ha-'Aliyah*.[61] What should be emphasized is that before the expulsion, Abulafia's Kabbalah was rejected by all the Spanish kabbalists. Hayyat, when he arrived in Italy, dismissed it with contempt. However, in Jerusalem, we now find a Sephardi adopting this rejected Kabbalah and creating work of his own in the same vein. Unquestionably, it was only because of the disappearance of the Iberian centre, with its centralist authorities, that the Sephardi kabbalists could free themselves from the inhibitions of two centuries. The Jerusalem centre, active for some few decades in the first part of the sixteenth century, included also three other outstanding kabbalists: Rabbi Abraham ben Eliezer ha-Levi, the messianic agitator mentioned above, Rabbi David ben Avi Zimra – for a few years – and Rabbi Joseph ibn Zayyah. All of them seem to have been of Sephardi origin and their contribution to the establishment of the Kabbalah as a major spiritual activity in the land of Israel still awaits detailed examination.

However, it was in Safed, the small Galilean town, that Kabbalah reached one of its most important peaks.[62] The encounters between some outstanding Sephardi kabbalists, Rabbi Shelomo ha-Levi Alqabetz, Rabbi Joseph Caro, Rabbi Moses Cordovero, Shlomo le-Veit Turriel and Rabbi Yehudah Hallewah, opened the way for an extraordinarily creative period. There is no doubt, in my opinion, that it was the opposite of that homogenous atmosphere characteristic of Spain since the fourteenth century that catalyzed the rapid development of Kabbalah in Safed. The coexistence of Ashkenazim, Italians and other nationalities induced an exchange of ideas and traditions that was very productive also for the Spanish kabbalists. Moreover, the probable existence of ecstatic kabbalistic books and traditions that had been current in this region since the end of the thirteenth century fertilized the Spanish Kabbalah in a significant manner; Cordovero and his disciples practised ecstatic techniques in order to achieve prophecy and indeed, according to the evidence of an Italian kabbalist, actually succeeded.[63] Cordovero himself regarded the ecstatic Kabbalah as a very important one and it was well represented in the most authoritative *summa* of pre-Lurianic Kabbalah, his *Pardes Rimmonim*.[64]

It seems that only in North Africa did the Sephardi Kabbalah retain its 'pristine' forms, since no major cultural force was combined with the texts that the exiles brought with them.[65]

Jewish philosophy

Jewish philosophy, like Kabbalah, benefited from the transition from one geographical area to another. The fifteenth century had been a conservative period in religious thought. Criticism and commentary on Aristotle, and by implication Maimonides, was combined with a concentrated effort to elucidate the dogmas of Judaism.[66] Philosophy, though only rarely creative from the point of view of ideas – the only significant exception being Rabbi Hasdai Crescas[67] – was still a major form of activity among the Jewish elite. But the two main figures to continue the Jewish philosophical tradition both derive part of their significance from contact with a new environment.

The first was Rabbi Isaac Abravanel. Though he wrote most of his works in Italy, he must be counted as the last outstanding medieval philosopher of Spanish Jewry. Although his thought is to be understood as part of the Hispanic speculative tradition, which was, as mentioned above, mainly conservative, he was relatively open to the new speculative literature being translated in Florence. Abravanel quotes, for example, hermetic writings in a manner that makes it obvious that he had read them in Italy.[68] Both his openness towards ancient historical traditions (e.g. Josephus) and his positive attitude to learned magic, betray a cultural orientation characteristic of the Italian Renaissance.[69] However, the main thrust of Abravanel's philosophy is exegetical and eschatological, and he particularly emphasizes messianic themes. Indeed, the importance of the expulsion in his oeuvre is undeniable.[70] This connection comes through again in the fact that Abravanel, more than any other Jewish philosopher of medieval Spain, pays special attention to political philosophy. However, even in the case of an apocalyptic writer like Abravanel, scholars have easily discerned traces of influences of much earlier astrological-messianic discussions, like those of the twelfth-century thinker Rabbi Abraham bar Hiyya.[71] It should be mentioned, however, that Abravanel was by no means typical of Jewish philosophical thought. The writer who was, philosophically speaking, closest to him, also an exile – Rabbi Isaac Arama, a famous preacher and one of the sources of Abravanel's thought[72] – explicitly opposed any messianic speculations, especially attempts to calculate the date of the Messiah's advent, believing that the redemption would come suddenly, as the result of divine intervention.[73] Jewish philosophy was rather indifferent to messianic eschatology, a fact demonstrated even by the nature of the philosophy of Abravanel's son.

This son, Yehudah Abravanel, better known as Leone Ebreo,[74] is the second great post-expulsion philosopher. Though he mastered Hebrew and Jewish sources, he was ambitious of finding a larger, i.e. Gentile, audience and therefore wrote in Spanish or Italian. His famous *Dialoghi d'Amore* was not only a best-seller of Renaissance thought, but also a piece of speculative literature that combined knowledge of general philosophy, Arabic and Christian, with a proud attitude toward the speculative legacy of medieval Judaism. His own family circumstances – he was himself expelled from Spain and his son, a small child, was detained there by the Spaniards – seem not to have influenced his thought in any discernible way.

The expulsion brought together Jewish medieval classical philosophy and general Renaissance thought, an achievement that would have been impossible if the Jews had remained in Spain. The openness of the Italian intellectual ambience contributed to the emergence of one of the classics of Jewish thought.

Inner exile

As we have seen in Chapter 4, one of the most dreadful consequences of the decision to expel the Jews from the Iberian Peninsula was to augment the existing numbers of conversos. Faced with the depressing alternative of either leaving the Peninsula or converting to Christianity, many of the Jews preferred water to wandering. The extent of the conversion, like the question of the numbers of Jews who left the Peninsula, is still a matter of debate between historians. What is certain, however, is that after the expulsion the conversos became a major problem for both Jews and Christians. For Jews, who left family members or friends in Spain and Portugal, the conversion of their relatives remained a painful wound; even so, there is no doubt that contact was maintained.

The Christians, through the Spanish (and later also the Portuguese) Inquisition, tried to ensure the complete divorce of the neophytes from their former religion. And since conversion was only rarely a *bona fide* act, the conversos secretly adhering to Jewish practices, the Inquisition had an excellent *raison d'être*. Instead of the external exile of their brethren, the conversos had to enter an inner exile, usually just as terrifying and fateful as that embarked upon by the refugees.

The tensions of this inner exile, this double life forced upon them through fear, created a state of mind that encouraged messianism. Indeed, the most intensive form of messianic expectation is found not in the Sephardi Diaspora, but in the Iberian Peninsula itself. Recent studies by Haim Beinart have revealed the fervour of messianic hopes and their social dimensions.[75] Though probably ignorant of many of the higher achievements of Jewish culture, the conversos cultivated an intense mood of expectation and reacted dramatically whenever a rumour surfaced relating to the possibility of redemption. An interesting illustration of the depth of these expectations is the way David Hareuveni was seen by the Portuguese conversos. His three-year stay in Portugal and negotiations with the king, Juan III, excited the imagination of many of the conversos, who were eager to project on him, perhaps even against his will, a messianic image and an imaginary eschatological mission.[76] This is particularly evident in the case of Diogo Pirez, who converted to Judaism as Shlomo Molkho in the belief that both he and Hareuveni had been given a messianic mission.[77] Messianic expectations were far stronger among conversos and persons related to them than among the Jews who left the Peninsula and had the opportunity to rebuild their religious life abroad.

However, it seems that with the passage of time, the conversos began to adapt to their new situation. Messianic expectations subsided and some of them began to interpret Judaism in a rather rationalistic manner. In the seventeenth century, cultured conversos who returned to Judaism preferred a philosophical understanding of their religion to a mystical one. Though some of them, for instance Rabbi Ya'aqov Hayyim Zemah[78] and later Abraham Michael Cardoso,[79] made important mystical contributions, it was the philosophical mode of thought that primarily attracted them. Uneasy about some aspects of the oral law, some former conversos developed a religious approach that is reminiscent of that of the Karaites, as some of their critiques have already intimated.[80] On the other hand, the critical attitude to the oral law also apparently encouraged a sympathetic reception of the messianic Sabbateanism, with its strongly antinomian overtones.[81]

Conclusion: rebuilding against despair

There can be no doubt about the tragedies that affected thousands of individuals during the two expulsions. Nevertheless, as happens from time to time, the reactions and adaptations and tensions did also have a positive side, which in the new cultural environment contributed to the creation of major writings in Kabbalah, philosophy and Halakhah. These were, in my opinion, basically not the result of despair, but of a sustained effort by the Sephardi Jews to rebuild their religious and social life in new centres. Certainly, the large literature produced by the Sephardi thinkers contributed substantively to the strength of Jewish culture in general in the following decades. In the above discussions, instead of putting the usual emphasis on trauma, despair and hope, I opted for the importance of the cultural encounters which the expulsions from the Iberian Peninsula made possible. The widely accepted assumption that the mystical interpretation of the event of expulsion by kabbalists was the major response to the crisis, does not explain the surge of creativity that came in its aftermath.

In my view, despair can paralyse much more than energize or invigorate and, though I cannot deny the obvious fact that there was despair among the exiles, I wonder whether it was those who despaired who contributed to the rebuilding of Jewish life in their new centres.

In the conventional view, the kabbalists, indeed the Jews in general, are seen as merely contemplating events, passive pieces in a game that they have to explain in order to make sense of it for those who would otherwise utterly despair – the explanation consisting of a new theological interpretation. I should like to put forward another reading of the situation. In my reconstruction of events the protagonists are not those who tried to overcome their despair by inventing new mystical theories, but rather those who were able to bear the vicissitudes of history and rebuild their lives in other countries or continents on the basis of continuity of and devotion to the major forms of traditional Jewish life. Sixteenth-century Jewish thought is only marginally a dialogue with a history which provoked a crisis of identity; it is much more an effort, more comprehensive than any earlier ones, to strengthen Jewish religion by exploring the spiritual implications of its traditions. The expulsion led to confrontations between different versions of Jewish life and thought, resulting in both frictions and syntheses which would have been almost unthinkable in Spain and Portugal.

Although I have proposed these general lines as an alternative to Scholem's general explanatory paradigm, I should still like to issue a warning against investing such generic concepts as 'Kabbalah', 'Spanish Jewry' and 'rebuilding' with too great a significance. I prefer less sweeping, more diversified answers to such large-scale processes, which take into account the particularities of different groups and circumstances. Scholem's thesis focuses on a crisis or a rupture in Jewish history of which the messianic-kabbalistic interpretation is a result.[82] The fact that this crisis or rupture in Jewish religious life is not seen as central in the early sixteenth-century documents, and sometimes not even mentioned in the later literature, seems not to bother those who support this theory. In Scholem's model of the history of religion, 'the Kabbalah of the sixteenth century is the movement where Judaism found the religious answer for the expulsion from Spain'.[83]

My analysis assumes that cultural developments should be studied as far as possible through the documents. The huge body of literature produced by the exiles can be described in terms of the general anthropology of religion. Spanish Jewry, especially in its mystical works but also in its extensive halakhic treatises, opted in the aftermath of the expulsion to move 'in the direction of more differentiated, comprehensive and . . . more rationalized formulations';[84] Judaism was understood as the 'general order of existence', to use C. Geertz's phrase.[85] Moreover, this more comprehensive order is to be sought not only in kabbalistic books but also in the halakhic literature that abounded in this period. No less than the all-embracing Lurianic Kabbalah, the comprehensive halakhic *summa* of Luria's compatriot Rabbi Joseph Caro exemplifies this tendency to offer broad systematic explanations of the various aspects of the Jewish tradition. To put it another way: Scholem saw the solution to the terrible rupture with the past in an eschatological improvement in the future, and focused therefore upon the kabbalistic literature as the core of the response of 'Judaism'. The present is a merely instrumental pause. But it is possible, on the other hand, to see the answer to the destruction of the past in a more vigorous and moral attitude to the present. Indeed, I see the importance of the renewal of Kabbalah in the sixteenth century not so much in its theological innovations, which seem to me to be relatively few, or in its eschatological historiosophy, but precisely in a strong and detailed interpretation of the Jewish *modus vivendi*, both in matters of Kabbalah – Isaac Luria's emphasis on precise behaviour – and in matters of Halakhah, in the composition of the most detailed halakhic compendium of the period, Rabbi Joseph Caro's *Shulhan Arukh*. Instead of resorting unilaterally to destabilizing factors as crucial for the understanding of the processes of the period, I wonder why we do not pay more attention to the impressive flourishing of the halakhic literature and to the conservative interpretation of Jewish ritual by Kabbalah. In newly established centres it would be counter-productive to encourage messianic movements. Indeed, in the great centres of Sephardi refugees – North Africa and the Ottoman empire – messianic propaganda was not so evident or so successful as it was, for example, in Italy, where both Italian and Ashkenazi Jews were more attracted to messianic figures than were the Sephardim themselves.

The event of expulsion served as an excuse for Scholem to argue that history had invaded kabbalistic thought under the guise of mystical historiosophy and messianism and, later on, in the Sabbatean movement, Jewish mysticism was portrayed by him as invading Jewish history.[86] This move of Jewish mysticism to the centre of historical events is a unique case in the history of mysticism in general and it assumes, as Scholem has explicitly indicated, the uniqueness of Jewish mysticism as a literature rich in historical symbolism.[87] However, my feeling is that the overemphasis on the role of Kabbalah in general and of the eschatological aspect of the theology of history in particular, has created a rather biased image of what happened in the spiritual life of the sixteenth-century Jews.[88] I have preferred to examine closely evidence that has so far been neglected by most modern scholars, such as pre-expulsion messianism, the whole range of post-expulsion kabbalistic literature (instead of only a very selective part of it which emphasizes the, in my opinion, marginal role of messianism) and, last but not least, to describe the whole period in a more subtle way, taking into account the balance between different forms of Jewish expression.

Chapter Six

Spain after the Expulsion

JOHN LYNCH

The Inquisition and its work

Spain specialized in expulsions. The expulsion of the Jews in 1492, the expulsion of the moriscos in 1609, the expulsion of the Jesuits in 1767. Few countries have punctuated their history with such uncompromising decisions, each variously motivated, secretly planned, and effectively executed, and each a sign of the continuing intolerance of the Spanish state, its enduring absolutism, and, when the cause was urgent, its compelling efficiency. Religion was not the only, or even the prime motive. The moriscos were hybrids but not heretics. The Jesuits were nothing if not Catholics. As for the Jews, no doubt they were the victims of anti-semitism of a religious kind but this was not the only reason for their expulsion, for Jews could live in Italy, France and other Catholic countries, free, or relatively free, of the extremes of persecution prevalent in Spain. Evidently further reasons and special conditions operated in the Peninsula.

The Jesuit historian, Juan de Mariana, writing in the reign of Philip II, observed that religion and ecclesiastical power were 'often a cloak used by princes to cover their actions and even to disguise great deceits', and that 'nothing has more power to move the people than the pretence of religion, behind which great deceptions are concealed'.[1] In the name of religion, he argued, strange things were done, such as the pressure on Jews in Portugal in recent decades to accept baptism: 'the extraordinary decision to force men to become Christians does not conform to Christian laws and custom, nor is it right to deprive them of the freedom which God gave them'.[2] As for the practices of the Inquisition, he thought, 'what appeared most strange was that children suffered for the sins of their parents'. Mariana was an eloquent if lone witness against intolerance, one who knew it from experience; he had learnt, too, not to take policy statements at their face value.

While economic motives were not decisive in the expulsion, economic calculations were certainly present. The Jews in medieval Spain filled a significant role in finance, commerce, and in the retail side of a number of industries. Yet they were expelled without severe economic disruption.[3] Expulsion had been preceded by the pogroms of the years 1391–1415, when many Jews decided that conversion was preferable to death and then eased their way back into finance, revenue collection, and the bureaucracy, and even procured preferment in the Church. For many Jews, and perhaps for the crown itself, the decree of expulsion was a further inducement to conversion, and one which enabled Spain to retain Jewish entrepreneurial skills. If there was a gap, this was soon filled by Italian and other merchants. The crown calculated between the demands of religion to expel and the needs of the economy to retain, expelling a minority and forcibly converting the rest. In the following two centuries orthodoxy was balanced against solvency: when the government needed revenue, the Jews were more tolerated. Thus the decree of expulsion was a scourge but not a final solution, either for the Jews or for Spain. Iberian Jews entered a time of migrations, changes of religion, economic adversities, and family dramas, but they survived. The first reaction was to negotiate their way out of the worst consequences of expulsion, helped by experience and contacts in high places. The crown itself was prepared to compromise. On 10 November 1492, within months of the expulsion, it issued a '*carta de amparo*' to all Jews who wished to return from Portugal 'first having converted to Christians', and ordering the restitution to them of goods sold on expulsion.[4] So a return movement began, with the encouragement of the crown and under favourable conditions. Conversion in itself, however, was not a guarantee of immunity.

The Catholic Monarchs, propelled by a surge of popular prejudice and clerical fanaticism, and sympathetic to anything which reinforced their own central power, responded positively to the idea of an Inquisition, one which would be a national, not a papal or episcopal institution, and would involve strong state control. Soon after it began its operations in 1480, the Spanish Inquisition acquired an Inquisitor-General nominated by the crown, and a *Suprema*, or Supreme Council, under royal control. By giving their blessing to the persecution of conversos, Ferdinand and Isabella gained support among the popular masses and the clergy, while at the same time they increased the power of the state. The Inquisition was 'popular' in a way. It expressed the prejudices of most Spaniards about religion and race, and their resentment of successful conversos. It became part of the institutional landscape, a familiar and reassuring body, one which understood the world of regional interests and local elites and knew how to survive in their midst.[5] It recruited a large corps of unpaid officials, the *familiares*, and so associated itself with representatives of a broad cross-section of provincial society, many of them drawn from the non-privileged sectors, especially *labradores*, peasant farmers, who were thereby able to enhance their status and prestige.[6] In this way the

Inquisition acquired a network of clients and supporters in the most important towns and villages, and the descendants of Jews found themselves isolated among an army of informers.

The Spanish Inquisition was established primarily to investigate conversos, who for the next three centuries were universally suspected of being crypto-Jews. The truth of the matter became a problem for the Inquisition and for later historians. Were the conversos secret Jews and therefore legitimate targets, or were they true Catholics persecuted for other reasons – race, greed, politics? Inquisitors had few doubts. Historians are not so sure. One argues that conversos remained Jews: 'the conversos were, and remained, Jews at heart, and their Judaism was expressed in their way of life and their outlook'.[7] Another insists that when the Inquisition was established most of the conversos were not Jews but 'detached from Judaism, or rather, to put it more clearly, Christians'.[8] A third maintains that the conversos, or some of them, formed a religious tendency of their own, neither Jewish nor Christian.[9] Valencia presents a more complex picture. When the Inquisition began its operations in the mid-1480s it found three categories: those who were Jewish in all but name; those who practised both religions simultaneously; and those who held themselves to be complete Catholics.[10] In the first group hundreds were executed. Those in the second group were also executed. The third group contained Christians with inherited remnants of Jewish ways, subsequently abandoned; but if they failed to confess they were prosecuted and could be executed.[11] Informers and witnesses were often servants who had been mistreated, or others with a grievance against the accused. So the Inquisition provided the community with a powerful weapon of social control, by permitting them to settle disputes at the expense of outcasts, and to frustrate the ambitions of conversos.

The social composition of judaizers was predictable. In the period 1478–1530 they were a middle class of merchants, money changers, and shopkeepers, together with a popular sector of artisans. Social position gave no protection. The tribunal established in Ciudad Real in November 1483 drastically reduced the converso community and then moved on to Toledo in 1485.[12] From 1485 to 1500 more than 99 per cent of its cases involved converted Jews. In 1490 alone 433 persons were sentenced. In Valencia in 1484–1530 91.6 per cent of the accused were conversos; and between 1488 and 1505 1191 of the 1199 persons reconciled by the Barcelona tribunal were conversos.[13] These early tribunals imposed harsh punishments. Of the 1997 persons sentenced at Valencia between 1494 and 1530, 909 or 45.5 per cent were given death sentences and of these 754 were actually executed. In some tribunals the percentage was even higher.[14]

Repression on this scale has a dual significance. On the one hand it points to the large number of crypto-Jews in Spain and the tenacious resistance of the generation which had been educated in Judaism before

1492. The first wave of persecution decimated the conversos, then there was a pause halfway through the reign of Charles V. But there was a revival of persecution from the later years of Charles V and during the early part of Philip II's reign. Extremadura, for example, became the scene of a radical extermination of conversos in 1560–70, especially in the region of Albuquerque, where a whole middle class community of traders, artisans, doctors, and lawyers was wiped out or scattered in an action more complete than expulsion.[15] In the second place, the repression reveals the Inquisition as an agent and a creature of Spanish anti-semitism. Many of its officials were automatically suspicious of conversos, no matter how Catholic they were, and some inquisitors carried out campaigns of terror against alleged Jews.[16] Race prejudice had consequences beyond the action of the Inquisition. It was one of the ingredients feeding the mania for aristocratic status in Spain. In the sixteenth century a number of prominent businessmen were undoubtedly of Jewish extraction. This fostered a bias against the whole entrepreneurial class and caused many of its members, including some with Jewish ancestry, to buy their way out, to procure land and ennoblement, and thus to make their social status impeccable.

By 1550, the first stage of Inquisition history, with its relatively autonomous regional tribunals, frequent violations of procedure, and an obsession with judaizers, was coming to an end. These violent persecutions had destroyed the main centres of crypto-Judaism in Spain, and new generations of conversos were less loyal to their Jewish past. At the same time excesses led to greatly increased intervention by the *Suprema* in the affairs of local tribunals. As a result procedure was reformed and standardized, and the *Suprema* began to review cases on a regular basis. The judicial autonomy of local tribunals was curbed even further by forcing them to refer to the *Suprema* before torturing a suspect and by requesting the submission of sentences for review in a variety of cases. The restructured Inquisition took its place among the legal institutions of Spain: it compared favourably with other courts, secular and ecclesiastical: it was relatively inexpensive to use but also impossible for plaintiffs to manipulate; strict rules of evidence and numerous internal controls ensured relatively high standards of procedure.[17] Between 1540 and 1559 judaizers comprised a mere 5.9 per cent of the 29,584 accused before all tribunals, while in Saragossa they were only 4 per cent of the 481 cases.[18] This lull in the persecution of converted Jews ended only when a large influx of Portuguese New Christians provided new targets for informers and new victims for the Inquisition.

Purity of blood

After its frenzied campaign against the conversos the Spanish Inquisition assumed a more routine existence and turned its menacing eye on the Old

Christian population, looking for Protestants, heretics of any kind, sexual offenders such as sodomists and bigamists, and acting as one of the arms of the Counter-Reformation. As such it was a means of protecting religion from fraud and superstition, and occasionally a vehicle of enlightenment. Witch belief was as firmly entrenched in Spain as in the rest of Europe in the seventeenth century; the secular authorities supported the prejudices of the populace and sought to burn witches, an attitude shared by many local inquisitors. It was the existence of a minority view within the Inquisition, together with the centralized methods of its administration and the authority of the *Suprema*, that made it possible to enforce a more enlightened policy and effect a suspension of witch burning a century before the rest of Europe changed its policy.[19] Other practices of the Inquisition, however, were not so enlightened.

Between 1540 and 1700 49,092 cases were tried by the Inquisition.[20] Many of these concerned *limpieza de sangre* ('purity of blood'). The expulsion of 1492 is sometimes seen as an invitation to convert and stay. The interpretation is not entirely convincing, for, as the Jews well knew, to stay was to encounter another form of expulsion, an expulsion from Spanish society. This took place when those alleged to lack purity of blood were barred from holding public office, carrying arms, exercising certain professions, and wearing particular styles of clothing. For the expulsion of 1492 left the state with a security problem, self-inflicted and to a large extent imaginary. How could it protect orthodoxy from the remnants of Judaism?

The statutes of purity of blood represented a mixture of religious fanaticism, race prejudice, social ambition, exclusivism, and political monopoly, all expressed and given further impetus by the Inquisition. From 1483 religious and educational institutions began to exclude descendants of Jews and of those condemned by the Inquisition; the movement began in Andalusia, where bitter antagonism raged between Old Christians and conversos, especially those prominent in commerce and the guilds, and in the Basque country where the entire province of Guipúzcoa closed itself to conversos. Colleges and universities, military and religious orders, cathedral chapters, and of course the Inquisition itself, began to close their doors, so that by 1547, when the cathedral chapter of Toledo adopted a statute of *limpieza*, there were few careers in Church and state open to conversos. Toledo was significant both for the controversy of the decision, in which there were twenty-four canons for, ten against, and for the aggression of the Cardinal Archbishop, Juan Martínez Siliceo, a man of humble origins and high attainments who saw his Old Christian lineage as a qualification, an asset, and a model. According to his defence of the measure, most of the parish priests of his archdiocese were descendants of Jews; in the last fifty years over 50,000 conversos had been punished by the Inquisition, yet still they flourished and were now trying to dominate the Church. Of the ten who had voted against the statute, no less than nine were of Jewish origin. In fact not all those entitled to vote had been present, and not all those against were conversos. At least six hostile canons were Old Christians and, unlike Siliceo, were *hidalgos*.

The dissenting canons drew up a protest, arguing that the statute was against the law, scripture, reason, and defamatory of 'many noble and leading people of these realms'. As Siliceo and his opponents knew, few members of the nobility were untouched by converso ancestry. By promoting *limpieza*, therefore, the archbishop was obviously claiming for his own class a racial purity which the nobility could not emulate.[21] Despite the opposition, the statute was confirmed in Spain and, against its better judgment, by the papacy. Toledo was a breakthrough: Jaén, Seville, León, and Oviedo followed, though Burgos, Salamanca, and Zamora did not. Philip II supported *limpieza*: 'all the heresies which have occurred in Germany and France have been sown by descendants of Jews, as we have seen and still see daily in Spain'. The king led his people in invincible prejudice, and the Inquisition had the support of Church and state to defend the practice. But not universal support. Even where it was applied, there were exceptions, and conversos managed to study and to teach in universities, and there were still institutions where conversos were admitted. The Jesuits resisted *limpieza* for many years, though they were harassed by the Inquisition and eventually compromised.

As Mariana said, it was difficult to defend the principle that the sins of fathers should be visited on sons and grandsons, but it was defended. If it were proved that an ancestor had been punished by the Inquisition, or was a Moor or Jew, the descendant could be branded as impure and disqualified from office. Applicants for many posts had to present genealogical proofs of purity of blood. Investigators examined the record, called witnesses, and admitted 'common rumour' as evidence. The opportunities for fraud, bribery, extortion, and blackmail were obvious. In a society where genealogy was a passport to office, racism was institutionalized and baptism counted for less than blood. Honour was based on religion and race. The opposite of honour, infamy, was deliberately perpetuated in the collective memory, and a family's flaw was displayed generation after generation, as the penitential garments, the *sanbenitos* hanging in church, gathered dust and derision until the end of the eighteenth century. Even when the Inquisition took action against anyone who unjustifiably slandered a person as a converso, this was a further slur on Jews.[22] According to some of the critics of *limpieza*, such allegations could also be socially subversive, when mere commoners challenged the lineage of the noble, wealthy and powerful, and when an artisan or peasant could use his status as an Old Christian to question the ancestry of the noblest families.[23]

Limpieza gave rise to fear, suspicion and perjury, and its persistence increased the voices of protest. By the end of the sixteenth century a movement gathered pace to abolish or modify the *limpieza* statutes as divisive, corrupting, and harmful to the state. Fray Agustín Salucio, a leading opponent of the statutes, justified his position by arguing that 'in general' the conversos were 'Christians at heart'.[24] The Inquisitor-Generals of the time, usually outside appointees, were also concerned at malicious allegations and added their weight to those advocating reform. Even Philip II was persuaded to set up an inquiry, and his last inquisitor, Pedro Portocarrero, was a known reformist. Reform was also advocated by those who valued the political collaboration of the conversos; Lerma, who had no converso ancestry, and Olivares, whose family was not so untouched, both spoke out against *limpieza*.[25] But little came of the campaign; the statutes remained in force, less invoked perhaps but still capable of being reactivated.

Ironically, in spite of the ingrained hostility of many inquisitors, the Inquisition itself proved to be a channel through which conversos could evade *limpieza* and become assimilated to Spanish society. When it was necessary to raise revenue to cover its extensive payroll, the Inquisition was quite capable of ignoring its own statutes. In return for cash it would commute sentences, relieve disabilities, and even allow a few conversos to enter the tribunal, mostly as *familiares*.[26] For the conversos it was money well spent; wealthy and influential converso families, at least those from the third generation onwards, were able to obscure their origins and even pass for Old Christians, integrating themselves fully into Spanish society, and qualifying for entry into the ecclesiastical and bureaucratic hierarchy.

The New Christians of Portugal

The repression of the Spanish conversos was not the end of Spain's Jewish history. Crypto-Judaism survived more vigorously in Portugal than it did in Spain.[27] Portugal had no Inquisition until the 1540s, and its activities were not severe until 1580. The Portuguese conversos, or New Christians as they were often called, consisting largely of those who had made a conscious decision to leave Spain in 1492 rather than accept baptism, were more loyal to their past than those who preferred to conform and remain. In Portugal, New Christians were barred from offices and honours even more effectively than they were in Spain itself; they did not assimilate as did those in Spain, but preserved their religion and culture and, in spite of further migration, maintained their numbers at about 50,000. But Portugal was not always a haven, and the possibility of returning to Spain, sanctioned by the Spanish crown itself from November 1492, was something the New Christians remembered. From time to time, according to the attitude of the Inquisition in Spain and the crown in Portugal, there were movements back and forth, which increased once the Portuguese Inquisition, responding to popular and clerical pressure, hardened its own operations from 1580. The result was that nationality differences between Spanish and Portuguese conversos largely ceased to exist, to be replaced by a racial and religious definition distinguishing Jews from non-Jews.[28] At the same time repression by the Inquisition and the constant threat of an *auto de fe* forced the New Christian community to develop a strategy of survival, a subtle combination of practices of conformity, concealment, and dissimulation in religious and in economic life, to become a community constantly on guard against its surroundings and its neighbours, and driven to make of each family group a small secret society. This was the price of preserving its identity.

Significant migration to Spain began in the 1560s and increased after 1580, following the union of the crowns and the increasing violence of the Portuguese Inquisition. Several thousand New Christians now settled in Madrid, Seville, and Málaga, and began to earn a living in the wool trade and in commerce with the Indies. Not all were prosperous financiers. In La Mancha there was a well-organized community of New Christians centred on the towns of La Roda and Santa María del Campo, people of modest to poor prospects, petty agricultural producers, wholesalers and retailers of farming and artisan products, linen and woollen merchants, some of them part of a commercial network embracing Madrid, Seville, and Córdoba, but many integrated into the rural community of La Mancha.[29] For the New Christian elite, however, the characteristic vocation was finance. Spanish imperial finance had long depended on Italian bankers, who had the capacity to handle the transfer of funds from Spain to the Low Countries. Anxious to escape the hard settlements imposed by the Genoese, especially after the state bankruptcy of 1575, and to open the system to wider competition, Philip II's government was ready to consider an alternative set of bankers, even if they were Jews and were accumulating their capital on the margin of legality. The union of the crowns in 1580 and the surge in transatlantic traffic in the late sixteenth century opened up commercial opportunities that the Portuguese New Christians were quick to exploit. Some made vast fortunes trading in Asian products, investing in the Brazilian sugar industry, and supplying slaves to both Brazil and Spanish America; others reexported commodities from northern Europe to America outside or inside the Seville monopoly.[30] Their growing resources earned them further protection from Philip III and his ministers, who wanted loans for use in various parts of Europe and wanted them from outside the Italian network; these needs eased conditions for New Christians in Spain and Portugal, and procured them government contracts for military and naval supplies and appointments as tax farmers. There was some official anxiety, especially over their skill in manipulating returns from the Indies trade, in receiving contraband silver, and in trading with it to northern Europe. But in fact they were known and accepted in Seville, paying their *indultos* (fines) like any Christian contrabandist.[31]

In Spain the New Christians retained their identity and assimilated less readily than Spanish conversos. While many of the Portuguese immigrants were content to live as good Catholics, many were crypto-Jews who developed links with Sephardic groups in other parts of Europe.[32] Spaniards tended to view the whole group with profound misgivings, their anti-semitism aggravated by social and economic resentment. But the real impetus to persecution came from the Inquisition itself, which though it responded to social prejudice, should not be confused with it. The Inquisition had its own logic, and once it moved there was no stopping it. It began to move in the 1590s, when it relentlessly pursued the New Christian community in La Mancha. The Portuguese were arrested by the Cuenca Inquisition for secretly reverting to Judaism; they were denounced by servants, priests, and debtors, and even by members of their own families under torture. In short they were the victims of a classic Inquisition process leading to *autos* or imprisonment. Others, nearer the sources of power, were more fortunate.

The growing wealth of the New Christians drew the attention of Philip III and his penurious government. Freedom and protection had to be paid for, in loans to the treasury and bribes to ministers, but the rewards were considerable. In the years 1607, 1608, 1610 and 1611 not a single converso was judged by the Inquisition. The advent of Olivares seemed to promise even greater opportunities. He was known to dislike *limpieza*. He declared before the Council of Castile on 1 November 1625 that the laws of *limpieza* were 'unjust and impious, against divine law, natural law, and the law of nations ... in no other state in the world do such laws exist'.[33] Olivares was ready to welcome New Christians into economic collaboration: the government wanted their financial services, while the prize they particularly sought was a legal entry to the Indies trade. In the event Philip IV granted them complete freedom to travel anywhere in the empire as well as naturalizations to participate in the Indies trade.[34]

New Christian bankers also became key agents in the Spanish system of international payments. In 1626–27 Olivares awarded financial contracts to a group of leading converso businessmen. It was a mutually convenient arrangement. By issuing a pardon for relapses into Judaism committed before 1626 and guaranteeing immunity from Inquisition confiscation of all *asiento* investments (contracts with financiers, often involving their supplying money to the crown), the crown provided the incentive for the Portuguese to compete on favourable new terms with their Italian rivals. Because of their international contacts in America and northern Europe, the New Christians were able to establish an efficient mode of investment, exchange and transfer, which was cheaper for the crown and served the military needs of the empire. Between 1626 and 1640 their share of the *asiento* contracts rose from 5 per cent to well over 50 per cent, providing the necessary funds for Spain's fighting forces in the years 1631–40. Highly competitive as they were, these Portuguese *asentistas* made sufficient profits in the export of bullion to enable them to continue backing the crown's debt even after the crisis of 1640. By 1647 their services had undoubtedly saved the crown large sums of money and preserved its military capability in an age of so-called decline.[35]

Exposure involved risks. From about 1622 the greater presence and higher profile of the New Christians drew retribution as well as reward. Municipal councils and Spanish merchants who were ousted from tax farming opportunities resented the loss of revenue and profits. Opponents of the Olivares regime saw the Portuguese as a protected and favoured client group. Merchants at both ends of the Indies trade saw them as competitors.[36] The Spanish Inquisition had never reconciled itself to the new deal for Portuguese conversos and it maintained its vigilance in spite of government restraint. Yet even its own ranks were penetrated. Pressed for financial contributions by Olivares, it sold offices to raise revenue. In the Inquisition of Granada, where substantial sums were raised in the period 1629–44 from sale of office, it was suspected that many purchasers were simply anxious to improve their social status, 'clear up doubts about their purity of blood', and cover up converso origins.[37] In 1633 Juan de Santaella, who had purchased an Inquisition office in Granada and been responsible for the detention of 133 people accused as judaizers, was himself charged with the same offence on the accusation of some of his relations among the detained.

The Spanish Inquisition renewed its vigilance. Between 1560 and 1614 the 1759 judaizers made up only 5.5 per cent of the 29,584 cases tried by the Inquisition, but between 1615 and 1700, a period of relative decline and bureaucratization of Inquisition business there were 3171 persons tried for judaizing, more than 20 per cent of the 15,326 cases tried during that period.[38] Most of them were concentrated in Toledo and a few other towns; in the course of an *auto de fe* in Córdoba on 2 December 1625, of the forty-five condemned thirty-nine were of Portuguese origin.[39] On 4 July 1632 the Inquisition held a celebrated *auto de fe* in the Plaza Mayor of Madrid. Among the seven who were burned as judaizers, six were Portuguese, and among the spectators were their protectors, Philip IV and Olivares.[40] This was a prelude to an attack on the crown's financiers. The Toledo Inquisition arrested Juan Núñez Saravia and others, accused them of judaizing, contraband, murder, and other crimes, and used torture to try to extract confessions; but the accused maintained their innocence, and other *asentistas* closed ranks. The government appeared helpless before the Inquisition and its supporting interests, impotent to intervene on behalf of its collaborators; Saravia and others were condemned and heavily fined, and their *asiento* careers brought to an end. Further cases came before the Inquisition in a campaign which reflected widespread hatred and envy of the wealth and influence of the New Christians. Olivares subsequently did his best to protect them. In 1634 he probably engineered the appointment of a moderate Inquisitor-General, Fray Antonio de Sotomayor; and in 1637 he intervened to persuade the Inquisition to drop a case against another *asentista*. But the Inquisition could not be halted completely. It was a political force and an interest group, competing with others in Spain and America.

In spite of the dangers, and the fall of Olivares in 1643, the Portuguese *asentistas* survived and continued to serve the Spanish state, providing 60 per cent of all *asientos* in 1626–47. The Portuguese of Seville, Lisbon and Madrid, with their contacts throughout Spanish America and northern Europe, were strategically placed to move American bullion and to undertake remittances without export licences. Through their factors in America, posted originally for purposes of the slave trade, the Portuguese of the Peninsula organized clandestine trade in merchandise and bullion that bypassed Seville and the Spanish market and successfully tapped the mining economies of Mexico and Peru. Without the ability of the Portuguese *asentistas* to call on these sources of ready money, it is likely that Spain's massive foreign payments from 1631 and the maintenance of Spain's military power in the Netherlands and elsewhere would have been compromised long before 1640. The Portuguese were responsible for vast bullion transfers to northern Europe, 15 million ducats in 1636–45, 22 million in 1641–45.[41] This was the peak. Spanish military and naval disasters in the Atlantic and the north in the period 1638–46 undermined the usefulness and the credit of the Portuguese *asentistas*, while the secession of Portugal severed their peninsular connections. They were also hit by the state bankruptcy of 1647, in which they incurred heavy losses and were forced to settle for less advantageous terms. So their capital began to flee the Peninsula, and with it went a new wave of emigrants.

The downfall of the Portuguese New Christians was popular in Madrid, and no attempt was made to protect them from renewed investigation. To judge by the records of the Cuenca Inquisition, which processed many of the cases denounced in the capital, the 1640s saw a very low number of judaizing trials, 13 per cent of total trials compared with an average of 32 per cent over the whole reign. But the succeeding two decades amounted to an era of sustained persecution, twice the average at 64 per cent. A great *auto* was held in Toledo early in 1651, with others following at regular intervals. A combination of intimidation and financial loss caused an exodus of the financier conversos from Spain in the years 1645–65, most of them making their way to the Dutch Republic, the Dutch Caribbean, Italy, England, and France.[42] In the reign of Charles II the attacks on the Portuguese bankers continued. In the *auto de fe* in Granada on 30 May 1672, out of 90 victims 79 were judaizers, and 57 of these were Portuguese. Luis Marquez Cardoso, director of the tobacco monopoly, and his wife were arrested by the Inquisition in 1669. In 1680 an *auto de fe* was celebrated in Madrid before Charles II and his court, where twenty of the twenty-one condemned to death were Portuguese New Christians who, before they died, heard themselves denounced from the pulpit as 'perfidious Jews... God's worst enemies'.[43] In 1691 three leading bankers were arrested and sentenced.[44]

Meanwhile Portuguese conversos had also penetrated Spanish America.[45] Since 1580 Spanish and creole merchants in Peru had felt the rivalry of Portuguese contrabandists in the Río de la Plata and Upper Peru, and since 1628 the legitimized competition of Portuguese merchants installed in Seville. The Portuguese in Peru also dominated the growing Lima trade in the Pacific, which supplied Asian commodities by way of Manila and Acapulco. Whether smuggling on the Atlantic or Pacific, or trading legally through Seville, the Portuguese beat the Spaniards. By evading customs duties and *alcabala* (Castilian sales) taxes, they could sell their contraband cheaper than the official monopolists. In the legal trade the Portuguese advantage over the Spaniards lay in their direct access to the textiles and hardware of northern Europe and the spices and luxuries of Asia that made up the bulk of American cargoes.

Merchants of the Lima *consulado* (merchant guild) and their allies in municipal government complained to Madrid of the damage done to the monopoly, but obtained no satisfaction. Although few of Peru's resident Portuguese had permission to settle or trade there, neither the crown nor the viceregal government seriously attempted to exclude them, as each received a share of Portuguese profits. But the Inquisition of Lima, served by familiars among the Spanish *consulado* merchants, began to strike at the Portuguese and prosecuted more and more from 1600. Then in a backlash comparable to the anti-converso campaign in the Peninsula itself, the Inquisition unleashed a violent campaign in Peru. In 1634, to break up an alleged crypto-Jewish conspiracy of major proportions – the so-called *complicidad grande* – it rounded up numerous Portuguese Jews in Lima and Cartagena who were involved in the slave trade, mining, Atlantic and Pacific trades, and contraband on the Venezuelan coast, and subjected them to trial resulting in large confiscations of silver and money. From then until 1640 the Portuguese were harassed on all sides, burnt at the stake, imprisoned, fined, and stripped of their property. The Seville end of the Portuguese network was badly affected; as the New Christians lost capital in America, so they cut back on their investments in fleets, and thereby left a large gap in the transatlantic trade. Their insecurity grew worse with the rebellion of Portugal in 1640, as they were now rebels as well as judaizers. Meanwhile in Mexico too the Inquisition had been pressing on the Portuguese since the 1620s. The peak of their wealth and influence coincided with a power struggle between their protector, the duke of Escalona, viceroy of New Spain (1640–42), and Juan de Palafox y Mendoza, bishop of Puebla, a contest which ended in a coup against the viceroy and the denouncing of a judaizing community among the Portuguese. From 1642 the Mexican Inquisition carried out a series of *autos* culminating in the large ceremony of 11 April 1649 at which there were 109 penitents, all but one of whom were convicted of judaizing, and thirteen of whom were executed.[46]

Inquisition and Enlightenment

The century of Enlightenment began badly for the conversos. The frenzy of the Inquisition during the late seventeenth century continued unabated in the following decades, and judaizers were still the first targets. They continued to live dangerously, tempted back into public life by the new opportunities for tax farming available under the Bourbon regime, no less insolvent than its predecessor, and the Inquisition was waiting to strike. In the period 1701–45 of the crimes punished in *autos de fe* 1149, or 78.8 per cent of the total, were for Judaism, and of these 950 occurred in the years 1721–25. The remaining victims were a minor assortment of Muslims, Protestants, blasphemers, sorcerers, and bigamists.[47] In 1701–45 217 people were burnt as judaizers, constituting 96.5 per cent of all those burnt. In one year alone, November 1721 to November 1722, 405 people were tried for judaizing, of whom 29 were burnt at the stake; some of them were burnt alive, but the majority were strangled first.[48] In Valencia between 1701 and 1750 Inquisition activity increased dramatically to 1323 cases (many of them judaizers), as opposed to the 451 recorded in 1651–1700.[49] This was the last major campaign of the Spanish Inquisition, a kind of final offensive against the Jews, when the tribunal aroused itself from the inertia imposed by the War of Succession in the Peninsula and asserted its autonomy against the perceived pressure of Bourbon absolutism. The Inquisition looked for its traditional victims and took a cruel revenge, its pride satisfied only by convictions, executions, imprisonments, whippings through the streets, confiscations of property, and the humiliation of entire families and their descendants. And it was a rapacious revenge, for the inquisitors were not blind to the possibilities of profit from confiscations and fines. The victims were merchants, shopkeepers, lawyers, medical doctors, teachers, and students, tax farmers and collectors of revenue, in all an incipient if faint middle class, caught between the prejudices of the traditional elites and the fury of the masses. If one judaizer were caught the whole family was usually netted, for a prisoner often incriminated others. These trials, like their predecessors, showed that it was the women of the households who were the stalwarts, preserving the Jewish religion and handing it on to their children.

The Spanish Inquisition, therefore, with the support of Philip V, made a political and financial recovery during the first decades of the eighteenth century. After 1725, it is true, the number of trials declined. Yet as late as 1755 the Inquisition of Toledo dug up the case against Diego Ventura Pastor, a humble country dweller and livestock dealer; they tortured him, extracted a confession, and sentenced him to confiscation of half his goods, three years in prison, and the wearing of a *sanbenito*, probably the worst punishment of all, for it frequently got him stoned in the streets.[50] Between 1792 and 1820 the Valencia tribunal dealt with six cases of judaiziers, some of them Jews from Gibraltar.[51] Of the more than 5000 cases coming before all tribunals in 1780–1820, only sixteen involved judaizing.[52] So thoroughly had the Inquisition done its work that by the middle of the eighteenth century judaizers were a rarity in Spain. The last accused to come before the Inquisition, one in Seville in 1799, the other in Toledo in 1801, were mentally sick rather than judaizers.

The growing moderation of the Inquisition, now more closely controlled and increasingly marginalized by a crown determined to assert its absolute power and to decide public policy in departments of state, was attested not only from its own records but also by foreign observers. According to Henry Swinburne, Jews could travel the length and breadth of the Peninsula staying at the homes of other Jews without being molested.[53] And Joseph Townsend regarded the Inquisition as more benign than in previous times, even if its bureaucracy was still in place.[54] Jews had little to fear from the Inquisition of Charles III and Charles IV, though the legacy of anti-semitism ensured that their entry into Spain was still prohibited and severely controlled; when other foreign workers were admitted, Jews were still specifically excepted.[55] In 1797 the minister of finance, Pedro Varela, urged the king, now that 'ancient prejudices have passed away', to allow Jewish merchants to return to Spain to help the crown improve its finances and particularly to assume the task of liquidating the *vales reales* (state bonds), one of the financial headaches of Charles IV's government. The proposal was not adopted, and the prime minister Manuel Godoy later claimed that it was the Inquisition which opposed the measure.[56] Yet individual Jews could still reach the top, if they had enough money to buy a title, as did the duke of Losada in 1759, or if they had a special talent, such as that of the court painter to Charles III, Antonio Rafael Mengs, son of a minor Jewish artist.[57]

The great campaigns were over. The crypto-Jews had been exterminated, the moriscos expelled, the Protestants terrorized. There only remained the philosophers and the critics of the Inquisition itself. It took the Inquisition some time to get to grips with the Enlightenment. It spent the first half of the eighteenth century preoccupied with Jansenism and adjacent doctrines, and firmly aligned with the Jesuits and traditionalists.

In 1756 it showed its first clear reaction to the Enlightenment, when it condemned works by Montesquieu, Voltaire, Rousseau and others, though this did not prevent their entrance into Spain. Further condemnations followed, Helvetius in 1759, the *Encyclopédie* in the same year, further works by Voltaire in 1764, Diderot and Rousseau in 1766. The trial and condemnation of a leading official, Pablo de Olavide, not for anything he had written but because he was an admirer of the *philosophes* and vaguely anti-clerical, was a victory for the Inquisition and a warning to its critics; the most intolerant sectors of Spanish society were encouraged, while the rabble sang a popular song incorporating the entire demonology of traditionalist Spain: 'Olavide is a Lutheran, a freemason, an atheist; he is a heathen and a Calvinist, a Jew and an Arian'.[58]

Ministers had to be careful. The count of Campomanes campaigned not to abolish the Inquisition but to restrain its jurisdiction, curb its independence and subordinate it to the state. He protected himself by presenting all his criticism in the form of a defence of the civil power and the regalian rights of the crown, and Charles III refused to grant the inquisitors the permission they wanted to prosecute his minister. The campaign of Campomanes against the Jesuits, leading to their expulsion and dissolution, was seen as an attack on all such corporations, including the Inquisition, whose ranks were filled with products of the Society. Again, the Inquisition found it difficult to challenge a policy which invoked the regalist power of the crown. The count of Floridablanca wanted to abolish the statutes of *limpieza* as contrary to the spirit of the Church and the interests of the state, but he failed to do so. In the *Instrucción Reservada* written for the guidance of the cabinet council he referred to the infamy suffered by the families of *convertidos* (no longer the historic conversos),

> whereby the greatest and holiest action of man, conversion to our holy faith, is visited with the same punishment as the greatest crime, apostasy, for the converted and their descendants are regarded as equally infamous as those convicted or punished for heresy and apostasy.[59]

An assembly of theologians chaired by the Inquisitor-General was summoned to consider measures to rid Spain of these prejudices, but little was done. The official apparatus of *limpieza*, now totally irrelevant, continued to function and to outrage enlightened ministers. As for the Inquisition itself, Floridablanca was circumspect:

> It is important to favour and protect this Tribunal, but care has to be taken that it does not usurp the regalian rights of the Crown... or depart from its proper function which is to persecute heresy, apostasy and superstition, and to enlighten the faithful in these matters with charity.

Floridablanca saw the Inquisition as a threat not to freedom but to absolutism.

The leading light of Spanish intellectual life, Gaspar Melchor de Jovellanos, regarded the persecution and expulsion of the Jews as acts of 'superstition carried to the point of fanaticism', and he wrote for Charles IV a brief history of the Inquisition with barely concealed hostility.[60] He himself had experienced its latent venom. His *Informe de ley agraria* (1794), a moderate project of agrarian reform, was denounced to the Inquisition as subversive. The tribunal's investigators condemned its most important conclusion, that ecclesiastical and noble entail was an evil, and recommended that the treatise be prohibited as an attack on the two principle props of the monarchy – the nobility and the Church – and an incitement to ideas of equality in the ownership of property and land. But Jovellanos had strong defenders at court, and the Inquisition decided to suspend the case, though it kept Jovellanos in its sights.[61] And he remembered his tormentors. When he was appointed minister of justice in 1797 he attempted to restrain the Inquisition's jurisdiction and to restore to bishops the rights of censorship 'usurped' by the tribunal. But he knew that minor reforms were no substitute for abolition, which would be the salvation of Spain: 'What a boon for literature that would be! What an improvement of morals! How fewer hypocrites we would have'.[62]

In Spanish America the eighteenth century was a time of decline for the Inquisition even more marked than in the Peninsula itself. The Lima tribunal was inactive, absorbed by its own internal problems of appointments, salaries, income, disputes between officials and between the Inquisition and the colonial administration. The institution had become an end in itself, a purely bureaucratic machine, and one in need of repair. In the period 1700–50 the Lima tribunal held only seven *autos de fe* and its 268 cases led to only four sentences of punishment. In 1750–1804 there were four *autos* and fifty-one cases.[63] During the whole of this period no more than seventeen of the cases concerned judaizers, the rest being a mixture of minor delinquents – heretics, bigamists, criminous clerks, and sorcerers. The prosecution of Manuel Lorenzo de Vidaurre in 1793 was evidence of the penetration of the Enlightenment but not that it caused a major impact or a severe reaction.[64] In Mexico the tribunal was equally inert, preoccupied with its own bureaucratic existence, and more or less indifferent to the intellectual and moral affairs of the viceroyalty. In the years after 1789 it became what it had often been accused of being, an instrument of state, when it was prodded into activity to stem the flow of news from France; its role in the Spanish counter-revolution in Mexico after 1810 was vindictive but not decisive.[65] The fact was that the history of the Mexican Inquisition and its record of repression closely reflected the measure of crypto-Jewish activity, and this was not a feature of the eighteenth century. The story was the same in

Cartagena. There the Inquisition was in a state of decline in the eighteenth century, and the tribunal found it difficult to fill posts, to make ends meet, to resolve its internal disputes, and to evoke respect.[66]

Approach to toleration

The fall of the Spanish Bourbons in 1808 was followed by a surge of liberalism during which the Cortes of Cadiz abolished the Inquisition in 1813. For the next two decades the fate of the tribunal followed the fortunes of liberalism and royalism. It was restored by Ferdinand VII, abolished by the constitutional revolt of 1820, and revived again by the French-imposed restoration of 1823, though it no longer actually functioned. By now it had outlived its usefulness, even to the traditionalists, and it was formally abolished by the queen regent, María Cristina, on 15 July 1834. *Limpieza*, the great divider of Spanish society and the enduring agent of social stigma, was a separate issue and even survived the abolition of the Inquisition. In 1811 the Cortes decreed that purity of blood was no longer necessary for entry to military and naval colleges. In 1824 Ferdinand VII restored it for entry to public institutions. Official sanction for it was withdrawn on 31 January 1835 but it was still necessary for entrance into the corps of officer cadets. In the Constitution of 1837 and subsequent constitutions it was decreed that all Spaniards were eligible for public office, and in the law of 15 May 1865 *limpieza* was specifically suppressed. At last the status of *infamia* and *inhabilidad* was ended; for many Spaniards this was one of the greatest gains of the nineteenth century.

The death of the Inquisition, whose prime reason and role had been to root out Jews and judaizers, meant that the Jewish question ceased to be a priority and was relegated to a lower level of Spanish consciousness. Masons and liberals were now the demons of conservatives, and if Jews were added it was through ignorance of what they were. A few Jews survived from the old regime and made their fortunes in the new world of the nineteenth century. Alejandro María Aguado, banker to the court of Ferdinand VII, and the financier Juan Alvarez Mendizábal, were Jewish by race, Catholics in religion, throw-backs to the converso bankers of Philip IV. While the progress of liberalism in Spain in the early nineteenth century swept away many of the old prejudices and obstacles, it could also produce a conservative reaction. Mendizábal, a liberal entrepreneur and politician, and prime minister in 1835, was an orthodox if anti-clerical Catholic, but the Jewish origins of his family excited the anti-semitism of his opponents. In caricatures he was portrayed with a tail and the motto 'Come on boys, after the Jew. Pull the tail of Juanillo'.[67]

Jews entered the world of mythology as well as of politics. One of the typologies was the heroic Jew. Disraeli's novel *Coningsby* portrays a character, Sidonia, descendant of a noble Aragonese family of conversos who had made their way high in Church, State, and the Inquisition itself, kept their titles and estates, and migrated to England after the Peninsular war: 'No sooner was Sidonia established in England than he professed Judaism; which Torquemada flattered himself, with the fagot and the San Benito, he had drained out of the veins of his family more than three centuries ago'. He had his son educated by a tutor, Rebello: 'A Jesuit before the revolution of 1820; since then an exiled Liberal leader; now a member of the Spanish cortes; Rebello was always a Jew'.[68] A character of fiction, Sidonia was part of the folklore of European Jews with a family history that was possible if not exact. In Spain itself Jews were more likely to be depicted as base and ignoble, associated with all the hate-figures of traditionalists, alongside Protestants, masons, and liberals. These prejudices were perpetuated by conservatives and preached from the pulpit. The association of liberal and Jew was especially prevalent in the conflict over the abolition of the Inquisition. Traditionalists and Catholics in the Cortes of Cadiz almost automatically denigrated liberals as Jews. Not that Spanish liberals were free of anti-semitism. The Cortes of 1812 agreed that Jews could return to Spain, but its attitude was grudging rather than generous.

While there was still hostility to Jews in popular mentalities, the authorities were trying to liquidate the past. The small Jewish community in Spain, seconded by their coreligionists in France, began to request rights of religion similar to those enjoyed by Protestants. The revolution of 1868 dethroned Queen Isabella II and brought to power first General Francisco Serrano as regent, then General Juan Prim as prime minister with a project to establish a constitutional monarchy. The constituent Cortes drafted a constitution which embodied some of the principles of Spanish liberalism. The Jews thought it opportune to seek a place in Spanish legislation and they petitioned Serrano to revoke the edict of 1492, if only as a symbolic gesture. Serrano was evasive, arguing that as the revolution had proclaimed freedom of religion, the Jews could take advantage of this in the same way as any other minority. The Cortes, however, went further. There were passionate debates on the religious issue, in which the sufferings of the Jews were recalled by the more radical deputies. The constitution of 1869, while still acknowledging Catholicism as the state religion, tolerated other religions, and the famous article 21 guaranteed the right not only of private but of public exercise of any religion.

This was an obvious liberal truth, but something which traditional Spanish Catholics found difficult to accept. Those who hesitated to attack the principle of religious liberty instead derided the alleged economic objects of the concession, the attempt to attract Jews and Protestants and bring in more capital and industry. Even Juan Valera, the novelist, suggested that Jews were the last people from whom to expect the economic revival of Spain:

> They are intelligent but hardly industrious, less industrious than we are, less suitable for any physical task; they monopolize and attract wealth to themselves, but they do not create it. They are great musicians, poets, philosophers and bankers, but not manufacturers or agriculturalists.[69]

If the intellectual elite thought in stereotypes, what could be expected of popular opinion? In fact, as far as Jews were concerned little came of the constitution of 1869, and only a few migrated to Spain in its wake. But the political environment was changing. Even the more conservative constitution of 1876 retained freedom of religion. And later in the nineteenth century, as the Jews experienced persecution in Russia and eastern Europe, and requests were made on their behalf to enter Spain, the Spanish government declared an open door and placed no obstacles in their way. If few Jews took advantage of the opportunity, it was less because of the perennial cry of the ultra-traditionalists, '*el peligro judío*', than because Spain offered poorer economic prospects than other countries.[70]

The dictatorship of Primo de Rivera was not a fascist government and the general himself was not anti-semitic. A synagogue existed in Madrid and remained unmolested throughout the 1920s. A decree of 20 December 1924 offered to the Sephardim eligibility to become Spanish subjects, if they took it up before 31 December 1930. A few Jews from Salonica and elsewhere accepted the offer, but the majority were not interested. From the subsequent republic Jews had little to fear. The republican constitution enacted by the constituent Cortes in 1931 separated Church and State and made the Catholic Church an association equal to other religious associations and subject to the law of the land.[71] The dictatorship of Franco, on the other hand, had some affinity with the Axis powers, though it did not specifically subscribe to the anti-semitism of Nazi Germany and Fascist Italy. Spanish consulates in occupied countries took steps to protect Sephardim and other Jews known to be of Spanish origin, and the Burgos government made it clear that there were no legal obstacles in the way of entry of Jews into Spain, especially if they had the means to help the state financially.[72] But there were a number of racists in the Burgos government, and the regime did not publicly dissociate itself from the policies of its allies of the civil war.

Catholics in Spain, as elsewhere throughout the world, were accustomed to intone in the liturgy of Good Friday: 'Let us pray for the perfidious Jews'. Pope John XXIII removed the word 'perfidious' in 1959. Meanwhile Spain had followed its own path of reconciliation. In the late 1940s the Franco regime sought to establish diplomatic relations with the new state of Israel, not from any sense of guilt but as part of an attempt to escape from diplomatic isolation after the Second World War. Israel rebuffed these overtures, again not because of the memory of 1492 but because of Franco's association with Nazi Germany.[73] Diplomatic relations between Madrid and Jerusalem were eventually established on 17 January 1986. Ministers and the media spoke of the opening of a new chapter, to end a historical cycle begun five centuries previously in 1492. This was hyperbole. There was no logical connection between the expulsion of the Jews at the end of the fifteenth century and the more recent relations between two sovereign states, Spain and Israel, in the second half of the twentieth century. If Spain had any historical debt to pay, it was to the Jewish people, not to the state of Israel. This debt was gradually paid from the early nineteenth century, when the Spanish state began to show a sympathy towards the Jewish community which gradually increased, and which eventually encouraged them to return to Spain.

The perspective of history

Historians adjusted to new times, sometimes leading, sometimes following. In general they began to treat Jewish history more objectively, as a subject of historical research rather than an exercise in polemics. A start was made in the years around 1850, when Adolfo de Castro published a short history of the Jews from medieval times to the early nineteenth century, which he prefaced by a statement that he did not belong to the Jewish race but simply wished to record their history.[74] José Amador de los Ríos published a similar book, the work of a Catholic but one who expressed admiration for medieval Jews.[75]

Marcelino Mendéndez Pelayo did not allow his sympathies for traditional and Catholic values to distort his treatment of Jewish history in Spain, and if he was anxious to rescue the Inquisition from its detractors he did not disguise the fate of its victims.[76] He took issue with those who assumed that the past and present decadence of Spain could be traced unmistakably to religious intolerance. In this view the Inquisition became the unique cause of every national defect. Menéndez Pelayo caricatured such an attitude in a well-known passage:

> Why was there no industry in Spain? On account of the Inquisition . . . Why are Spaniards lazy? On account of the Inquisition. Why are there bull-fights in Spain? On account of the Inquisition. Why do Spaniards take a siesta? On account of the Inquisition . . .[77]

Against this obsession with intolerance as an historical cause, Menéndez Pelayo made a plea for sanity and a sense of proportion. But he seems also to have believed that he had a religious duty to defend the Inquisition.

This assumption came to dominate the writing of ecclesiastical history in Spain and frustrated its development. Menéndez Pelayo appreciated that there were more problems in interpreting the Inquisition than he accounted for in his major work, *Historia de los heterodoxos españoles*, but he himself propagated new myths. He writes:

The Inquisition was not a cause of intolerance, but an effect. Moreover, historically considered it has a distasteful and repugnant side to it... the fanaticism of blood and race, which we probably owe to the Jews, and which was then hideously turned against them.

Again,

There is nothing more repugnant than this internal race conflict, the principal cause of the decadence of the Peninsula... The question of race explains many events and resolves many of the enigmas of our history.[78]

These misleading suggestions, in which the Jews are made at least partly responsible for their own tormentor, were echoed by Américo Castro in his *Structure of Spanish History*, where he argues that 'the Inquisition had been in the making since the beginning of the fifteenth century', helped largely by 'deserters from Israel', and that converso intellectuals, while creative were also conflictive and through their Jewish background aroused the suspicions of the Inquisition.[79] In this view Spanish intolerance was a kind of hereditary disease which the Jews played their part in implanting. It is true that some conversos, anxious to protest their own orthodoxy and to protect themselves against the suspicions of the Old Christians, denounced not only Jews but also fellow converts, and that some officials of the early Inquisition were descended from conversos, as were some intellectuals of the sixteenth century. But what do these things prove? The fact remains that Jews and their descendants were victims of the Spanish Inquisition and preserved their identity by hiding it, not contributing it.

Liberal historians, too, have been prone to excess in interpreting Jewish history, and they too have found it difficult to overcome their Spanish and national sympathies. How otherwise can we account for Salvador de Madariaga's explanation of the fall of the Spanish empire in America, which he attributes to an international conspiracy of Jews, Freemasons and Jesuits? In this unholy alliance, the Jews were motivated by encyclopaedism and gain; the Freemasons by hostility to Church and crown; the Jesuits by resentment of their expulsion; and all three 'driven to cooperate... in the destruction of the Spanish Empire'.[80] This is one of the more curious interpretations of the origins of Spanish American independence, a new variant of an ancient demonology. But it illustrates the difficulties which Spanish historians of that generation created for themselves in placing recrimination before research. A new approach to the Inquisition and the Jewish past was signalled in 1976, when Ricardo García Carcel showed that original research and objective interpretation were necessary and possible, and that measurement could take the heat out of history as well as clarify its results.[81] Soon others followed, and Spanish historians took their place alongside their British, French, and American colleagues, in the revision of Inquisition history and the rediscovery of the Spanish Jews.

Chapter Seven

The Sephardim in the Ottoman Empire

ARON RODRIGUE

The rise and decline of the Ottoman Sephardim (fifteenth to eighteenth centuries)

The expulsion from Spain in 1492 and the forced mass conversion of the Jews of Portugal in 1497 heralded the end of open Jewish life in the Iberian Peninsula. This constituted a momentous development in Jewish history as it spelled the demise of the most important and brilliant of all medieval Jewish communities. It also represented the culmination of a long process of expulsions in western Europe; Jews had been expelled from England in 1290, from France in 1394, and from many German cities by the mid-fourteenth century. By the end of the fifteenth and the beginning of the sixteenth centuries, western Europe, with the exception of certain areas in Germany and Italy, was empty of Jews. The accompanying migration shifted the centre of gravity in the Jewish world east, to Poland-Lithuania and to the Ottoman empire. Ashkenazim congregated in Poland-Lithuania, while the Ottoman empire came to provide a safe haven to the majority of the Sephardi exiles.

The Ottoman Turks had gone from strength to strength in the fourteenth and fifteenth centuries, expanding a small tribal principality on the Byzantine frontier in Anatolia into an empire that controlled much of the Balkans in the course of the fourteenth century, finally conquering Byzantium itself in 1453. They ended Mameluke rule over the Holy Land and Egypt in 1516/17, and came to dominate most of the Middle East and North Africa by the middle of the sixteenth century. They appeared as a formidable, invincible force to the rest of the world.[1]

Jewish communities were one of the many numerous religious and ethnic groups that came under Ottoman rule. Greek-speaking Jews of the Byzantine lands, known as Romaniotes, were to be found in the Balkans and in Asia Minor. South and east of Anatolia, Arab-speaking Jewish communities inhabited most of the Fertile Crescent. Karaites lived in Egypt and Constantinople. Small-scale Ashkenazi migration from central Europe into the empire had taken place in the course of the fifteenth century, most of the Ashkenazim settling in Balkan towns under Turkish rule. Some Sephardi Jews had already made their way into the Ottoman empire in the decades that followed the pogroms of 1391 in Spain and the ensuing mass conversion of thousands of Jews.[2]

The Ottoman policy towards the Jews followed the classic Islamic pattern laid down by the *dhimma*, the covenant that regulated relations between Muslims and non-Muslims which stipulated toleration and protection of Christians and Jews while keeping them socially and juridically inferior to the true believers, the Muslims. Hence, non-Muslims were allowed extensive freedom in the practice of their religion, and in the running of the internal affairs of their communities, in return for which they paid special taxes, such as the *cizye*, the poll tax, and the *harac*, the land tax, as well as many other less important levies. They were subject to certain vestimentary regulations, to restrictions in the building and repairs of houses of worship, and to disabilities vis-à-vis Muslims in Muslim religious courts. The discriminatory aspects of the *dhimma* were designed to erect and maintain social boundaries with the infidel and emphasize the latter's inferior social status. But, like under many other Muslim regimes, these lines of social demarcation remained fluid in the Ottoman empire and were maintained with varying degrees of strictness according to the circumstances of the moment, or to the whim of the rulers. The most important parts of the *dhimma* remained the special taxes paid by the non-Muslims which constituted an important source of revenue to the Sultan.[3]

The Ottomans introduced two new policies that were to be of importance for the non-Muslims. They developed the *devshirme* system whereby in many areas, most notably in the Balkans, Christian boys were forcibly recruited into the army after conversion to Islam and came to constitute the elite military corps known as the janissaries. They also used *sürgün* extensively, a policy of transferring population to designated areas for primarily economic reasons. While the *devshirme* system was never applied to the Jews, the *sürgün* came to affect certain Jewish communities in the course of the fifteenth and sixteenth centuries. Many Jewish families of Edirne (Adrianople) and eventually the whole community of Salonica were transferred to Constantinople in the years following its conquest as part of a policy of repopulating the city. Salonica was hence devoid of any significant Jewish presence when the Sephardim began to arrive after 1492. While not used as a punitive measure, it is clear that such compulsory moves caused major hardship and disruption in many communities. The use of the *sürgün* declined during the course of the sixteenth century just as the *devshirme* was discontinued after the seventeenth century.[4]

The juridical and social contours of Jewish existence under the Ottomans that were to last until the nineteenth century were hence all in place before the mass arrival of the Sephardim after 1492. And it is important to realize that in spite of the many restrictions that prevailed in the Ottoman realms, these paled in comparison with the recent experience of the Jews in Spain and elsewhere in Europe. A new triumphant force offering a safe haven, the Ottoman empire constituted to many a Sephardi Jew a powerful magnet, and its rise and victories were even interpreted in messianic terms by some in the Sephardi religious elite as presaging the beginnings of redemption dawning in the East.[5]

Upon hearing of the expulsion of the Jews from Spain, Sultan Bayezit II (1481–1512) is said to have attempted to attract them to his lands as a matter of policy:

> So the Sultan Bayezid, king of Turkey, heard of all the evil that the Spanish king had brought upon the Jews and heard that they were seeking a refuge and a resting place. He took pity on them, and wrote letters and sent emissaries to proclaim throughout his kingdom that none of his city rulers may be wicked enough to refuse entry to the Jews or expel them. Instead, they were to be given a gracious welcome....[6]

Furthermore, he is said to have uttered: 'Can you call such a king wise and intelligent? He is impoverishing his country and enriching my kingdom.'[7] These attributed statements all come from Jewish sources and have no counterparts in Ottoman ones. The Sephardi Jews were indeed greeted as a useful addition to the population by the Ottomans. Nevertheless, these apocryphal statements are more revealing of the Jewish frame of mind at the time rather than characterize a conscious Ottoman policy. They reflect intense Jewish hopes and expectations attempting to transcend the tremendous shock of the expulsion, which would continue to feed a messianic undercurrent that would rise to the surface a century and a half later with the emergence of Sabbateanism.

One can discern two distinct waves of migration of Sephardim into the Ottoman empire. The first was composed of the expellees of 1492 from Spain and of those who managed to leave Portugal after the forced mass conversions of 1497. Many indeed did not arrive in Ottoman lands immediately but stayed for a few years in various parts of Italy before gradually making their way further east, either by overland routes from the Adriatic into the Balkans and Asia Minor, or by sea to some of the principal Ottoman port cities. The second wave, much more episodic and smaller in numbers, was the marrano (converso) immigration, primarily from Portugal after the definitive establishment of the Inquisition there in 1547, a migration which in trickles was to last well into the seventeenth century. The route taken by the marranos, while often following the first one over the Mediterranean, came also to include a more circuitous trajectory via the Spanish Low Countries in the north.

The increase in the Jewish population of some major Ottoman cities in the early sixteenth century as a result of these migrations is amply reflected in Ottoman statistics. While a Turkish register of 1477 shows 1647 Jewish households in Istanbul, a similar census in 1535 listed 8070 households in the capital city. Salonica, which had no Jewish population represented in the census of 1478, had 2645 Jewish households by 1520–30.[8] Similar increases were the case in many Ottoman centres in the Balkans and Asia Minor.

This immigration from outside the empire, as well as internal migrations within, such as a major Jewish influx from Salonica into the newly ascendant port of Izmir in Asia Minor in the late sixteenth century, eventually came to form the new Sephardi heartland in the Ottoman empire. Four major cities, Istanbul, Izmir, Salonica, and Edirne constituted the axes on which were aligned smaller satellite communities following the important trade routes of the area. The Sarajevo, Monastir (Bitola), and Uskub (Skopje) communities linked Salonica Jewry to the Adriatic and to Venice. The communities of Phillipopolis, Sofia, Nikopol, and Widdin dotted the overland trade route from Istanbul via Edirne to the Danubian basin and from there west to central Europe and north into Poland. Izmir was the terminus of the major trade routes from Asia into Anatolia and the life of the Jews of Aydin, Tyre, Manisa, and Bergama revolved around this major entrepot. While Jews of Iberian origin also came to settle in Safed, Jerusalem, Aleppo, Damascus, Cairo, and Alexandria, the demographic weight of Sephardi Jewry in the Levant rested overwhelmingly on the first four cities and on their hinterlands.

Relations between the Sephardim and the autochthonous Romaniote Jews remained tense and conflict-ridden for decades. Major differences in interpretations of Jewish religious law (Halakhah), in custom, in culture, in way of life in general, set the two communities apart. Istanbul bore the brunt of this endemic friction, as it was here that the bulk of Romaniote Jewry was concentrated. Moshe Capsali was appointed as the Chief Rabbi by Mehmet II after the conquest of Constantinople in 1453 to represent the Jews as a collectivity, and he was succeeded by the renowned scholar Eliyahu Mizrahi in 1498. Both were Romaniote Jews. No Chief Rabbi replaced Eliyahu Mizrahi upon his death in 1526 because of power struggles between Romaniotes and the Sephardim, and the main task of tax gathering which had been entrusted to the Chief Rabbi fell to a lay Sephardi leader. The authority of the Chief Rabbi had never extended beyond Istanbul and the institution was discontinued until its revival in the nineteenth century.[9]

Eventually, Sephardim gained the upper hand and had succeeded in imposing their authority over the Romaniotes by the late sixteenth and early seventeenth centuries. The Romaniotes gradually underwent a process of Hispano-Judaization, and with the exception of a few isolated centres such as Ioannina in the Epirus,[10] assimilated completely into the numerically superior Sephardi group.

The struggles between Sephardim and the Romaniotes, and the ending of the institution of the Chief Rabbinate point to the fact that while eventually there came into being a united Judeo-Spanish culture area in the Ottoman Balkans and Asia Minor, this was never a political unit. Each community maintained its own leadership and its own intermediaries with the authorities. Each community remained independent. The Jewish tradition did not have a religiously sanctioned hierarchy, and the Ottoman rulers appear to have seen no inconvenience in dealing with their Jewish subjects in a decentralized manner, through local Jewish intermediaries. The latter could sometimes be rabbis, but were more often than not lay leaders. This in fact followed the Ottoman pattern of rule, whereby many a conquered area had its leadership left intact and established its relationship with the centre through particular and specific laws and provisions. There was no centralized system of governance in the Ottoman territories until the onset of westernizing reforms in the nineteenth century.

Indeed, Sephardi communities remained internally fragmented for many decades after their arrival. Congregations (*kehalim*) formed according to geographical places of origin, new immigrants joining or creating congregations with other Jews stemming from the same areas in Spain, Portugal, and other lands. Each congregation maintained its own rabbis, synagogues, and charitable organizations. Schisms within congregations led to the creation of new ones. Rabbinical sages in certain cities, such as Samuel de Medina in Salonica (1506–89) who had highly respected halakhic authority, acted as agents of unity by dispensing widely accepted legal rulings. Nevertheless, divisions within communities continued to be a major problem in most Sephardi centres until the seventeenth century. Gradually, differences in origin faded and circumstances such as fires, plagues, and increased exactions in taxation led to a relative unity and the emergence of one *kehillah* (community) within each city, with its leadership in charge of dealings with the authorities, the law courts, and taxation.[11] But there never came into being an empire or region-wide united Jewish leadership until the appointment of the last Ottoman Chief Rabbi, Haim Nahum, who after 1909 attempted to enforce authority over all the Jews of the empire.[12]

The communities enjoyed a certain degree of internal autonomy. The Jewish court of law, the *bet din*, applied Jewish religious law whose jurisdiction covered all areas of life. Litigation between Jews and Muslims had to be conducted in Muslim law courts where the Jews were under a considerable disadvantage, as Islamic law favoured the testimony of Muslim witnesses over that of non-Muslims. Nevertheless, even many cases involving only Jews were tried in Muslim courts in spite of the fact that this was severely disapproved of by the rabbinical leadership. There is considerable evidence to suggest that the decisions of Jewish courts of law did not have the wholehearted sanction of the state and many took their cases to the Muslim courts to obtain clear rulings and prevent the overturning of cases later. The juridical autonomy of the Jewish community, though substantial by modern standards, should be characterized as a relative one at best.[13]

Communal councils made up of the most influential members of the community, together with the rabbis, were responsible for the collection of the poll tax as well as other levies which they presented as a lump sum to the authorities, assessing the contribution of each taxpayer according to his means. This was also the case for internal communal capitation taxes paid by individuals, known as the *pesha* in Salonica and the *kitzbe* in Istanbul, which were used for the maintenance of communal institutions such as the schools (*Talmudei Torah*), academies of higher learning (*yeshivot*), charitable organizations, and various funds for the ransoming of captives and aiding the Jews of the Holy Land. Indirect taxes for the same purposes were levied on cheese, wine, and meat.

The whole system of Jewish self-governance relied upon the economic well-being and achievements of the individual members of the community. The intellectual and social Golden Age of the Sephardim in the Ottoman empire paralleled closely their rise to prominence in the Ottoman economy in the sixteenth century. The urban skills brought by the Jews from Europe were well suited to the gaps that existed in the economy. The Sephardim were well connected to trade circles in Europe, links that were strengthened and replenished by the ongoing arrival of marranos. Don Joseph Nasi (*c.* 1524–79) and his aunt Gracia (1510–69), wealthy marrano financiers and merchants who managed to transfer most of their wealth to the empire, illustrate this trend. Joseph Nasi played a very important role in the finances of the empire under the rule of Sultan Suleiman the Magnificent (1520–66) and Sultan Selim (1566–74), was active as tax farmer, banker, and trader, and used his knowledge of the European economy and political system not only to his own advantage but also for the sultans' benefit.[14] Many other Sephardim, conversant in European languages and way of life, worked as intermediaries between the locality and the world markets.

Commerce with Italy, especially Venice, was particularly important in this respect. Sephardim dominated Ottoman trade with Venice. Spalato (Split) on the Dalmatian coast became a free port in the late sixteenth century upon the instigation of a wealthy Sephardi Venetian financier, Daniel Rodriguez, and emerged as the entrepot of the overland trade route through the Balkans and Macedonia which was controlled by the Sephardim.[15] The Jews of Salonica established a flourishing textile industry, and woollen textiles, as well as lead, hides, wax, pepper, linen, and cotton were exported from various parts of the empire to Venice.

In fact, in a paradoxical way, the very Sephardim who had been expelled, and their descendants, having risen to great economic heights under the Ottomans, became thus desirable commodities in the West. The economic 'utility' of the Levantine Sephardim drove rulers to more lenient policies vis-à-vis the Jews as a whole. Venice and Livorno gave them relatively liberal charters in 1589 and 1593 respectively and encouraged their presence. This argument from 'utility' which was to underpin mercantilist policies towards the Jews in the Europe of the seventeenth century, and influence their toleration in and readmittance to areas from which they had been expelled, was linked directly to the appreciation of real or perceived Jewish success in the Levant.[16]

Ottoman Sephardim were also active as translators, merchants, money-lenders, tax farmers, provisioners to the army, and were an important source at the mint. The Hamon family constituted a dynasty of doctors at the court, gaining the ear of the sultans and acquiring great wealth and influence.

The textile industry of Salonica, and to a lesser extent that of Safed, employed thousands of Sephardim.[17] The production of cloth was considered of such great importance by the authorities that the poll tax to be paid by the Jews of Salonica was transformed to a tax in kind in 1568 to be paid in set amounts of cloth to the janissaries every year. Jews were, of course, active in many other areas of the economy as artisans, shopkeepers, pedlars, small-scale traders, etc.[18]

This variegated and successful economic profile of the community provides the background to its rich intellectual life in the sixteenth century. Sephardim established the first printing press in the empire in Istanbul in 1494. The cities of Istanbul, Salonica, and Edirne emerged as very important centres of Hebrew publishing. The same cities together with Safed rose to become the principal centres of Jewish intellectual life. Important *yeshivot* and *Talmudei Torah* were established in all these centres. The great *Talmud Torah* of Salonica attracted students from as far away as Poland. Great halakhic sages such as Joseph Mitrani, Jacob ben Habib and his son Levi ben Habib, Samuel de Medina, Joseph Taitazak, Josef Levi (Bet Halevi) taught in these institutions and produced numerous works of Jewish religious law. Joseph Caro moved to Safed after teaching in Istanbul, Edirne, Nikopol and Salonica and wrote the celebrated and authoritative Jewish law code, the *Shulhan Arukh*, which became the standard accepted code for Jewish communities in the empire and in Europe. Kabbalistic thought also rose to prominence, most notably in Safed where Moses Cordovero, Salomon Alkabez, Isaac Luria, and Hayim Vital studied and taught.[19]

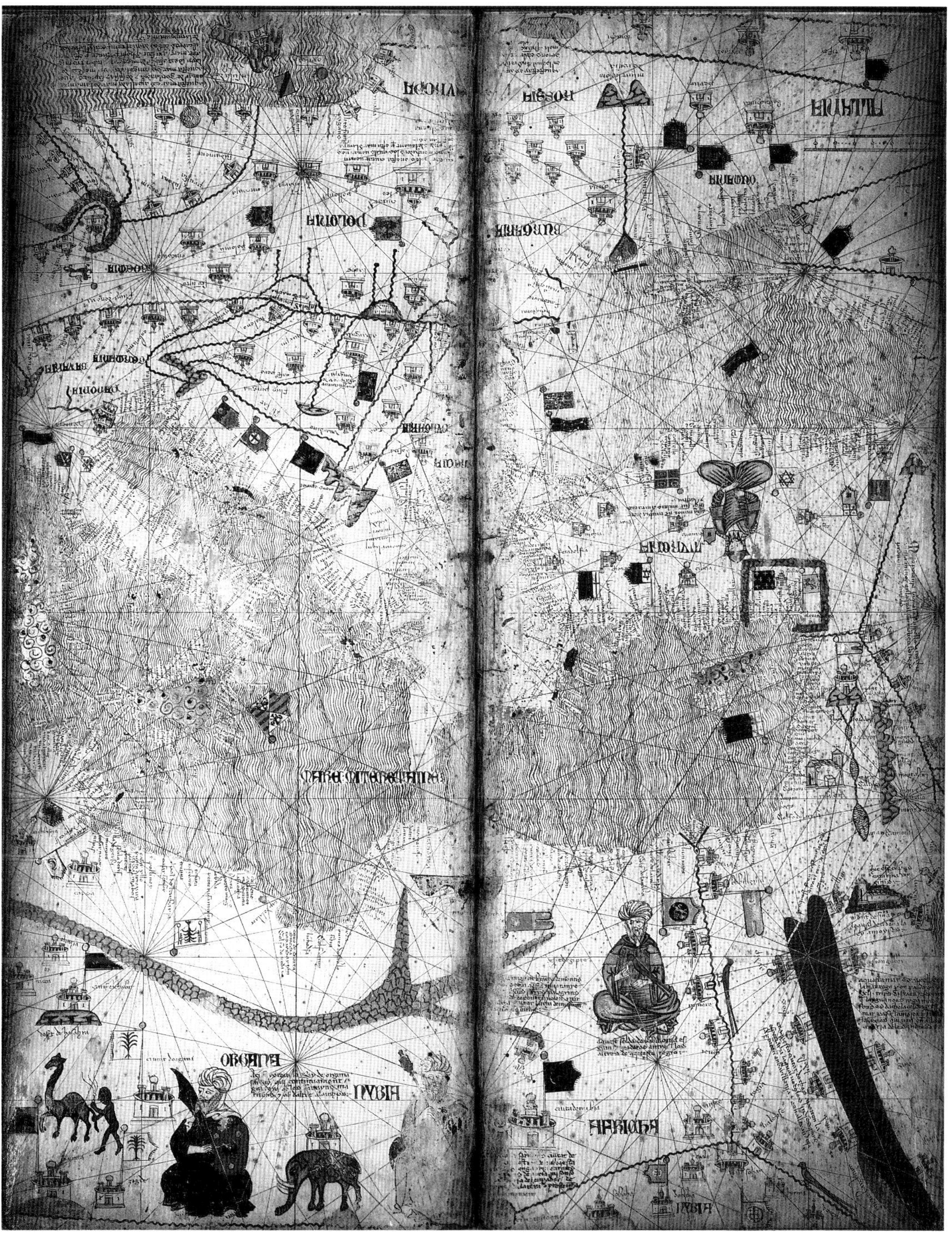

Map of the Eastern Mediterranean by the Jewish cartographers Abraham and Judah Cresques, late 14th century. Africa is at the bottom, with the Mediterranean Sea, Italy, Greece, Turkey and Palestine, and the Red Sea bottom right. To many of these lands the expelled Jews made their way.

The Ottoman empire was for many of the Jews the safest refuge. By 1535 there were 8070 Jewish households in Istanbul (above) as against only 1647 in 1477.

The Messianic movement, nourished by Kabbalah, won many adherents after the expulsion. In 1665 Sabbetai Sevi, who came from the Sephardi community in Izmir, proclaimed himself the Messiah and attracted a following all over Europe. This illustration is from a book published in England. Under threat of death, he renounced Judaism and converted to Islam.

A Jewish doctor in Turkey during the 16th century. The Hamon family practised at the court of the sultan.

Doña Gracia Mendes was the head of a powerful Sephardi family trading with Istanbul. She helped many refugees on their way there via Italy.

A middle-class Sephardi family in Salonica, c. 1890. The husband wears the Turkish fez, the women Western-style clothes and the older woman Greek dress.

In the Netherlands the Sephardi community flourished. Its Amsterdam synagogue, inaugurated in 1675, was the most splendid in the world. Designed by a Dutch architect, it still stands within an enclave of its own.

Opposite: Rembrandt's 'Jewish Bride' commemorates the wedding of a Sephardi couple whose names have not survived.

Rabbi Menashe ben Israel, a Kabbalah scholar instrumental in the return of the Jews to England.

The philosopher Baruch Spinoza, excommunicated for his rejection of traditional Jewish teachings.

Above: Isaac D'Israeli, man of letters, pillar of the London Sephardi community (until he quarrelled with them and left) and father of the future prime minister.

Moses Montefiore, a successful businessman, became the effective leader of the English Sephardi community in the 1830s. Right: with his wife entering Jerusalem in 1839.

Opposite: interior of the Bevis Marks Synagogue, London, built in 1700 and still intact. The huge brass chandeliers were donated by the Sephardim of Amsterdam.

דע לפני מי אתה
עומד
אנכי ה'
לא יהיה
לא תשא
זכור את
כבד את
לא תרצח
לא תנאף
לא תגנב
לא תענה
לא תחמד

The picture began to darken for the Sephardim from the end of the sixteenth century onwards and the community as a whole began a slow but steady process of decline in most areas, a decline that was to last until the nineteenth century. In many ways, the fortunes of the Sephardim followed those of their Ottoman overlords. The empire had reached the height of its expansion at the end of the sixteenth century and was stopped militarily by European powers on land and at sea. The price inflation that affected Europe with the introduction of Spanish bullion into the markets spilled into the Ottoman empire, seriously disrupting the financial system, leading to increased reliance on the part of the Ottomans on rapacious tax farmers who exploited the taxpaying population for their own ends. The janissaries, deprived of booty with the halt in the expansion of the empire, became an unruly element that added to the growing anarchy. The sultans and the centre began to lose control over the distant provinces, and local overlords to emerge in the peripheries, sapping central rule.

The Sephardim were adversely affected by these changes. Jews historically always suffered with the decline in central authority and this case was no different. Local governors increased their exactions. Fortunes were arbitrarily confiscated, affecting severely the process of capital accumulation. Even the fortune of Don Joseph Nasi did not escape this fate upon his death in 1579. Increased taxation, disasters such as fires and plagues caused serious problems for most communities. The Salonica textile industry, embroiled in local difficulties stemming from these developments, could also not compete with the new English cloth flooding the market and went into a serious decline, surviving as a pale shadow of its former self until the nineteenth century.

The central causes of the decline of Sephardi Jewry, however, lay in some serious structural economic changes that affected the whole area. The opening of new trade routes to the East that went around Africa rather than through the Mediterranean led to the decline in importance of trade in the Mediterranean. Italian cities such as Venice lost their preeminence in this trade with which the Jews had been intimately associated, being replaced by the English, the French, and the Dutch who soon became the dominant elements thanks to the capitulations treaties signed by the Ottomans, beginning with the French in 1535. These treaties granting extensive concessions and preferential treatment to the European signatories made it very difficult to compete with them. Furthermore, the weakening of the Italian connection for the Jews was not replaced by the forging of major ties with these new forces on the scene. The Greeks and Armenians whose elites began to develop close relations with Europeans and frequently sent their children to study at universities abroad, slowly came to replace the Jews as intermediaries in the lucrative trade with the West, becoming the preferred local interlocutors of European merchants.[20]

In the USA, the Sephardim came largely from South America. One of their oldest surviving buildings is the Touro Synagogue (called after the first cantor) at Newport, Rhode Island, begun in 1759.

The Sephardim lost the central advantage that they had enjoyed over their competitors in the Levant, their links with western economic interests, and their up-to-date knowledge of developments in European economy and politics. The immigration of marranos into the empire slowed down substantially in the seventeenth century, the new centres of trade such as Amsterdam, London, and Hamburg, around which the ascendant Atlantic economy revolved, attracting them more than Levantine cities. Just as western Europe began to rise economically and politically, Sephardi Jewry slowly became more eastern, more inward-looking, buffeted by the winds of chaos and anarchy that threatened it from within and from without.

This context proved ripe for the bursting forth of the greatest messianic movement in Jewish history. The study of the *Zohar*, the most important book of Jewish mysticism, had become quite popularized in the course of the sixteenth century. Developments in kabbalistic thought taking place in Safed and the emergence of the Lurianic Kabbalah gave a great impetus to esoteric contemplation and calculation. This and the undercurrent of messianism that had been with the Sephardi exiles since the expulsion fused in the person of Sabbetai Sevi to produce a messianic explosion that affected most of the Jewish world. A Sephardi Jew from Izmir, Sabbetai Sevi claimed to be the Messiah in 1665 and announced the beginning of redemption. He attracted a huge following from all sections of the Jewish population inside and outside the Ottoman empire, being greeted with extraordinary mass enthusiasm wherever he travelled. Many stopped work and sold all their belongings in preparation for the ingathering of the exiles in the Holy Land. While at first the authorities ignored the movement, its revolutionary implications were brought to their attention by some of its opponents. They gave Sabbetai Sevi a choice between conversion to Islam or death in 1666, whereupon he chose the former. A stunned Jewish world woke up from its dreams, though substantial numbers continued to believe in Sevi, many even choosing to follow him in his conversion to Islam. These formed the *dönme* (from the Turkish word to turn) sect which was to survive until the twentieth century in Salonica.[21]

While Sabbateanism was undoubtedly linked to internal developments in Jewish thought and practice in the sixteenth and seventeenth centuries, and especially to the popularization of the Kabbalah, the economic and social crises that had become endemic in the Sephardi world with the onset of decline provided an important impetus for the search for radical solutions. Sabbateanism was a symptom, a response to the malaise, and in return contributed powerfully to it. The tremendous psychological letdown that followed in its aftermath was compounded by a growing rigidity on the part of the Sephardi rabbinate as a whole, fearful of new uncontrollable outbursts of messianic fervour. Intellectual decline came to accompany the economic one even more closely in the course of the eighteenth century, with very few original or revolutionary rabbinical works being written in the major Sephardi centres.

However, the decrease in religious knowledge among the masses led in response to a new cultural development that was to have important consequences. Rabbi Jacob Houlli (Culi) embarked upon the writing of a vast popular compendium of commentaries and of religious lore in Judeo-Spanish in order to educate and bring moral teaching to the masses. The first volume, on Genesis, was published in Constantinople in 1732 under the title of *Me-am Loez*. The work was continued over the years until the end of the nineteenth century by many rabbinical scholars, covering most of the books of the Bible, and constitutes a veritable encyclopaedia of Jewish and more specifically Sephardi thought and legend. It enjoyed a huge success and the individual volumes of the *Me-am Loez* became the most read and studied of all books in the Sephardi communities, each household owning a well-worn copy.[22]

Judeo-Spanish had remained primarily an oral language until the publication of the *Me-am Loez*. The Sephardim had clung tenaciously to the Spanish that they had brought with them since the expulsion. While this language remained close to the Spanish of the Iberian Peninsula in the first half of the sixteenth century, it gradually grew apart as contact with Spain declined. The fact that it was written in Hebrew characters also contributed to this development. Loan words from Hebrew, Turkish, Italian and Greek set their own distinctive stamp on the language. Like Yiddish, it eventually developed into a separate language, though remaining much closer to Spanish than did Yiddish to German.[23]

In the first two centuries after the expulsion, relatively little was published in Judeo-Spanish. Whatever was published consisted, with the exception of a few works, of translations of sacred Hebrew texts, such as the translation of the Pentateuch which appeared in Istanbul in 1547. The prayer book as well as the Passover *Haggadah* were also translated. The latter acquired the sacred character of the originals, remaining fixed and immutable. As the language evolved over the centuries, these translations and the language that they contained became more and more archaic for the masses. Rabbinical and scholarly writing proceeded always in Hebrew and was inaccessible to the majority of the Sephardi population.

Hence the revolutionary importance of the *Me-am Loez*. For while it had a religious-moralistic aim, the work was a major and lengthy publication in the language of the masses. It legitimated the usage of Judeo-Spanish in intellectual discourse and set a powerful precedent for the emergence of a significant secular Judeo-Spanish literature and press in the nineteenth century.

Looking at the picture on the eve of the modern period, it can be said that the Sephardim of Ottoman Asia Minor and the Balkans, with smaller communities in Syria, Palestine, and Egypt, formed a distinct group in the mosaic of religions and ethnicities that made up the Levant. Deeply embedded in the Ottoman milieu, and adopting many of the eating habits, dress, and customs of their surrounding societies, they nevertheless, like other groups in the area, remained apart. Judaism as a religion, and a deeply held identity revolving around the Judeo-Spanish language, formed the core of their self-definition. Outside influences remained weak and uneven, and declined as the community grew more inward-looking in the aftermath of the Sabbatean debacle. Whatever came from the outside such as food or music was filtered, domesticated, and Judeo-Hispanicized to form part of the Sephardi tradition. Both the Ottoman policy of keeping groups apart, and a strong sense of Judeo-Hispanic consciousness resulted in the making of a clearly demarcated and separate Sephardi identity.

Renewal and change in the twilight years of the Ottoman empire

This Judeo-Hispanic community, numbering close to 250,000 by the end of the nineteenth century, and in deep economic decline, was profoundly affected by the rise to dominance of the West in the economic, cultural, and political life of the Ottoman empire from the end of the eighteenth century onwards. Both the modernizing reforms instituted by the Ottomans and the creation of new states in areas where Ottoman rule fragmented were the result of the massive incursion of triumphant western might into the region. The fundamentals of political, cultural, and economic life had to rise to the challenge of growing western domination and undergo radical change. Whether in its acceptance or rejection by local groups, the impact of the West became the determining factor in most areas of the public life of the Levant in the nineteenth century.

Of all the features of western power, the one that proved most irresistible to old and new political elites was the modern state, especially the French nation-state. The strong post-revolutionary Napoleonic French state that evolved in the course of the nineteenth century, highly centralized, rationalized and bureaucratized, emerged as an ideal model for all the elites interested in political change in the region.

The Ottoman officialdom adopted western state-building practices to strengthen the power of the central administration. This affected all the inhabitants of the empire, including the Jews as well as other non-Muslims. The reforms known collectively as the *Tanzimat* which began in 1839 promised the guarantee of the life, honour, and property of all the subjects, irrespective of religion. The reform decree of 1856 granted formal legal equality to Ottoman Jews together with other non-Muslims, hence spelling the end of the *dhimma*. This was further elucidated in the new citizenship law of 1869 which formulated explicitly the new conception of Ottoman citizenship which included all the subjects of the Sultan. The Ottomanist agenda of the reformers implied a united citizenry loyal to the Sultan with religion and ethnicity retreating to the realm of the private. This obviously made the existing legal autonomy of the various non-Muslim groups undesirable.[24]

Hence, as in the West, legal emancipation of the Jews was accompanied by a serious erosion of the legal autonomy of the Jewish community. Criminal, civil and commercial litigation were subject from 1856 onwards to new codes introduced in the middle of the century. In 1850 the French commercial code and in 1858 the French penal code were adopted, and since these now were not based on Muslim religious law, they were made to apply to all subjects of the empire. Indeed, for all intents and purposes, the autonomy of the non-Muslim groups in civil, criminal and commercial matters came to an end in 1856. The decree gave them the option of continuing to use their own courts in cases involving family, inheritance, and divorce litigation. Juridical autonomy in matters concerning personal status was all that remained to each group.[25]

The decree of 1856 also called upon the non-Muslims to reform their communal administrations. The term *millet* (the Turkish word for a religious group that soon was to have connotations of 'nation') had come to be used increasingly to designate the Greeks, Armenians, and the Jews. New regulations re-organizing *millet* bodies prepared by the non-Muslims came into effect in the decade following the decree.[26] The new administrations were explicitly hierarchical organizations with the laity having a major say in the running of communal affairs. The religious leaders of each group, in the case of the Jews, the Chief Rabbi, were now formally the juridically recognized leaders of the communities and acted as their representatives in affairs that were of concern to them. The new organs appear to have been mainly confessional bodies, with most matters outside the religious realm falling outside their purview. Nevertheless, the very fact that each *millet* administration still functioned as a representative body vis-à-vis the authorities, added legitimacy to group identity and jeopardized the creation of a united Ottoman citizenry.

The Ottomanist agenda of the reformist officialdom failed. Several factors contributed to this. Western interests interfered incessantly, preventing any development that might hamper their freedom of action, and using the safeguarding of the protection of the various privileges of the Christian groups of the empire as pretexts to erode the effectiveness of the centralizing measures of the state. Traditionalist Muslim groups resisted newfangled ways and resented the growing equality given to the infidel. Various non-Muslim elites, seeing new options and alternatives, threw their weight into separatist nationalist policies. And last but not least, the cultural implications of Ottomanism remained vague and ambiguous. It was unclear whether the ideal aimed for was a culturally uniform Ottoman-Turkish speaking citizenry. The reformist bureaucracy was remarkably slow in developing a unitary Ottoman education system. It was only in 1869 that secular Ottoman primary schools began to be established, and this very slowly. In 1895, only eighty non-Muslims were attending these schools in all of the empire.[27] When the Young Turks adopted Turkicization as the goal after 1908, it was already too late. In spite of various efforts to increase control over the separate education systems of the various *millets*, these survived intact until the end of the empire. Few non-Muslim schools taught Turkish effectively, and few instilled great loyalty in the Ottoman state.

Hence until the end, the empire remained a mosaic, a patchwork of ethnic and religious groups, all pulling in different directions, all with separate agendas. Not only did particularist identities not weaken, but the uneven growth of state power stemming from the ineffective adoption of the centralizing measures of the western state contributed to the exacerbation and intensification of ethnic and nationalist sentiment.

In this multi-ethnic, polyglot setting, the failure of the Ottomanist agenda blunted any real cultural Turkicization of the Sephardi community. Instead, the cultural realm was left open to the massive involvement of western Jewry in the affairs of Ottoman Jews through the action of the Alliance Israélite Universelle.

An organization founded in Paris in 1860 by French Jews, the Alliance played a very significant role in the history of Sephardi Jewry in modern times. It was active in defending the rights of the Jews throughout the world. But its real work was to be in the field of education. Emancipated and increasingly acculturated French Jews at the head of the Alliance saw European culture and modern europeanized Judaism as superior to the culture and achievements of eastern Jews. A westernized educational system appeared as the panacea for all the ills facing the Sephardim.

Starting in 1862 in Tetuan in Morocco, the Alliance opened elementary, and eventually secondary schools for Jewish boys and girls throughout North Africa and the Middle East. By 1913, it had established a network of 183 schools with 43,700 students in an area ranging from Morocco in the west to Iran in the east. Generations of Sephardim were educated in these institutions which provided an essentially French instruction with the addition of Jewish subjects such as Jewish history, religious instruction, and Hebrew to the curriculum. The Alliance played a crucial role in the westernization process of Sephardi Jewry.[28]

The first school in a major Turkish centre was established in Edirne in 1867. This was followed by schools for boys and girls in Istanbul and Izmir in the 1870s. By 1914, each Sephardi Jewish community in the Ottoman empire had an Alliance school. After often rocky beginnings, the schools slowly became accepted by the local communities. At first, they began as private establishments, with very few students. Eventually they gained in popularity. Opposition from the traditionalist camp, itself in deep crisis, was soon overcome. For the first time in the history of Sephardi Jewry, girls also began to attend the schools. Indeed, this was perhaps the most revolutionary development that followed the establishment of western education in the Sephardi communities. It became normal and desirable for girls to receive an education, and this eventually opened new paths for Jewish women, not only in the professional realm, but also in contributing to the social advancement of women within the family, and within society at large.

The Alliance institutions expanded particularly rapidly at the turn of the century. Large centres such as Istanbul, Izmir and Salonica had more than one school each for boys and girls. In many cases, what began as elementary establishments slowly became secondary ones. Accountancy classes were added. Vocational training schemes were established to teach new trades. Many youth clubs, alumni organizations, mutual help groups, libraries were set up around the schools. The language used in all these centres was of course French, although Hebrew was not ignored, though it was taught mainly for the purpose of enabling the students to read and understand the Bible and the prayer book. By 1914, it can be said that in the Judeo-Spanish speaking communities of the Ottoman empire, the Alliance was the force with the greatest influence on all the Jewish educational establishments, and came close to establishing a monopoly on Jewish education.[29]

But the importance of the schools should also be interpreted in the context of the economy of the region and the economic and political rivalry between the non-Muslim groups of the empire. The nineteenth century saw a massive incursion of European economic interests into the Levant. The Anglo-Ottoman trade convention of 1838 heralded the beginning of free trade with the West, with the lowering of taxes on trade, and the abolition of state monopolies. Accompanied by the introduction of the steamboat to the Mediterranean, commerce with Europe had increased dramatically by the middle of the century.[30] The Greek and Armenian commercial classes, by now the traditional intermediaries with the West, benefited tremendously from this growth.

It was French that had emerged as the *lingua franca* of all trade and commerce in the Levant, and its acquisition was essential for success in the international and indeed local marketplace now dominated by western economic interests. The popularity of the Alliance schools in Turkey was the result of this larger development. A European orientation in general, and knowledge of European ways and languages in particular, were considered crucial by the Sephardi commercial elite in order to compete effectively with the Greeks and Armenians, and to improve the lot of the desperately poor masses. With Jews flocking to Alliance schools, and eventually, in much lesser numbers, even to other establishments such as

Catholic and Protestant schools set up by missionaries, a major cultural opening to Europe took place in the decades that preceded the First World War. In the context of the reforms undertaken by the state and the domination of the economy by Europe, western education came to constitute for the Jews a major tool for the re-establishment of economic links with the West that had been lost in the previous two centuries, and thus for their elevation into the ranks of the predominantly non-Muslim mercantile classes.

This was nowhere more in evidence than in the port city of Salonica which became the most important entrepot of trade with Europe in the nineteenth century. The Jews constituted close to half of the population of Salonica and the process of westernization contributed directly to their gaining control of the economic life of the booming city by the end of the century. Firms such as those of Gattegno, Burla, and de Boton played an important role in trade with Europe. The exportation of grain, wine and beer production, textile and tobacco industries all attracted Jewish capital and know-how. The Allatini, Modiano, Fernandez, and Morpurgo families were active in banking and in industry.[31]

The fact that it was French instead of Turkish which became the language of instruction for the Sephardim of the empire had important consequences, especially in the cultural realm. French came to pervade all aspects of cultural life. Many upper-class families abandoned the usage of Judeo-Spanish at home, preferring to adopt French as their principal language. Judeo-Spanish itself underwent a dramatic change, succumbing to the invasion of hundreds of loan words from French. The language of the 1900s had become quite different from the language of the 1840s.

The opening of the horizons of Sephardi Jewry to the West, especially to France, led to an explosion of journalistic and literary activity. Given the fact that the mass constituency was still largely Judeo-Spanish speaking, writings emerged primarily in this language. Istanbul, Izmir, and Salonica became centres of Judeo-Spanish publishing. David Fresko's *El Tiempo* and Izak Gabay's *El Telegrafo*, newspapers founded in the 1870s in Istanbul, propagandized aggressively for modernization. They became dailies in the 1880s and continued to publish until the 1930s. Aron Hazan's *La Buena Esperansa* and Alexander Ben Giat's *El Meseret* in Izmir, and Saadi Halevi's *La Epoca* in Salonica also developed to become important Judeo-Spanish newspapers.[32]

This press was crucial in the forging of a Sephardi political culture. It was also instrumental in introducing the masses of Sephardi Jewry to European literary genres. Most of the French classics were translated into Judeo-Spanish in feuilleton form in newspaper columns, providing a powerful impetus to the emergence of a secular Judeo-Spanish literature. The novella, adapting the themes of European classics to the local setting, emerged as a favourite genre by the twentieth century. Elia Karmona and

Alexander Ben Giat were especially prolific authors, and published between them close to one hundred novellas in the first two decades of the twentieth century.

The efflorescence of the Judeo-Spanish mass-media and literature was a direct result of westernization. Although the language of instruction and that of high culture had become French, the language of the masses, the language used in daily speech had, by and large, remained Judeo-Spanish. It was this mass of Sephardi Jewry which remained the natural public for the journalist and the author. Western ideas could be popularized only through the medium of Judeo-Spanish. Nevertheless, by the first decade of the twentieth century, the number of those completely at home in French had become sufficiently large to allow the creation of a viable French press. *Le Journal de Salonique* of Salonica and *L'Aurore* of Istanbul were particularly significant in this respect.

The state had now begun to create many more institutions of secondary and further education, and public careers were becoming open to those Jews with a good knowledge of Turkish. Applying the western model of the nation-state to the Ottoman empire, many Jews began to propagandize in favour of the necessity of the adoption of Turkish as the mother tongue of the Jews. Societies for the propagation of the language emerged at the turn of the century and especially after the Young Turk Revolution of 1908 which appeared to promise new vistas to all the citizens of the empire.[33] Nevertheless, the movement in favour of Turkish remained largely ineffective. French remained popular as the language of civilization *par excellence*. Although a relatively large number of Jews were now continuing their education after the Alliance schools in Turkish institutions, the majority of the Jewish population remained satisfied with the Alliance. The multi-ethnic nature of the empire, the existence of many different educational systems associated with the different religious and ethnic minorities, the relative weakness of the Ottoman education infrastructure, all contributed to the relative slowness of Turkicization among the Sephardim. The strong sense of a distinct Sephardi identity remained intact.

In fact, the acquisition of French, far from weakening Sephardi ethnicity, simply marked it even more. French became domesticated, Judaized, Hispanicized. The ethnic boundaries shifted and accommodated French and western ways, and emerged strengthened. A strong Jewish identity and ethnicity, though now more secularized, remained paramount in the self-definition of the group.

This facilitated the receptivity of many to the Zionist movement that began to affect all the major Sephardi communities after the Young Turk Revolution. Zionism went from strength to strength in communal politics in the years just prior to the First World War and expressed in a modernized form the aspirations of westernizing Sephardi intellectuals and masses that continued to perceive the Jews as a distinct and specific collectivity in the Levant.[34]

At the same time, unlike other non-Muslim nationalist movements, Jewish nationalism in the empire does not appear to have favoured its dissolution. Rarely was there talk among Sephardi Zionists of an independent Jewish state in Palestine. The latter was seen rather as a land that would serve as a safe haven for the persecuted and would become a national home of the Jews under the rule of the Ottoman Sultan.

The interests of the Jews were well served by the continuation of the empire as a multi-ethnic entity. Like their Habsburg counterparts, the Jews were one of the few loyalist groups in the Ottoman empire at a time when separatist nationalisms had made deep inroads into the non-Muslim populations, and the ruling Turks themselves had begun to abandon Ottomanism for a more exclusive Turkish nationalism.

Sephardi participation in Ottoman politics remained low. There appears to have been a brief flurry of activity at the time of the Young Turk movement. There was considerable support for the Young Turks among the Jews in the years 1908–09.[35] Individual Jews such as Albert Fua, Emmanuel Carasso, and Nissim Mazliach were active in Young Turk politics. But there was no real mass involvement of Jews in the public arena. Centuries of marginality within the political process, and the long tradition of separation between the ruler and the ruled that marked Middle Eastern power relations did not predispose the Sephardim to activity in the public sphere.

However, this did not preclude a genuine loyalty felt by all sections of the Jewish population towards the Ottoman fatherland. There was no convergence culturally, and weak political participation remained the norm. Nevertheless, Jews counted on the continued existence of the Ottoman state. With the rise of nationalism among the various groups of the region, inter-ethnic conflict had started to reach major proportions and the Jews were often at the receiving end. From 1840 onwards, blood libel accusations by the Greeks and Armenians emerged with great frequency, followed by riots and mob attacks on the Jews.[36] The re-emergence of this medieval accusation was closely tied in with growing economic rivalry between the groups, but was also fuelled by the perception among the Christians that the Jews and the Turks were both together opposed to their aspirations. And indeed, it was always the Turkish authorities that intervened to protect the Jewish community in periods of crisis engendered by the blood libel accusation.

There was a certain element of truth behind the perception that the Jews were strong supporters of the Ottoman state. A reformed westernized empire with its policy of tolerance and non-intervention vis-à-vis the Jews was clearly preferable to the new intransigently nationalist states that were coming into being, where the Jews would constitute a small beleaguered minority under the rule of their traditional rivals. Whenever given the chance, Jews worked to the utmost to prevent the collapse of Ottoman rule in contested regions.

This is particularly clear in Salonica in 1912–13, when the entry of the Greek army was met with great alarm by the Jewish population in the town. The Jews of Salonica appealed with great urgency to leading Jewish personalities and organizations in Europe to use their influence with the great powers to prevent Salonica's annexation by the Greeks and to maintain Turkish rule, and failing that, to internationalize the city into a free port so that it would not fall under Greek control. And European Jewry did intervene, though to no avail.[37] As a result, over 10,000 Jews migrated to Turkey in the year following the Greek conquest, and many others began to move to Europe and the Americas. This trend was amplified after the First World War, leading to the continuous haemorrhaging of a great community that, facing serious economic and political difficulties under its new masters, went into a steep decline until it was completely annihilated during the Holocaust.

On the eve of the conquest of Salonica by the Greeks in 1912, the Sephardim of the empire had been an integral part of the Ottoman social fabric for centuries. Forming a distinct group, they had preserved substantial elements of their Iberian heritage, most notably in custom and in language. After a long period of decline, the last century had seen a major improvement in their condition as a result of westernization. The latter process had altered their cultural, social, and economic profile dramatically, re-integrating them successfully into the complex structure of relationships between the West and the Levant.

The Ottoman empire, itself in the throes of westernizing reform, with a long tradition of relative toleration of the Jews, appeared to promise the best option for the Sephardim to survive and flourish in the Levant. The new nation-states of the Balkans emerging as a result of the fragmentation of Ottoman power, intransigently nationalistic, promised nothing but problems. And indeed, the retreat of the Ottoman empire in the nineteenth century and its definitive collapse after the First World War was to lead to the most revolutionary, dramatic, and often catastrophic changes in Sephardi life since the departure from the Iberian Peninsula.

In November 1912, Joseph Cohen, a teacher at the Alliance school in Salonica sent the following letter to his superiors in Paris, describing the situation that followed the entry of the Greek army into the city:

> It is done... and no sooner has the Turk abandoned the city than anti-semitism has reared its ugly head, with the entry of the first Greek soldiers into town.
>
> One must say that the Jew in great sadness has no time for the celebrations taking place in the city. He has adopted the correct and dignified attitude that is

proper to the vanquished. He cannot greet with enthusiasm the victor who tramples upon his most cherished sentiments. It is when one loses what one has that one appreciates its true value, and the Jews who had always recognized the rare qualities of tolerance and good will of the Turkish people, feel today that they have lost in this terrible cataclysm their strongest and surest protectors. The simplest among the people have come to me with tears in their eyes saying that they cannot reconcile themselves to the ruin of the Ottoman fatherland. And even I who have often complained of the petty bureaucratic problems created for the schools by the old administration, even I feel devastated when I see our poor soldiers wander aimlessly in the streets without arms, in search of shelter and a piece of bread. The Greeks have invaded the barracks and our soldiers are in the street.... Today terrible rumours circulate in the streets. There have been accusations against the Jewish merchants that they have been selling poisoned drink to the Greek soldiers.... A long and painful experience has taught us that anti-semitism always begins like this, always takes this form that eventually leads to massacres.[38]

Joseph Néhama, the director of the Alliance school ended his own letter reporting the same events with the following premonitory note:

What will be our fate in the new circumstances in which we find ourselves? One fears the worst. Many speak of total ruin and of a mass exodus from Salonica as a result of anti-semitism and of the new economic conditions engendered by the war.

Bakalum [let us see], as would say our old masters, and let us add, like them, always wise and confident, *Allah kerim* [God is kind].[39]

These sentiments reflect faithfully the attitude of Sephardi Jewry towards the Ottoman empire in its twilight years, marked by the realization that the world it had known for the last four centuries was in collapse, and was being replaced by an infinitely more dangerous, sinister, and unpredictable Middle East and Levant.

Chapter Eight

The Sephardim in the Netherlands

JONATHAN ISRAEL

The Sephardim of Antwerp: a commercial elite

For four centuries the Sephardi presence in the Netherlands, and especially in Amsterdam, has been of far-reaching significance for the rest of Sephardi Jewry, the Jewish world as a whole, and also for the Netherlands itself. Organized Sephardi communities based on normative Judaism did not come into being in the Dutch context until the early years of the seventeenth century. Yet decades before this occurred, groups of crypto-Jews of Iberian background settled in various places in the Low Countries, especially in the city of Antwerp. From this precarious toehold in what was then the Spanish Netherlands, crypto-Jews of Sephardi origin went on to play, by the late sixteenth century, a substantial role in the international commerce and financial activity of a country which, at that time, was the hub of the entire European and world economy.

At the time of the expulsion of the Jews from Spain in 1492, Iberian Jewry, including those who had been forced into baptism, as yet had little or no connection with northern Europe. The Jews (and forcibly converted Jews) of Spain and Portugal were then only just beginning to participate, through investment and in other ways, in long-distance voyages of exploration and trade. It was essentially during the half-century following the mass forced baptism of all the Jews – including the great mass of recent Spanish immigrants – in Portugal in 1497, that the conversos of Lisbon and Oporto (most of whom remained loyal to the religion of their ancestors in their hearts and in their private lives, even while publicly acting as Christians) captured a major share in the overseas and colonial commerce of Portugal. By the middle of the sixteenth century, the crypto-Jews of Portugal included a large and sophisticated semi-Christianized business elite, experienced in financing long-distance voyages and merchandizing in East Indian products, including diamonds and pearls from India, and the products of West Africa and the Portuguese West African island of São Tomé. After 1550 they also captured a growing share in handling the sugar shipped from Madeira, São Tomé, and, from the 1570s onwards, increasingly also from Brazil back to metropolitan Portugal. In the secular sphere, it is this conspicuous and energetic involvement in capital-intensive, transoceanic business enterprise, dealing in new and costly commodities from Asia, Africa, and the New World, which most clearly distinguishes the role of Iberian crypto-Jewry in the life of the Peninsula and of Europe as a whole from that of the pre-1492 Jewish and crypto-Jewish populations of Spain and Portugal. Transoceanic commerce and investment was not just an impressive extension of previous activity but by 1550 was the mainstay, the basis of the economic and social existence of Portuguese crypto-Jewry. The commodities of Asia, Africa and Brazil also provided the material basis on which the emerging colonies of Portuguese crypto-Jews, precariously established in other parts of western Europe outside the Iberian Peninsula, took root and grew. These outlying colonies which arose in the sixteenth century then in turn became the nuclei around which modern western Sephardi Jewry emerged and developed. The modern Sephardi communities of the Netherlands, Hamburg, France and England – and several of those of Italy – all arose in this indirect way.

By and large those Iberian crypto-Jews who left the Peninsula – usually Portugal – for northern Europe during the sixteenth century were not seeking places of refuge and security where they might, without hindrance, or at least without risk of severe persecution, revert to normative Judaism. The movement northwards was not religiously motivated, whether or not this can be said of much of the simultaneous migration of Portuguese crypto-Jews to Italy and the eastern Mediterranean. For while liberty of conscience and worship was on offer in the Ottoman empire, including the Balkans, and in some places in Italy (at any rate until the 1550s) the Spanish Netherlands was the place where religious intolerance and persecution of what the Catholic Church regarded as heresy was most prevalent. Under the Emperor Charles V, who was ruler of the Netherlands from 1506 to 1555, a rudimentary form of Inquisition was established in the 1520s and the machinery of religious persecution became gradually more oppressive. The vast majority of those arrested, interrogated, tortured and executed for heresy were Protestants of one sort or another, especially Anabaptists, but a not inconsiderable number of crypto-Jews suffered too. Nor was there any opportunity for the open practice of Judaism. Just as most Protestants in the Spanish Netherlands from the 1520s onwards confined their religious opinions, books, and practices to the most private parts of their homes, so did the slowly growing Portuguese crypto-Jewish community of Antwerp. Yet Antwerp was from the outset, until Amsterdam assumed this role in the 1590s, the unrivalled hub of Portuguese-Jewish cultural, intellectual and religious activity in the whole of Europe north of the Alps and Pyrenees.

The reason for this concentration of activity on Antwerp lay in the close economic and political links between the Spanish Netherlands and the Iberian Peninsula on the one hand and its colonial empires on the other. Antwerp was the general store-house and emporium for all Spanish and Portuguese colonial commodities in northern Europe. It is certainly true, even at this stage, that loyalty to Jewish tradition played a central and crucially important part in the lives of many of the conversos who migrated to northern Europe. But it was the economic role of the Portuguese crypto-Jewish communities which prepared the ground and created the conditions which made possible the emergence after 1600 of a secure and thriving northern European Sephardi Jewry. There had to be a viable material and social basis and there was no other way this could be achieved, given the fact that all traditional areas of commerce, finance and industry in northern European countries were fenced around by privileges, restrictive legislation and guild regulations designed to exclude outsiders of whatever description from gaining a foothold, except by bringing new commodities and trade links to the emporia of the north. Prospects for a successful extension of Sephardi Jewish religious, educational and intellectual activity to the northern parts of Europe in the sixteenth and seventeenth centuries would certainly have been much worse, and probably non-existent, without this new and vitally important economic dimension.

In 1511 there were still only a score or so 'Portuguese' living in Antwerp. In 1526, at a time of preoccupation with the Protestant threat, it had not yet been realized in official circles that along with the 'Portuguese' settlement, crypto-Judaism had taken root in the Spanish Netherlands. By the 1540s the 'Portuguese' community was playing a major part in the business life of a city which at that time outstripped London, Venice, and every other European commercial centre, not least as an emporium for colonial products. But mounting suspicion and indications of the crypto-Jewish nature of their beliefs and private religious activity aroused the hostility of the Emperor and the Church and, in 1549, an order was issued expelling from the city and the Spanish Netherlands all those Portuguese New Christians who had arrived since 1543. It took some years for the community to recover from this blow. With the rapid weakening of Spanish governmental control in the Low Countries following the departure of the new ruler, Philip II of Spain (1555–98) from the Spanish Netherlands to Madrid, in 1559, the Portuguese converso community at Antwerp recovered in numbers and, with the far-reaching gains achieved by the Protestants in the Low Countries in the mid-1560s, increasingly escaped from the close scrutiny of the past. The arrival of the Duke of Alva with a large Spanish army in the Low Countries in 1567 restored Spanish control temporarily, and led to five years of severe repression. But Alva and his regime had too much to do trying to contain the now massive increase in Protestantism in the country to pay any attention to the relatively small converso population which was still largely confined to Antwerp. In 1571, a year before the outbreak of the main Dutch revolt against Spain, the number of Portuguese New Christians in Antwerp was officially listed as eighty-five families and seventeen unattached individuals, suggesting a total community of around four hundred adults and children.[1]

It should not be supposed that all of these were carrying on Jewish observances and remaining loyal to Judaism in private. But a wide variety of evidence shows that many or most of them were. From 1530 onwards a series of Portuguese conversos residing in Antwerp were arrested by the authorities for judaizing. One of the most notable of those who was unquestionably loyal to Judaism, and to the cause of rebuilding Jewish life in the Netherlands, was a wealthy merchant by the name of Diogo Mendes (d. 1543) who was arrested in 1532 after living in the city for twenty years and having assisted a number of other crypto-Jews in a variety of ways. Mendes' nephew, João Miques, who assumed the name Joseph Nasi, has already been mentioned (Chapter 7, p. 167). Felipe de Nis (Solomon Marcos), born at Oporto, son of a famous converso physician, for twenty years lived as a factor for Lisbon merchants on São Tomé, before moving to Antwerp where he lived in the 1570s. Subsequently he migrated, still as a crypto-Jew, to Cologne, before finally settling as a practising Jew in the ghetto at Venice.

The crypto-Jewish community of Antwerp was at its height in the early 1570s before the sack of the city by mutinous Spanish troops in the so-called 'Spanish Fury' of 1576. After 1576, when part of the Antwerp Portuguese New Christian community left the city and scattered in various directions, some settling temporarily in Cologne, Middelburg, London and other places in northern Europe, others leaving for Venice, the community declined. Nevertheless, throughout the remainder of the sixteenth century and the first half of the seventeenth, it remained substantial both in terms of numbers and commercial importance. Not until the late 1590s did Amsterdam and Hamburg begin to outstrip Antwerp in significance for the Sephardi Jewish diaspora as a whole. In 1591 the Antwerp Portuguese converso community consisted of fifty-seven families plus some twenty or so unattached persons.

The move to Amsterdam

The northern provinces which broke away from Spanish rule in 1572 and set up what subsequently developed into the fully independent republic of the United Provinces, followed from the outset a very different religious policy from the Spanish Netherlands. Under the terms of the Union of Utrecht (1579), the founding constitutional document of the Dutch republic, it was laid down that the conscience of the individual living under the rule of the seven provinces was free and that no-one should be investigated or prosecuted on grounds of religion. Moreover, although the Catholic faith was officially suppressed and only the Dutch Reformed Church enjoyed full freedom of public worship, in practice Protestant dissenting churches and the Jews were free to organize private religious gatherings in their homes, as early as the 1570s and 1580s. Despite this, hardly any of the crypto-Jews living in Antwerp, and (before 1595) scarcely any crypto-Jews from elsewhere, chose to settle either in Holland or Zeeland, the two maritime provinces of the Dutch republic, or in fact anywhere in the newly born state. The main reason for this at first glance rather surprising state of affairs was that although the Dutch already played a large part in the shipping of bulky commodities around northern and western Europe, especially of Baltic grain and timber, and Iberian salt, they did not at this time offer a viable basis for the long-distance 'rich trades' or for processing and distributing the colonial products in which the Portuguese converso business class specialized. In this period the Dutch provinces seemed an unattractive haven, not only to the crypto-Jews but also to those Protestant refugees from the southern (Spanish) Netherlands who specialized in this sphere of activity. Most Antwerp elite merchants and sugar refiners, Christian as well as crypto-Jewish, preferred not to join in the great migration of Protestant refugees from the Spanish Netherlands to the United Provinces which culminated in the late 1580s following the reconquest of Antwerp by the Spanish troops in 1585.

After 1585 the Portuguese New Christians in Antwerp could in theory continue to operate in the Spanish Netherlands, under pretence of being Christians, on the same basis that they had before 1572. But while the Spaniards had recovered Antwerp and most of Brabant and Flanders, they failed to clear the Dutch rebels from the sea around the Scheldt estuary, which meant that the Dutch continued to control the flow of maritime traffic in and out of Antwerp and lost no time in subjecting it to heavy restrictions and taxes in order both to divert business to the United Provinces and cream off useful revenue. This meant that Antwerp's days as the dominant entrepot for the 'rich trades' were over, especially by the 1590s when the Dutch also tightened up their maritime blockade of the Flemish seaports, making it difficult for Antwerp merchants to bypass the Scheldt estuary by importing and exporting through Dunkirk and Ostend. The northern Netherlands did not benefit initially from the suffocation of Antwerp, however, mainly due to the rather grim military situation which prevailed there until 1590. Though most of the middling and poorer Protestant refugees from the southern Netherlands settled in Holland and Zeeland in the late 1580s, both the Protestant emigré business elite and the migrating Portuguese crypto-Jews still preferred Cologne and Hamburg to Amsterdam, Rotterdam and Middelburg. It was only from 1590 onwards, when Philip II switched his main military effort to France (where

Henry of Navarre – at that time still a Protestant and a declared enemy of Spain – seemed likely to emerge from the continuing civil war as king) that the strategic and economic situation of the northern Netherlands was fundamentally transformed in such a way as to make Holland and Zeeland attractive to merchants involved in long-distance, transoceanic commerce. During the 1590s the Dutch rapidly increased their military and naval strength, cleared the Spaniards from the great inland waterways, reopening the routes linking Holland with Germany, and made their republic secure. As the situation in Holland improved, key merchants, capital, and specialized skills such as sugar-refining, started to move from the German commercial emporia to Holland, especially Amsterdam, and the first Portuguese crypto-Jews likewise, as part of this wider trend. By the late 1590s Amsterdam had already outstripped Hamburg, as well as Antwerp and London, as northern Europe's foremost emporium for sugar, spices, and all other products from the Iberian colonial empires.

Before 1595 there was thus practically no enduring crypto-Jewish settlement in the northern Netherlands. But once the process began, it moved forward with such speed that within four or five years, the community in Amsterdam was already by far the most important nucleus for Sephardi Jewish settlement and activity anywhere in northern Europe, and had gained permanent control over a very large slice of Holland's traffic in colonial products. This is clearly illustrated by the first major international incident involving Portuguese crypto-Jews, when, for the first time, the Amsterdam burgomasters and council stepped in to protect the interests of the Amsterdam 'Portuguese' – they were not yet described as 'Jews' officially, nor did they yet call themselves Jews in their dealings with the Dutch authorities – in the international arena. In 1601 the English allies of the Dutch in the war against Spain arrested six richly laden Emden vessels returning from Lisbon carrying colonial commodities belonging mainly to merchants living in Amsterdam, especially Portuguese crypto-Jews. These merchants had employed Emden vessels because, since 1599, Dutch vessels were prohibited in both Spanish and Portuguese ports, Portugal (since 1580) being now a dependency of the Spanish crown. When the English admiralty authorities refused to release the cargoes, Amsterdam warned the federal assembly of the United Provinces, the States General, to take firm action, maintaining that if the 'Portuguese' residing in Amsterdam were not protected by the Dutch state from such occurrences and losses, and the community was ruined or driven away, Amsterdam herself would suffer serious loss. Sixteen Portuguese merchants residing at Amsterdam, virtually all those of any consequence then living in Holland, were affected. The cargo included in the first place a large quantity of sugar loaded in Lisbon but originally from Brazil and São Tomé. There were also some ten packets of diamonds and pearls from India, a considerable quantity of cinnamon from Portuguese Ceylon, and smaller quantities of green ginger, indigo, and cotton wool as well as olive oil from metropolitan Portugal. It is significant that the load did not include pepper, nutmeg, cloves, or mace, these all being spices which the newly set-up Dutch East India Company (an organization in which the Portuguese conversos in Holland played very little part in the first half of the seventeenth century) could obtain in quantity and ship back in its own vessels from the East Indies. The business niche which the Portuguese crypto-Jews had carved out for themselves in the highly competitive Dutch milieu was confined exclusively to those colonial products which the Dutch could not (yet) obtain for themselves and which were available to the Dutch entrepot only indirectly via the Iberian Peninsula, principally Lisbon and Oporto. In the case of products originating in Asia this meant that the crypto-Jews living in Holland in the years around 1600 played a major part in the traffic in cinnamon which came only from Ceylon and Malabar (both of which were then firmly under Portuguese control), Indian diamonds and pearls, and ginger, but not in pepper and other East Indian spices. Dutch Sephardi Jewry continued to play a significant part in the importing of products from Asia into the Dutch republic only during the first three decades or so of its existence; for in the 1620s the Dutch East India Company broke into the China trade, ending the monopoly of Portuguese Macao over Chinese exports to Europe, and in the 1630s commenced its conquest of Portuguese Ceylon, ending the Portuguese monopoly over the cinnamon trade.

The synagogue revived

It is no accident that the key personalities of the crypto-Jewish community of Amsterdam in its early years – those who contributed to the emergence of Sephardi Jewish religious practice, institutions, education and welfare – were among the merchants who set up the trade in colonial products in Amsterdam and were involved in the 1601 incident. For the importing of colonial products from the Iberian Peninsula, in the early period mainly from Portugal, was the only possible material basis on which Sephardi Jewish settlement and religious institutional development could thrive. The 'Portuguese' were welcomed and protected only because they were bringing new strands of commerce which had not previously been present and which the Dutch town councils were keen to encourage.

Among the leading merchants involved in the incident of 1601 was James Lopes da Costa, whose Jewish name was Jacob Tirado. It was in his house that the first of the Amsterdam synagogues was established and it was after him, presumably, that the *Beth Ya'acov* congregation was named. A silver torah breast-plate which he had cast in Amsterdam in 1610 for the use of his congregation survives today as one of the principal early relics of Dutch Sephardi religious life. Another key merchant involved in the 1601 episode who played a major part in establishing normative Judaism in Amsterdam was Duarte Fernandes whose synagogue name was Joshua Habilho. He was one of the leaders of the first abortive attempt to build a 'public' purpose-built synagogue in Amsterdam in 1612 and it was he who took the lead in setting up, in 1615, the organization known as the *Santa Companhia de Dotar Orphas e Donzellas*, a charitable dowry society, based on a similar society set up at Venice a few years previously, one of the main aims of which was to encourage poor girls of New Christian background still in the Iberian Peninsula and even as far away as Brazil, to come to Amsterdam and marry as Jewesses in synagogue with dowries provided by the congregation. In addition to his commercial and communal activity, Duarte Fernandes had close links with the New Christians in Antwerp, and also played an important part during the Twelve Years' Truce between Spain and the Dutch (1609–21) in the murky world of secret Dutch-Spanish diplomacy. He was entrusted with several clandestine missions and, in 1611, when the court favourite of King Philip III of Spain, the duke of Lerma, tried to tempt the Dutch leader, Johan van Oldenbarnevelt, into concluding a permanent settlement with Spain on the basis of total Dutch withdrawal from the Far East and all parts of the 'Indies east and west' which they had penetrated, it was Fernandes who conducted Lerma's secret emissary, a Portuguese New Christian friar called Martin del Espiritú Santo, to the house of the Dutch leader in The Hague.

The main trend amongst the Portuguese crypto-Jews who settled in Holland in the 1590s and the first decade of the seventeenth century was to return with some enthusiasm to the laws, life-style, beliefs and culture of the synagogue. However, by no means all of the Portuguese crypto-Jewish merchants who came to Holland at this time were as committed to the rebuilding of organized Judaism as were Lopes da Costa, Fernandes, and a number of others. One important Portuguese trader in early seventeenth-century Amsterdam, Manoel Carvalho, who was given the synagogue name Moseh de Casseres, admitted in 1643 that although he had been living in the city for many years, he had not professed the Jewish religion until as late as 1616. There is no doubt that many were reluctant or half-hearted about giving up a life of ambivalence and non-commitment, suspended between Judaism and Christianity, for an open, undisguised return to Jewish observance. The first decade of the seventeenth century was decisive for establishing a normative Jewish framework as the dominant tendency amongst the Portuguese crypto-Jewish community in Amsterdam, and by the second decade of the century the main stream had succeeded sufficiently to be generating the sort of pressure that sufficed to suck in many, or most, of the reluctant and half-hearted.

The demographic and economic impetus behind Sephardi settlement in the Netherlands in the 1590s, and the first part of the seventeenth century, derived chiefly from Portugal itself and in the second place from Antwerp. It was quite otherwise, however, with regard to the momentum behind the new community's spiritual, cultural and institutional development. The arrivals from Portugal and Antwerp provided the population base and material success for the early development of Dutch Sephardi Jewry, but such immigrants – even while their leaders provided the resources and initiative for a mass return to normative Judaism – could not provide the models, or specifically religious leadership, which were required. They had little or no knowledge of Hebrew, Jewish law and synagogue ritual, and no means of forging a Jewish religious educational framework. The guidance and impetus for developing this aspect of early Dutch Sephardi Jewry could come only from the organized Sephardi diaspora in Italy and in Muslim lands. In fact Venice was the main source of inspiration and guidance.

The first religious teacher available to the Portuguese crypto-Jewish community at Amsterdam was an Ashkenazi rabbi from Emden named Moses Uri Halevi, who arrived in Amsterdam, together with several Portuguese converso families, in 1602. He served the community as rabbi, mohel, teacher and ritual slaughterer and, in 1604, took part in the negotiations with the Alkmaar city council, which some of the more committed amongst the Portuguese in Amsterdam initiated, hoping to be allowed to establish Jewish life on a freer basis there than was then permitted in Amsterdam. Shortly after Halevi's arrival a group of Sephardi immigrants had arrived from Venice and from the Levant via Venice and these newcomers, coming from a religious background very different from that of the immigrants of Portugal and Antwerp, reacted with impatience and aversion to the laxity, indiscipline and half-heartedness which they encountered amongst the Portuguese community in Amsterdam. At the same time that negotiations were initiated with Alkmaar, other towns were approached. A group of recent immigrants to Amsterdam applied, also in 1604, to the Haarlem city council, asking to be allowed to establish a 'public' synagogue there, at the same time undertaking to establish commercial links with Venice and the Levant. This group, interestingly, described themselves as belonging to the 'Portuguese and Spanish nation descended from Levantine and Ponentine [Western] Hebrews, or Jews, living and professing the Jewish religion in Italy and various places in Turkey'.[2] In the economic sphere the links with Venice and the Levant remained of only very marginal significance compared with the commercial connections with Portugal, Spain and the Iberian empires in Asia, Africa and the New World. But in the spiritual and cultural sphere, Dutch Sephardi Jewry – as early as 1604 – formed a clear dichotomy: on the one hand there was the vague, often half-hearted allegiance of converso immigrants from lands where the formal observance of Judaism was prohibited; on the other, there was the rigorous, fully-fledged Judaism brought by a mixture of Portuguese and Spanish-speaking Sephardim from Venice and the Levant.

The earliest Sephardi rabbis in Amsterdam were a certain Jeuda Vega, about whom virtually nothing is known, and Isaac Uziel (d.1622), the son of a rabbi of Fez, who, after a brief spell at Oran, moved to Amsterdam in 1606, becoming the rabbi of the second of the three synagogues which were established in private houses there in the early seventeenth century, the congregation called *Neveh Shalom*. The third Sephardi rabbi arrived in 1608. This was Joseph Pardo (d.1619) who came originally from Salonica, but had been living at Venice since before 1589, serving there as rabbi of the so-called 'Levantine' synagogue. From 1609 until his death, Pardo served as rabbi of the *Beth Ya'acov* congregation. Although it seems likely that *Neveh Shalom* was stricter than the *Beth Ya'acov* congregation in matters of ritual and observance, and that Pardo therefore was in some respects more liberal in religious matters than Uziel, we may be sure that all the early Sephardi rabbis in Amsterdam inveighed ceaselessly against the dithering, backsliding, and lukewarmness of many of the converso arrivals who had come direct from the Peninsula.

A major concern was to establish a Jewish burial ground for the use of the two Amsterdam Sephardi congregations. In 1606, and again in 1608, petitions requesting permission for the city burgomasters for the acquisition of land in the vicinity of the city for use as a cemetery were rejected. It was for this reason that the burial ground acquired by the short-lived Alkmaar Sephardi community adjoining the village of Groet, some forty kilometres from Amsterdam, was appropriated, in July 1607, by the Amsterdam community. Until 1614 those Amsterdam Sephardim who were given a Jewish burial – some of the Portuguese in Amsterdam were at that time still buried in non-Jewish cemeteries – were buried at Groet. In 1614, with the help of an immensely wealthy new arrival from Venice, Don Manoel Pimentel, the Amsterdam congregations finally acquired the relatively nearby burial ground on the Amstel river, at Ouderkerk. The purchase price of the land was 2700 guilders.

Pimentel who, on his death the following year, became one of the first congregants to be buried at Ouderkerk was a remarkable personality. He was certainly the richest Jew in Amsterdam during the short time that he lived there. He made several handsome donations to the *Neveh Shalom* synagogue, the congregation favoured by the Venetians and Levantines, and left a legacy of 250,000 guilders, reportedly to his children. He had a brother, Alvaro Pimentel, who was a rabbi at Constantinople and his family was reckoned one of the most select of the Portuguese Jewish diaspora. In his days as a New Christian he was said to have spent some years as a courtier to King Henry IV of France and had the reputation of being the 'king of gamblers'. Out of gratitude for his gifts, the congregations recited after his death a special memorial prayer every sabbath.

A few of the immigrants from Venice and the Levant were wealthy; most were poor men who, like Joseph Pardo, had failed in business or else been relatively unsuccessful. Those who migrated from Venice had remarkably varied backgrounds. One of the most colourful personalities was Jacob Pelegrino who lived in Venice for thirteen years before migrating to Amsterdam at some point before 1609. In 1611 he sailed on a Dutch vessel to West Africa where he remained for several years as the factor of Sephardi merchants in Amsterdam and Venice as well as Pisa. The proceeds of his trading activity, mainly gold and ivory, were shipped back partly to Holland and in part to Italy.

In so far as there was any continuing tension between the *Beth Ya'acov* and *Neveh Shalom* congregations this had, by 1618, been overshadowed by a growing quarrel within *Beth Ya'acov*. The wrangling was partly to do with personalities but also concerned *kashruth* and other matters of ritual and observance. In 1619 what is taken to have been the more orthodox element split away, under the leadership of *haham* Joseph Pardo, and set up the *Beth Israel* synagogue, the third of the early Amsterdam Sephardi congregations. As the warring parties were unable to negotiate a division of the congregational assets, the burgomasters intervened to adjudicate, enforcing a division of money, premises, ritual objects, and books which was heavily favourable to the original *Beth Ya'acov* synagogue. However, it would be wrong to assume that *Beth Ya'acov* subsequently developed in a markedly different direction religiously from the other two congregations. The dominant figure in the *Beth Ya'acov* synagogue after 1618 was Saul Levi Morteira (*c*.1595–1660) who had learnt his Judaism in Venice and who arrived in Amsterdam from Paris in 1616 bringing the remains of the celebrated physician and controversialist Elijah Montalto. Morteira was uncompromising in his orthodoxy, and a stern critic of converso laxity and backsliding, and was later, during the second quarter of the century and the 1650s, to become the leading theological controversialist of Dutch Sephardi Jewry, writing numerous tracts, in the Montalto tradition of polemicizing against Christianity and Christian beliefs, which had to remain in manuscript but were widely circulated.

Holland was geographically remote from the main centres of Sephardi life during the first century after the expulsion from Spain. There was no Sephardi community adhering to normative Judaism in the Low Countries before the first decade of the seventeenth century. Yet, within the space of just a few years Dutch Sephardi Jewry, and especially that of Amsterdam, acquired such great importance that it rivalled and soon overtook Venice as the hub of the western Sephardi world. This was partly to do with economic developments and patterns of commerce. The whole of the European commercial system was becoming, by the late sixteenth century, more orientated towards the Atlantic. But it also had to do with the exceptional degree of religious and personal freedom which was available in the United Provinces, which meant that living conditions for Jewish immigrants were more favourable in the Dutch context than elsewhere, including Venice. Another reason why Amsterdam so quickly assumed a position of leadership in western Sephardi life was the dominant position of the Dutch in the international book trade. Having cheaper supplies of paper and a more advanced technology of book production than other European countries, as well as unrivalled facilities for the export and distribution of books, it was probably inevitable that Amsterdam should very rapidly outstrip Venice, Constantinople, Salonica, and all other centres of Sephardi Jewish book production – and long retain its hegemony in the supply of Jewish books in Hebrew, Spanish and Portuguese to the entire Sephardi world, east and west. The very fact that the Sephardi Jewish world was so scattered and diffuse tended to encourage the overwhelming concentration of printing and book production at a single point. From the 1580s to around 1610 Venice was the unchallenged principal supplier of Jewish books to the Sephardi world. But from 1611 onwards a continuous stream of Jewish works, especially in Spanish, issued from the printing presses of Amsterdam, which soon eclipsed Venice as a centre for production of Jewish books in vernacular languages. Venice remained important as a centre of Hebrew publishing. But here too Amsterdam rapidly assumed the principal role.

Fluctuating fortunes: the Brazilian adventure

During the Twelve Years' Truce between Spain and the Dutch, Dutch Sephardi Jewry experienced one of the most explosively rapid periods of growth in its entire history. The Dutch economy as a whole acquired much new momentum from the lifting of the Spanish embargoes on Dutch trade with Spain, Portugal and the rest of the Spanish empire, and the crypto-Jewish population remaining in Portugal was, for the time being, able to maintain close communication with relatives and trading partners in the United Provinces. With hundreds of Dutch ships plying each year from 1609 to 1621 between the republic and the Iberian Peninsula, it was also relatively easy for refugees from religious persecution in Portugal and, to a lesser extent Spain, to emigrate with their families, and at least some of their possessions, direct by sea to Holland. By 1620 there were around 1000 Sephardim residing in the Dutch republic, the great majority in Amsterdam with a small community also at Rotterdam. To cater for the new immigrants, and strengthen the return to Judaism amongst recent arrivals and their children, various new welfare and educational institutions were established in Amsterdam at this time. In 1615–16, for example, the three Amsterdam congregations jointly established a day school, or *Talmud Torah*, for the education of their children.

But this unprecedented phase of expansion ended with the expiry of the Twelve Years' Truce in April 1621. The embargoes which had been in force in the years 1599–1608 were re-imposed and remained in force in the case of Portugal until that realm broke away from the Spanish crown in 1640 and in the case of Spain, the Spanish Netherlands and the rest of the Spanish empire, until 1647. This meant that for over two decades Dutch ships, goods, and commercial involvement were officially cut out of the Iberian kingdoms and their colonial empires. Although a certain amount of contraband traffic between Holland and the Iberian Peninsula continued, the previously flourishing commerce of the Dutch Sephardim, heavily orientated towards Portugal and the Portuguese colonial empire, was severely disrupted. A number of Dutch Sephardi merchants sustained an unbroken clandestine trade with Portugal and especially southern Spain, but the difficulties and risks were considerable. Not infrequently valuable cargoes consigned to Lisbon, Oporto, Málaga, or another Iberian port by Sephardi merchants in Amsterdam, using false papers and seals, and German, or English ships, or at least Dutch vessels disguised as German or English, were seized along with the ships by the authorities in the Peninsula. A particular speciality of Sephardi Jews was a new overland contraband route linking Madrid by road and mule-path over the Pyrenees to Bayonne in south-western France from where Dutch vessels chartered by Amsterdam Sephardi merchants carried to Holland the Spanish and Spanish American products, especially silver and merino wool, exchanged for the cloth and spices brought from Amsterdam to Bayonne – where there was now a flourishing Portuguese converso community – for the Spanish market. But this route too was blocked off in 1635 once France entered the Thirty Years' War against Spain, and closed the frontier at the Pyrenees.

The Spanish embargoes of 1621–47 squeezed the Sephardi community in the Netherlands both economically and demographically. Around 1621 a substantial number of Amsterdam Sephardim migrated, owing to the slump, to Hamburg and Glückstadt on the Lower Elbe from where it was easier at that time to maintain commercial contact with Spain and Portugal. The volume of trade handled by Dutch Sephardi merchants was drastically reduced. Whereas in 1620 no less than 114 Sephardi businessmen held accounts at the famous Amsterdam Exchange Bank, then the most important bank in northern Europe, a figure which represents 9.5% of the total number of Amsterdam Exchange Bank account holders, by 1625 only seventy-six Sephardim still held accounts, which now represented only 5.9% of the total. At the same time the increase in unemployment and hardship in the community meant that demands on the three congregations' welfare and charity institutions greatly increased. The synagogues were thus confronted with a veritable social crisis which they met by setting up, in 1622, a new joint welfare board called the *Imposta*, after the new special community tax which the three congregations agreed to levy on their congregants to provide the required additional finance. As well as supervising and improving the community's poor relief system, the *Imposta* strove to reduce the numbers of Sephardi poor on the community's books by subsidizing the emigration of some of the poor to distant communities in the Mediterranean. The success of this joint venture for regulating the community's social problems and the evident need for a common policy and regulatory machinery in the sphere of education, and in matters such as the provision of kosher meat, led to a gradual broadening in the functions of the *Imposta* and helped prepare the way for the merging of the three congregations and the creation of a single, all-embracing community structure for the whole of Amsterdam Sephardi Jewry. The constitutional arrangements were finalized and signed by the elders of the three former synagogues in April 1639. The new constitution consisted of forty-two articles. Under its terms, the three congregations united under the name *K(ahal) K(adosh) Talmud Torah* and services were henceforth conducted in just one central place of worship. As yet there was still not a 'purpose-built' synagogue. The community worshipped in a large converted warehouse which did not look, from the outside, like a place of worship, but which, in the style of the Venetian synagogues, was lavishly embellished within.

The rules and regulations which governed the life of the united Amsterdam Sephardi community were strict. The new board of seven elders, or *Mahamad*, co-opted from amongst the wealthiest and most influential lay members of the community, claimed and exercised authority over many other aspects of the life of the Sephardi community besides what actually went on within the synagogue and the school. The *Mahamad* ruled on matters of dress and social conduct and censored the writings of congregants, deciding what could and could not be published as well as what should not be read. Anyone who received charity from the community was likely to find his or her life governed by the communal authorities in all kinds of ways. There were even occasions when the *Mahamad* took it upon itself to make rulings concerning political matters, notably during the period of very tense relations verging on war between the United Provinces and Portugal over the fate of Dutch Brazil in the late 1640s. In cases where the secular interests of the community as a whole were affected, such as the seizure of Dutch Sephardi cargoes overseas by foreign governments, the *Mahamad* acted like a town government in representing the interests of the community to the Amsterdam burgomasters and, through them, to the States of Holland and the States General.

The great business slump affecting Dutch Sephardi Jewry continued until the 1640s. In 1641, the first year of Portugal's ports being re-opened to Dutch shipping, there were still only eighty-nine Sephardi account holders with the Amsterdam Exchange Bank, representing under 6% of the total number of account holders. The community continued to enforce the re-emigration of a high proportion of poor Sephardi immigrants as well as impoverished Ashkenazim fleeing the Thirty Years' War in Germany, on the grounds that the community lacked the means to support them. Nor was there any possibility of economic diversification since the guilds, shopkeeping and most areas of business remained closed to Jews. The one crucial change in the picture during the period 1621–47 was the effect on Dutch Sephardi Jewry of the Dutch conquest of the northern part of Brazil in the early 1630s. For about a decade, in the years 1635–44, the sugar plantations of Dutch Brazil throve, and under the auspices of the Dutch West India Company a large number of Dutch Sephardim emigrated to Brazil, mainly to Recife, and captured a large share in the sugar export business. Some Dutch Sephardim also briefly owned or managed sugar plantations in northern Brazil. As the outlook seemed promising and the West India Company granted Jewish emigrants who settled in Brazil much greater economic as well as religious and personal freedom than yet existed for Jews in the Dutch republic itself, the rush to Brazil assumed what for Dutch Sephardi Jewry were enormous proportions. By 1644 there were 1450 Sephardim living as Jews in Netherlands Brazil, a figure not much less than the total then living in Holland itself, and although a proportion of those in Brazil were former New Christians who had reverted to normative Judaism in Brazil, most had emigrated from, or at least via, the Netherlands.

By 1645 Dutch Sephardi Jewry was as dependent on the traffic in colonial commodities as it had ever been, especially sugar, but the community was now heavily orientated socially as well as economically towards Netherlands Brazil. During the decade 1635–44 Dutch Sephardi Jewry became an essentially transatlantic society with its attention firmly focused on what was happening in South America. Among those deeply preoccupied, on various levels, with Brazil at this time was the famous rabbi and printer Menashe ben Israel (1604–57), a member of the rabbinic staff of *Neveh Shalom* since 1622 and retained as a rabbi and teacher by the new united community after 1639. Besides his activity as a rabbi and scholar and, since 1626, publisher of Jewish books both in Hebrew and Spanish, Menashe also traded in books, exporting much of his output to Italy and elsewhere. Menashe was never regarded as a particularly outstanding rabbinic scholar in Jewish circles but, following the publication in 1632 of his *Conciliador*, a work resolving obscure and difficult passages of Scripture in Spanish, he enjoyed a considerable and growing reputation as a learned man amongst Christian clergymen and academics in England as well as Holland. From the 1630s onwards he showed a degree of interest in cultivating contacts with the Christian world, and especially learned men, which was highly unusual amongst rabbis in early modern times. Menashe was interested in the establishment of synagogues in the New World from a spiritual point of view. But he also took a keen interest in the business aspects of Sephardi settlement in Brazil. From the late 1630s onwards he invested heavily in the Brazil trade, collaborating with his brother, Ephraim Soeiro who went out and settled in Brazil. At one stage Menashe himself was on the point of doing so.

The optimism generated by the rapid progress of the Dutch Sephardi colony in Brazil proved shortlived. The whole venture, and the commerce linked to it, collapsed with the sudden revolt of the Catholic Portuguese in Netherlands Brazil in 1645. In a matter of months the hinterland of Dutch Brazil was devastated, the plantations burnt, the economy ruined. By the end of the 1640s many of the Sephardim who had settled in the colony had already returned to the Netherlands or moved on to find fresh opportunities in the Caribbean. When what was left of Netherlands Brazil finally surrendered to the Portuguese crown in 1654, the rump of the community in Recife was shipped off in its entirety. Many returned to the Netherlands, swelling the community at Amsterdam and establishing another at Middelburg, others migrated to the Caribbean area, including Barbados. One small group settled in New Amsterdam (New York).

The collapse of Netherlands Brazil was a disaster for Dutch Sephardi Jewry. But the disruption of Dutch commerce with Brazil happened just as the Eighty Years' War between Spain and the Dutch was drawing to a close, and when important new opportunities for Sephardi settlement were opening up in the Caribbean. As a result, the scattering of Sephardi settlers from Brazil in the years around 1650, settlers used to the tropics, skilled in sugar cultivation and expert in trading in a variety of New World products, had many positive as well as negative aspects. The Dutch-Spanish peace treaty of 1648 restored commercial links between the Dutch republic and Spain and resulted in the Spanish crown agreeing to allow Jews who were Dutch subjects to trade with Spain and Spanish America legally through Christian factors residing in Spanish ports. At the same time the deterioration in the position of the Portuguese New Christian merchants and financiers living in Madrid and Seville which commenced following the downfall of the Count Duke of Olivares in 1643, and the resurgence of Inquisition activity in Spain in the late 1640s, generated a sustained flow of immigrants and capital from Spain to the Sephardic communities in the Netherlands which continued from the late 1640s down to 1672.

This combination of factors – the restoration of links with the Spanish empire, the flow of immigrants and capital from Spain to Holland, the rise of new Caribbean plantation economies producing sugar, and also the collapse of Venice's trade with the Levant during the Venetian-Turkish war of 1645–69 – gave Dutch Sephardi Jewry the most flourishing and dynamic phase in the whole of its history. In the period from the lifting of the Spanish embargoes (1647) down to the French attack on the Dutch republic in 1672, the Amsterdam Sephardi community grew to reach its maximum extent, a total of around 3000 souls. A network of small subsidiary Sephardi communities arose, or were re-established at Rotterdam, Middelburg, Maarssen, Amersfoort, Nijkerk, and a little later at The Hague. At the same time thriving new Dutch Sephardi communities grew up on Barbados, from the late 1650s on Curaçao, in Surinam and Jamaica. Although Barbados and Jamaica were, of course, English not Dutch colonies, the Sephardi communities there were regarded as essentially 'Dutch', their trade links being more with Amsterdam than with London until late in the seventeenth century.

Overseas commerce mainly with Spain, Portugal and the Caribbean remained the basis of Dutch Sephardi economic life from the middle of the seventeenth down to the end of the eighteenth century. The range of occupations open to Dutch Sephardi Jews was significantly widened during the middle decades of the seventeenth century, however, due to the rise of semi-industrial activities connected with the processing of colonial products in which Sephardim specialized, and the rapid growth in the number of Jewish brokers and dealers who found employment in and around the Amsterdam Exchange and stock market. Particularly important in opening up employment opportunities for poor Sephardi as well as Ashkenazi Jews were the Sephardi-owned tobacco spinning and blending workshops and the diamond cutting and polishing establishments in Amsterdam. In the early 1650s when the influx from Brazil, Spain, and Venice was at its height and the new possibilities only beginning to become evident, Dutch Sephardi Jewry was permeated with anxiety and a sense of crisis. The various Dutch Sephardi projects for colonization which surfaced in the 1650s, settling groups of poor Sephardi Jews in the Guyanas, Curaçao and elsewhere, were one symptom of this mood. Menashe ben Israel's famous book, *The Hope of Israel* (1650), written in the midst of the Brazilian debacle, and his project for the resettlement of the Jews in England to which he devoted all his energies in the mid-1650s also reflected this urgent need, albeit in Menashe's case suffused with mystical yearnings for new perspectives and openings in every relevant direction.

During the second half of the seventeenth century Dutch Sephardi Jewry was at its height both in demographic terms and in terms of the importance of its economic role. It is arguably also at this time that the community was at its zenith in terms of cultural achievement, as this has been seen as the time of the most decisive religious and intellectual developments in its history. One of these developments was the short but sharp encounter with the radical biblical criticism and deistic tendencies introduced on the Dutch Sephardi scene in the mid-1650s by Baruch Spinoza (1632–77) and Juan de Prado. The ferment which they caused in the community should be considered against the background of a much wider furore over the relationship between philosophy and religious faith which was in progress in Dutch society at that time, the States of Holland issuing an unprecedented decree on philosophy and religion in the same year, 1656, that Spinoza was excommunicated from the community. This latter was the culmination of a community campaign against 'philosophical' rejection of rabbinic authority which reached back to the somewhat rigorous treatment meted out by the *Mahamad* and the rabbis to the undoubtedly heretical, and in some respects confused, but also tragic and lonely figure of Uriel da Costa who had committed suicide in Amsterdam in 1640 and whose key work, the *Examen dos Tradicoẽs Phariseas* (1624), suppressed at the time, has recently been rediscovered by scholarly research in the Royal Library at Copenhagen.[3] Spinoza, after leaving the Sephardi community, learnt to philosophize in Latin rather than in Portuguese, Spanish, or Hebrew, and went on to become the most important of all thinkers, Christian or Jewish, of the Dutch Golden Age. But he also remained a highly controversial and somewhat isolated figure, his rejection of the notion that the Bible is divine revelation leading to his being reviled during his lifetime and after by virtually all organized religious communities in the Netherlands and beyond.

Sabbateanism and its aftermath

During the 1660s the Dutch Sephardi community was convulsed by the messianic movement associated with the figure of Sabbetai Sevi (see chapter 7, p.178). During 1665 probably most of the community became caught up in the wave of mystical enthusiasm which was sweeping the whole of the Jewish world and especially the Sephardi communities. Some of the leading merchants at Amsterdam were reported to be preparing to sell up and migrate to the Holy Land as part of the ingathering of the Jewish people in preparation for the messianic age which was now supposedly dawning. The disillusionment which followed the news of the apostasy of Sabbetai Sevi, in 1666, proved profoundly unsettling, not least because in Holland, as in Italy and the Levant, there were those who refused to be disillusioned or to give up their millenarian yearnings, and who continued to believe that Sabbetai Sevi was the Messiah. Among those who refused to discard their Sabbatean beliefs was Daniel Levi de Barrios (1635–1701), the most notable of the poets and writers in the Spanish language during this half-century when Dutch Sephardi involvement with Spanish literature and secular literary activity was at its peak. Levi de Barrios, who had arrived in Amsterdam in 1662, was one of the new wave of immigrants from Spain, as was his friend Isaac Orobio de Castro (1620–87) who arrived in the same year via southern France, and who also came, like so many of the new immigrants, from Andalucia.

Orobio de Castro, Dutch Sephardi Jewry's most eminent lay writer on philosophy and theology in the late seventeenth century, adopted a very different, rather hostile attitude to this lingering Sabbatean tendency. Levi de Barrios' post-1666 Sabbateanism was particularly marked during the 1670s when his literary activity was at its height. His most significant compilation of poetry and prose, the collection named the *Triumpho del govierno popular*, was published in Amsterdam in 1683.

A notable feature of the secular culture of the Dutch Sephardi community during the second half of the seventeenth century was the high degree of interest shown in literature and the patronage of Sephardi literary activity by the wealthiest and most influential members of the community, men such as the Baron Manuel de Belmonte, 'Agent-general' of Spain at Amsterdam, the Baron Antonio (and his son Francisco) Lopes Suasso, great financiers with important links with the Spanish and Dutch governments, and Jeronimo Nunes da Costa (Moseh Curiel), 'Agent' of the crown of Portugal in the United Provinces and the most important Dutch Sephardi merchant trading with Portugal during the second half of the century. These men patronized individual writers and publications and they also encouraged the setting up of the two literary societies, or 'academies', in Amsterdam. The first, set up in 1676, was called *La Academia de los Sitibundos*, and had the same name as a parallel academy which was set up at Livorno in the same year. The second, *La Academia de los Floridos*, was set up (and probably did not continue long beyond) 1685. The lay leaders of the Dutch Sephardi community encouraged the cultivation of Spanish literature no doubt partly for its own sake. But they were also motivated by a desire to reflect the kind of sophistication in languages and literature which was expected of diplomats and noblemen in the European society of their day. Belmonte, Lopes Suasso, and Nunes da Costa regularly hosted Spanish, Portuguese and other diplomats and nobles in their homes and liked to adorn the dinners which they gave in their honour with literary conversation, just as they liked to show off their collections of rarities and fine town gardens. Orobio de Castro was particularly useful in this connection since he could also double as a physician if any distinguished guest became ill, as once happened, for example, when a German prince was staying in Nunes da Costa's house.

The expansion of the Amsterdam Sephardi community during the third quarter of the seventeenth century rendered the old synagogue of 1639 inadequate and obsolete. Once the Sabbatean frenzy was over, the lay leadership of the community also felt a need to reassert in the most emphatic way the community's rootedness in its Dutch context. In 1670 the decision was taken, with the broad support of the community, to raise the large sum that would be required to build a magnificent new synagogue together with adequate outbuildings to house the community's collections, stores, school-rooms and offices. An additional motivation for embarking on this major building project was a desire, for reasons of status and prestige, to outdo the Amsterdam Ashkenazim who had earlier obtained permission from the city council to build a large public synagogue and engaged the services of one of the leading Dutch architects of the time, Elias Bouman. The Sephardi community also engaged Bouman and the four corner foundation stones of the great new synagogue, intended from the outset to be the most imposing then existing anywhere in the Jewish world, were laid – the first by Jeronimo Nunes da Costa – in April 1671. Though it was intended that the construction work should be completed in 1672, work on the synagogue had to be suspended owing to the outbreak of the Franco-Dutch war and was not finally completed until 1675. The inauguration of the new synagogue in 1675 was regarded by the community's chroniclers as one of the most significant events in the history of Amsterdam Sephardi Jewry.

At the end of the seventeenth century the commercial importance and financial resources of the lay leadership of the Dutch Sephardi community were still vastly greater than those of the Dutch Ashkenazi leadership. The Sephardim at this time also exercised vastly more leverage than the Ashkenazim in the stock market. The Amsterdam stock exchange was in fact the first true modern stock market and it is striking that by the 1680s the majority of the dealers who handled the day-to-day business, which mainly involved shares in the various chambers of the East and West India Companies, were Sephardi Jews. On the whole this was accepted without much controversy but when things went badly wrong, and there were three major crashes when vast sums were lost in 1672, 1688 and 1720, there were sudden surges of anti-semitic comment and feeling, including (certainly in 1688) the accusation that the Jews were deliberately manipulating the stock exchange by spreading lies in order to strip honest Christians of their money. The Sephardim themselves regarded the stock exchange as a highly paradoxical, even dangerous phenomenon, and one of the most fascinating books written in Spanish by any of the group of Dutch Sephardi writers of the late seventeenth century is the famous description of the stock exchange, the *Confusión de Confusiones* (1688) by Joseph Penso de la Vega (1650–92), another whose family had fled relatively recently from Spain. Penso de la Vega's book was addressed specifically to the Sephardi community. He warned them to take great care in their encounters with the stock exchange, an institution which he considered more convoluted and scarcely less hazardous than the labyrinth of Crete.

The Dutch Sephardi patrician elite which was at the zenith of its wealth and power at the end of the seventeenth and beginning of the eighteenth century had no real parallel in other Sephardi communities. At Bayonne, Livorno and Venice there were also Sephardim of great wealth. But these lacked the diplomatic agencies and the titles and patents of nobility issued by European monarchs and princes which the Sephardi leadership at Amsterdam and The Hague possessed. The one family outside Holland which was of comparable status was that of Isaac Teixeira and his son, Diego Teixeira de Mattos, at Hamburg, where they acted as agents for Queen Christina of Sweden after her abdication, and performed financial services for various governments including the crowns of Denmark and Sweden. However, this family transferred to Amsterdam in 1698. It was also only the elite of Dutch Sephardi Jewry which was sufficiently intimate with governing circles in the host country to perform, on occasion, a role of real importance in general European politics. The most significant example of this is the involvement, through their close relationship with the Stadholder William III, of the Sephardi leadership in the Dutch intervention in Britain which triggered the Glorious Revolution of 1688. On that occasion Baron Francisco Lopes Suasso played a notable part in organizing the financial side of several aspects of that immensely bold and risky operation, including the forwarding of the marching costs of the 6000-strong Swedish army, which the States General hired from the Swedish enclaves in Germany. The two leading Dutch Sephardi military contractors, Moseh Alvares Machado and Jacob Pereira, supplied the bread and provisions both for the Amsterdam contingent of the invasion armada itself and for the Dutch reserve army under Prince Waldeck which was stationed on the inland border to prevent any French attempt to interfere.[4]

The eighteenth century: gradual decline

The process of gradual decline which characterized the history of the Dutch Sephardim in the eighteenth century was perhaps an inevitable result of the general waning of the Dutch overseas trading system and of the commercial and financial role of Amsterdam. It is true that in contrast to the Sephardim, the Dutch Ashkenazi community managed to grow in prosperity and economic importance during the eighteenth century despite the difficulties of the Dutch economy as a whole. But this was because the Ashkenazi business elite had the considerable advantage of a much larger and more pervasive internal Ashkenazi retailing and distribution network, reaching down to the level of the thousands of Jewish street-sellers and pedlars to be encountered after 1700 in all parts of the northern Netherlands. The Sephardi community remained always tied first and foremost to colonial and Iberian trade and, as the importance of Dutch commerce first with the Iberian Peninsula and then, after 1780, also with the Caribbean area waned, the role of Dutch Sephardi Jewry relentlessly contracted with it.

The most remarkable personality of eighteenth-century Dutch Sephardi Jewry, Isaac de Pinto (1717–87), was acutely aware of the decline of his community and the social, economic and cultural difficulties in which it now found itself. In one of his first works (and the only one which he wrote in what was still his community's vernacular language, Portuguese), a pamphlet entitled *Reflexoens politicas tocante a constitução da nação judaica* (1748), de Pinto presented the community leadership with a sombre analysis of the community's economic prospects and a gloomy assessment of the likely impact of what he predicted would be a steadily rising burden of poor relief. In his most important publication on economic affairs, the *Traité de la circulation et du credit* (Amsterdam, 1771), de Pinto reassessed the general contribution of commerce and finance to the well-being of society as a whole, a discussion in part intended as an antidote to the anti-commercial bias of the physiocratic economic concepts then prevalent, especially in France. In his published work de Pinto considers aspects of the social and economic decline of Dutch Sephardi Jewry. But at the same time, the uncompromisingly secular tone of de Pinto's life and work, and his religious attitude, tinged as it was with deism and a marked philosophical bent, mirrored also the decline in religious observance which characterized large sections of the Dutch Sephardi community during the age of the Enlightenment.

During most of the eighteenth century, the period 1713–95, Dutch Sephardi Jewry declined visibly and substantially in most respects – cultural, religious, economic, social and demographic. But this long phase of decline was also very gradual, albeit becoming steeper with the outbreak of the Fourth Anglo-Dutch War of 1780–84 when Britain attacked the Netherlands for giving too much assistance to her enemies, the American rebels and the French, swept Dutch shipping from the seas, occupied several Dutch colonies and, among much else, severely disrupted Dutch Sephardi trade in the Caribbean, the last major Dutch Sephardi overseas market. But with the fall of the federal republic of the United Provinces, and the invasion of the French revolutionary armies in 1795, there began fifteen years of unprecedented economic, communal, and cultural upheaval, disintegration as well as (in some respects) renewal. The dismantling of the former constitution and political and legal institutions of the old republic, was paralleled, for the Jews, by the ending of the Jewish communities' legal and educational autonomy. All at once, in the midst of exceptional social and economic disruption, Dutch Jewry was hurled into the modern world, shorn of its special characteristics of the past, being granted full political and social emancipation in September 1796.

The tumultuous twenty years of the revolutionary and Napoleonic period, 1795–1815, mark the great divide in Dutch Sephardi – and in all Dutch Jewish – history. Practically all the structures and forms of the past were broken up or radically weakened and replaced by more modern patterns. In the particular circumstances of the Netherlands, it was a change which left Dutch Sephardi Jewry a mere shadow of its former self.

The economic vitality of the Dutch Sephardim was largely destroyed by the collapse of the Dutch maritime trading system and the devastation of Dutch shipping under the relentless pressure of revolution and war, the British occupying virtually all the Dutch colonies – in some cases permanently. Dutch Sephardi-accumulated investments, funds and general affluence were drastically cut back by the collapse of savings and securities and in particular that of the provincial bonds of the now dissolved federal provinces and the liquidation of the shares of the former Dutch East and West India Companies in which Dutch Sephardim had held a considerable proportion of their savings. Sephardi poverty and pauperization in the Netherlands escalated but now ceased to be exclusively, or even mainly, a communal affair. The cultural autonomy of the community, and its traditional cultivation of Spanish and Portuguese literature and learning ended, the new Dutch governments after 1795 making strenuous efforts to integrate young Dutch Sephardi Jews into the same educational framework as the rest of the population and encourage the promotion of the Dutch language, in place of Portuguese, as the main spoken and written language of Dutch Sephardi Jewry.

The history of Dutch Sephardi Jewry as a major element in world Sephardi Jewry, playing a role of great importance in many different spheres of human achievement, ranging from commerce to philosophy and Jewish-Christian theological dialogue, was over. After the setting up of the modern kingdom of the Netherlands, in 1813, and the subsequent separation of Belgium from the Netherlands, in 1830, what remained of Dutch Sephardi Jewry, in the Netherlands and in Curaçao and Surinam, continued to decline both in numbers and in cultural and economic significance. The Sephardim in Amsterdam, and throughout the Netherlands, were now completely eclipsed by the Ashkenazi community in almost every respect. Only in the Dutch Caribbean, and Surinam, did the steadily shrinking Sephardi communities continue to constitute the main Jewish presence. Yet, as always, the past lived on, not least in the fierce pride in a long and great tradition displayed by the surviving Dutch Sephardi families, including those – and there were a number, even among those bearing the most distinguished Sephardi names – who decided to convert to Christianity. The most remarkable figure in this context, and perhaps the most significant Dutch national figure since Isaac de Pinto, to emerge from a Sephardi background, was Isaac da Costa (1798-1860). This highly controversial, as well as vastly creative, personality, was the son of a Dutch Sephardi wine merchant, descended from a distinguished family resident in Amsterdam since the seventeenth century. His wife, Hanna Belmonte, carried a still-famous Dutch Sephardi name. In 1822, they both converted to Protestant Christianity. Subsequently, Isaac da Costa became one of the most important Dutch poets, Protestant publicists, and opponents of the spirit of the French Revolution, of his century. At the same time, though, he was a notable antiquarian and historian of Dutch Sephardi Jewry.

The collective pride in a tradition reaching back to pre-1492 Spain was displayed above all in a series of commemorative events and publications of the nineteenth and early twentieth centuries. The last such lavish celebration occurred in August 1925 to mark the 250th anniversary of the inauguration of the Portuguese Synagogue in Amsterdam. It was on this occasion that the secretary of the community, A. Mendes da Costa, published his history of the Portuguese Jewish community of Amsterdam. A special commemorative medal was issued to mark the occasion, depicting the great synagogue, as had been done also to mark the 200th anniversary, in August 1875.

Chapter Nine

The Sephardim in England

AUBREY NEWMAN

The new community

The arrival of Sephardi Jews in England in the middle of the seventeenth century and their recognition as an organized Jewish community recreated an Anglo-Jewish community which itself had been expelled three centuries earlier. The group which returned and the community which developed from it were always small in number, but the pattern and tradition which were then created were to continue for many generations. Indeed in some respects this Sephardi pattern was to continue to dominate the much larger Anglo-Jewish (mainly Ashkenazi) community which appeared over the following three centuries, even though those newcomers were to have little or nothing directly or indirectly to do with Sephardi Jews.

Many of these founding fathers had not come directly from the Iberian Peninsula. They came rather from communities established as a result of the expulsions; however, during the rest of the seventeenth and the eighteenth centuries there was a constant inflow of refugees from Spain and Portugal, and the congregation still retained immediate links with the people, the land, and above all the language of the Peninsula. There was for some generations amongst the members of the community a lively realization of the dangers which many of them had faced. One list of 'alien' members of the community, deposited in the Synagogue Archives under the terms of the Aliens Act of 1803, includes the name of one who had come into England in 1767 'on account of the persecution against the Jews', while another on that list testified that he had come (at some unstated date) from Seville 'flying from the Inquisition my mother having been burned alive for Judaism'. There are also many eighteenth-century entries in the Marriage Registers of the congregation of marriages – or remarriages – of elderly couples, to which have been added the phrase *Vindos de Portugal* (refugees from Portugal). Individuals are known to have maintained contacts with the Peninsula, while a further formal recognition of the congregation's roots in the Peninsula can be seen by the retention into the nineteenth century of Ladino (Judeo-Spanish) as its official language.[1]

Details of how that Sephardi congregation in London came into being have been subjected to a great deal of examination by scholars. It has now been accepted that there had been in the late sixteenth and early seventeenth centuries individual groups of settlers who had enjoyed some measure of Jewish life more or less in secret. But it was in the middle of the seventeenth century that a group of marrano merchants in London was able to throw off its cloak of Christianity and affirm its Jewishness, and it is from that time that an organized community can be traced. At virtually the same time there had been a mission from Amsterdam to Oliver Cromwell in London, headed by Rabbi Menashe ben Israel, who sought on religious grounds to persuade Cromwell to permit Jews to return to England. Only when Jews had been dispersed to all four corners of the earth could there be a Restoration to Zion and even the arrival of the Millennium. There were many English Protestants who could be relied upon to feel very sympathetic to such arguments. Traditionally, permission to settle has been strongly linked with this mission; although scholars have disputed whether it was that or more long-term politico-commercial motives which determined the eventual decision (or even whether there was any formal decision at all made by the government), the existence of a cemetery and a place for worship during the Protectorate would seem to justify the belief. At all events, the date traditionally ascribed to the readmission has been 1656, even though at one stage the congregation itself seemed to ascribe its foundation to Charles II rather than Oliver Cromwell.[2]

The absence of any such formal decision to readmit the Jews would have had one further important result for Jews in Britain. If there was no formal 'readmission' there could be no formal terms laid down to govern the relations between these Jews and the 'State'. In consequence Jews were subject to no special laws but to exactly the same laws as any other group and, as a result, there was never to be any need for a movement requesting 'social' or 'economic' emancipation. The demands during the first half of the nineteenth century for 'political emancipation' were different in many ways from the apparently similar demands elsewhere in Europe. Those born in Britain acquired all the rights and privileges of any other native-born subject, while the community as a whole was in the same position as any other religious group which did not conform to the State Church, the Church of England. At a time when membership of that church was an essential prerequisite of a number of activities within the State, Jews were excluded, as were also Roman Catholics and Protestant Dissenters. In one area, however, Jews were to acquire special privileges; whereas most other Christian groups (with the exception of

Quakers) had their marriage ceremonies regulated by the Established Church, Jews were allowed to regulate and conduct their own as they saw fit. Thus, the only time when Jews as such were specifically excluded from participation in public life came after the 'emancipation' of these other groups in the early nineteenth century.

Numerically this early community was of little significance. In 1660 there were between thirty-five and forty families in London; in the early 1680s there seems to have been a total of 414 men, women, and children; and in the London census of 1695 there are 519 Sephardi names out of what seems to have been a total Jewish population of 716. The figure is confirmed by the details of the seating in the new synagogue erected in Bevis Marks in 1701, for it contained accommodation for about 400 men and 160 women. There was a constant flow of new arrivals, comparatively few coming from Spain and Portugal – although, as already indicated, there continued to be a number of refugees from there – but many more coming from various Sephardi communities in Italy and North Africa as well as a few from communities in America and the West Indies. In 1726 there seem to have been between 1050 and 1700 Sephardim in England, while in 1795 one estimate from the secretary of the congregation would suggest a total of some 2000. The largest number of Sephardim in London throughout the history of the congregation was probably never above 4000. The congregation did not ignore other Jews; there were some early traces of 'Tudesco' ('German', i.e. Ashkenazi) membership of the congregation, but there were never many of them, even before it was officially resolved that they should not be admitted in future. The community was originally established on the fringes of the City of London, choosing to live there because it was outside the control of 'The City' which had excluded Jews from its full privileges, and yet near enough to allow close links with its commercial activities. When at the end of the seventeenth century the authorities of the City decided to restrict the number of brokers who could operate on the Exchange, it was decided to give licences to one hundred English dealers, twelve 'Gentile' foreigners, and twelve 'Jew Brokers', many of whom were Sephardim.[3]

The heart of the congregation was its synagogue, and when in 1700 the original premises in Creechurch Lane proved inadequate it was nearby, in Bevis Marks, that a new synagogue was erected, the building still in use today, despite a threat to its survival in 1886. The building was to become a symbol to Anglo-Jewry as a whole. It was also a symbol of cooperation amongst various other denominations; the Quaker builder refused to accept any profit on his work, while there was a legend at one time that the devoutly Anglican Princess Anne, later Queen Anne, had donated one of the oak beams.

There was a great deal of interest in this new community amongst the Gentiles of London. The Princess Anne came to one Passover service, and the financial accounts for her visit still survive. There are also two descriptions of visits paid to the synagogue, both well known. One by Samuel Pepys (at the time of the Rejoicing of the Law) was scathing, but another by John Greenhalgh on an 'ordinary' Sabbath is longer and much more valuable. Such visits became so numerous and so disturbing to the decorum of the congregation that one of the earliest amendments to its constitution, the Ascamot, was a ruling forbidding any of the Yehidim (the ordinary members) from welcoming or even bringing non-Jewish guests to the services of the congregation. The first edition of the Ascamot was drawn up in 1663 and echoed the rules of the congregations of Amsterdam and Venice. It portrays a small community aware of the problems which might face it in the midst of a Gentile world, and the need to protect the community as a whole. At the same time the constitution of the community thus created remains basically in force till this day, and the basic structure given to the congregation still continues. The members of the congregation, the Yehidim, were responsible for choosing a number of Elders, and from them were then chosen the Mahamad, the ultimate governing body. Virtually absolute control was placed in the hands of the Mahamad, which had however to swear solemnly to exercise its duties 'with truth, justice, and the fear of God'. All members of the congregation had to pay an 'imposta', virtually a sales tax, and the congregation also received the proceeds of a tax on meat sold under the auspices of the synagogue. On the other hand, the congregation was bound to meet the needs of the poor, and indeed it was a proud boast for many generations that none of the poor of the community ever had to seek poor relief externally. The religious life of the community came under the supervision of its rabbi, the haham, but even he might come under the jurisdiction of the lay leaders. The opportunities for disagreement between individual members of the community and its haham were displayed most tellingly in the career of Haham David Nieto, accused of heresy in 1703. It is fair, however, to make clear that the opposition to Nieto came not from the official members of the congregation but from a dissident group within it, and that Nieto had always had the official support of the Mahamad.[4]

Probably the 'golden age' of the Sephardi community in Britain in terms of its collective wealth and influence in both the Jewish and Gentile spheres is to be found in its first century and a half. Members of the community took the lead in many fields of business and commerce, maintaining trade as a result of their family links with Spain and the Spanish and Portuguese empires as well as with the Mediterranean and India. They also played a large part in the development of government finance and the raising of large sums of money to enable Britain to play a prominent part in Europe. The activities of such financiers as Samson Gideon and Joseph Salvador, and the extent to which governments during much of the century relied on them and their successors, have been well documented. Equally much has been written about the activities of individuals in the social, scientific, and literary life of this period. Virtually every activity within the host community displays participation, indeed very active participation, by individual members of the Sephardim of Britain. Some of them stayed within the community and retained both their faith and their membership of the synagogue. Many more, however, did not, and a catalogue of their names here would serve perhaps to indicate the debt owed by the 'host' society to the existence of a Sephardi community in Britain but at the same time underline the loss they represented to that community.[5]

Sephardim and Ashkenazim

If some of the Sephardim were wealthy, the image of a highly successful rich Sephardi community, as set against a poor and struggling Ashkenazi one, would be far from reality. A survey of the 'community of the resettlement' shows extremes of wealth and poverty, and that, while some 17 or 18 members of the congregation could be regarded as having considerable means, over one third of the congregation's revenue went on charity for the poor. In order to try and deal with this problem attempts were made to reduce the numbers of poor entering the country and seeking relief from the community; instructions were given to grant them their fares back whence they had come, or to encourage them to emigrate, perhaps to the new debtors' colony of Georgia. The congregation also established a number of charitable and educational institutions. The Society for Visiting the Sick and Charitable Deeds was founded in 1665, although it proved shortlived and had to be either refounded or replaced several times during the following years; various schools for boys and girls made their appearance; and in 1747 there were founded a hospital and an old people's home, though this attracted a degree of scurrilous propaganda in the following year.[6]

The leading individual in the community, certainly the man who took the leading part in public life, was Joseph Salvador, known in the community as Jessurum Rodrigues. Prominent in the Sephardi community, he was equally well-known in government circles as a government loan-contractor. Perhaps not as significant in this respect as Samson Gideon, nor even as financially successful, he played a more important role within the community, of which he remained always a loyal member, and acquired an even greater reputation within Anglo-Jewry for his association with what was to become its representative institution, the Board of Deputies. He was also to become prominent in the abortive attempt to allow Jews who had not been born in Britain to acquire British nationality without having to become Christians.[7]

By the end of the eighteenth century, however, the Sephardi community in Britain had been overtaken in numbers and wealth by the more recently arrived Ashkenazi Jews. Even by the middle of the century the number of Ashkenazi synagogues had swamped the single Sephardi community, and many of the leading members of Anglo-Jewry were Ashkenazim rather than Sephardim. The leading history of the congregation, that by Albert Hyamson, in placing most of its emphasis on the eighteenth rather than the nineteenth century implicitly recognizes this, while his tale of internal feuds and disagreements would seem also to make the same point. Such disagreements could arise out of a variety of causes. One such was over finance. As a result of financial weaknesses in the community various attempts were made by its leaders to impose extra taxation upon the congregation by increasing the regular collective assessment, the *Finta*. These proved unsuccessful, and so they turned to an alternative method. Members of the congregation were elected to offices they were expected to refuse. Since the Ascamot had laid down that if any member did not take up such office a fine could be paid instead, this was obviously a way of increasing revenue. One of those who was thus elected was Isaac D'Israeli, a retiring gentleman of literary tastes who was not in any case particularly convinced of any religious truths. He declined office, continued for several years to pay his normal subscription, but refused to pay any fine. Eventually he determined to retire from the congregation altogether, whereupon a friend of the family persuaded him to have his children baptized. Thus Benjamin Disraeli left the Anglo-Jewish community, taking with him that spurious attachment to Judaism which appears in the character of Sidonia.[8]

And yet it was in this period that members of the Bevis Marks congregation were responsible for the most significant developments in Anglo-Jewry, one of the most outstanding contributions coming from Moses Montefiore. Montefiore was of a third-generation Anglo-Jewish family, although as it happens, he was born in Livorno during his parents' visit there in 1784. His mother was a Mocatta, the most senior Sephardi family in Britain. Later accounts have perhaps given an undue lustre to Montefiore's early business career, which seems to have been without much success, and indeed it has been suggested that it was not until he married the (Ashkenazi) sister-in-law of Nathan Mayer Rothschild that he really prospered. At the age of 42 he retired from active business life, and concentrated on an Anglo-Jewish career. He had been sponsored in office in the Sephardi community by his uncle Moses Mocatta: at the age of 20 he had been made a Yahid (a full member of the congregation; technically this should have been delayed until he was 21); one of the Lavadores (those members responsible for the burial of the dead) in 1808; and eventually Parnas, or Warden of the congregation. But it was on a wider field that he became significant. He was first elected to the Board of Deputies in 1828, but in 1835 he succeeded his uncle, Moses Mocatta, as President of the Board and as such he became embroiled in a number of controversies, some of which must be ascribed to his own actions.[9]

The origins of the Board have traditionally been found in 1761 in the mutual jealousies between the Sephardi and Ashkenazi congregations in London. On the death of George II the Sephardi community had sent a loyal address to the new king, George III, and to this the Ashkenazim had taken exception. It had then been agreed that in future all the synagogues should concert their actions and they had formed what was originally termed The London Committee of Deputies of British Jews. In practice the members of the group rarely met and even more rarely concerted their actions. It was not until the late 1820s, with a growing agitation for 'political emancipation', that there developed any element of regularity about their activities. But with the advent of Sir Moses as President there developed a regular constitution and a frequency of meetings, and this led to his election being perhaps regarded as a new foundation of the Board. His dominance of the Board was marked by his virtual monopoly of its presidency until 1874 when, at the age of 90, he declined being re-elected. Through and with that presidency he acquired a pre-eminent position not only in Anglo-Jewry but in world Jewry as a whole. Indeed he acquired a position in the non-Jewish world hitherto unattained by any British Jew and to that extent gave additional lustre to Sephardi Jewry in Britain. It might well be argued, however, that his position on the Board owed less to his being a Sephardi than to his connections through marriage with the leading families of Ashkenazi Anglo-Jewry. At all events, during the arguments in Anglo-Jewry over claims for full political emancipation, in which many of the leading members of the Sephardi community played a very active part, Montefiore was reluctant to make such demands upon the government of the day, perhaps because he had already acquired a status as the virtual representative of the wider Jewish community with both the British and foreign governments.[10]

Equally linked with the Sephardi congregation is the story of the emergence in the 1840s of the West London Synagogue of British Jews. Central to the laws of the Sephardi community had been the prohibition of services on a regular basis elsewhere than in the one central synagogue. This stemmed from the basic need to maintain cohesion within the congregation and to preserve the social institutions of the community, as well as the recognition that virtually all lived within close proximity to Bevis Marks. But as members of the community became wealthier many sought to live elsewhere, and an attempt was made to secure the foundation of a branch synagogue in the western part of London under the auspices of the congregation. That move was defeated, and as a consequence a number of very distinguished members of both communities broke away to form their own congregation with its own new forms of prayer and worship. Despite the presence of many of his own close relations within this breakaway group, Sir Moses Montefiore proved an obstinate opponent of any steps of reconciliation, refusing to recognize the existence of this new group or giving any consideration at all to its members.

The community of the mid-nineteenth century was one in which the Sephardim played a much less significant part. The Ashkenazim of London increased in numbers and in influence, and their creation of a unified synagogual structure meant that the Bevis Marks synagogue declined in importance. Technically, old partnerships were retained in such matters as the provision of kosher meat or of unleavened bread for Passover, but there could be no doubt as to where real authority increasingly rested.

The causes of this decline can be traced to a number of factors. Undoubtedly one of the most important was the absence for many years of a spiritual head of the congregation. After the death of Haham Raphael Meldola in 1828 no successor was found until the appointment of Dr Artom in 1866, and when he died in 1879 the congregation had further difficulties in finding a haham. In 1843 it had been suggested that the new Ashkenazi chief rabbi who was about to be appointed should include the Bevis Marks congregation amongst his responsibilities, but this had been rejected by the Elders. The suggestion was again made after the death of Haham Arton, but was averted with the election of Dr Moses Gaster as haham. There were those who pointed out in response to this that the Sephardim had had to choose a Romanian-born Ashkenazi to fill the post. The absence of a haham would have been less serious had there existed an active group of three Dayanim (Judges), qualified to give verdicts on religious issues; unfortunately it was not always possible to ensure continuity amongst them.

Another cause of decline was the loss to the community of many of its leading families, either through the secession which had led to the formation of the West London Congregation or through Anglicization and conversion to Christianity. One of those who left has already been mentioned, Isaac D'Israeli. Another was the economist David Ricardo, who left not out of religious conviction – or even lack of conviction – but out of a desire to marry the daughter of a Quaker neighbour. These were but two names out of very many who left Bevis Marks during this period, and whose careers enriched the life of Great Britain at large, even though they play no subsequent part in the history of the Sephardi community.[11]

When the tranquillity and structure of the Anglo-Jewish community of the mid-nineteenth century was rudely disrupted by the 'Great Immigration' out of eastern Europe during the last quarter of that century, the imbalance of numbers and power was further emphasized. A community in which Sephardim had amounted to perhaps three thousand out of a total of sixty thousand was transformed into one in which they had hardly increased but the total had risen sixfold or more. Whereas the Ashkenazim had been reinforced by a great influx from eastern Europe, the Sephardim who arrived from North Africa or from the Netherlands were few in numbers and more often than not represented a drain on the community which had very often to pay large grants to enable applicants to resume journeys overseas. The geographical structure of Anglo-Jewry had also been changed by this immigration, so that although the Sephardi community now had smaller daughter congregations in Manchester as well as elsewhere in London, the haham at Bevis Marks was set against an Ashkenazi chief rabbi who claimed the allegiance of congregations not only all over the United Kingdom but throughout the Empire as well. Within London very marked differences can be traced from details of occupations as well as places of residence, and it would seem that the Sephardim followed the same variety of occupations as the other Jewish communities, even to the extent of a geographical division between those still living in the East End and those who had moved to the richer areas of London.

What appears also at this time is a growing uncertainty amongst the leaders of the community as to their own future. One complaint to the Elders made by one of its members was not merely of a relative decline in numbers but of a clear division between the leadership and the bulk of the ordinary membership: 'We are absolutely devoid of that numerous and energetic and well-to-do middle class which constitutes the backbone of other congregations'. One further indication of this is perhaps the suggestion put forward at the time by the leaders of the community that the Bevis Marks site should be sold and new buildings be erected elsewhere. The appointment of Dr Gaster certainly gave new impetus to the congregation as did the opening of the new synagogue in Lauderdale Road.[12]

Anglo-Jewry today

It was the twentieth century which saw a remarkable regrowth within the community and a reestablishment of its place within Anglo-Jewry. Its numbers were maintained in part by a small but significant movement from the Ashkenazim (these recruits proving to be of very great value in many aspects of its life, not least in the study of its history) and in greater part by the arrival in Britain of Sephardi Jews from various parts of the Middle East, as Jews there came under increasing persecution from newly emergent Arab governments. Strictly speaking these were not Sephardi Jews, but rather representatives of that body of Jews who had already been living in various parts of the eastern Mediterranean before the arrival of the Sephardi diaspora after the expulsion from Spain; their culture had been overlaid by the Sephardi customs and ways of life. When they came to England they gravitated quite naturally to the Bevis Marks congregation. It was true also of the Jews from Iraq and Iran, that even though they had never come under direct Sephardi influence, they found a more sympathetic home in the Sephardi community rather than among that of the Ashkenazim. The influence of the Sephardi community was further upheld by the outstanding contribution of its ecclesiastical leaders to such causes as Zionism; Haham Gaster might have displayed all the pugnacity of contemporary Anglo-Jewish ecclesiastical leadership, but he (and his congregation) could certainly never be ignored by the larger body. And for their part the leaders of 'mainstream' Ashkenazi Anglo-Jewry saw the good sense of trying to carry the Sephardi community with them within the institutions of the wider community.

If by the end of the twentieth century the Sephardi community had declined to a considerable extent from its original highpoint, it could still look back with pride to the traditions it had created. From the beginning the community had established a pattern of 'looking after its own', of ensuring that those of its members who were in need did not have to look to the State for help. It had been responsible for the establishment of such bodies as the Board of Deputies of British Jews, which acted as the formal representative of the community. Above all, it had never been blind to the needs of other Jewish communities, whether they were in the Holy Land or in the lands of the dispersion, whether they were Sephardi or Ashkenazi. Its members have played a prominent part in the life of the Jewish and non-Jewish communities alike, so that they have fully repaid the confidence implicitly placed in them at the Resettlement.

At a time when Anglo-Jewry itself is undecided as to its future path it would be impossible to try and determine the future of the Sephardim of Great Britain. They have been spared many of the intellectual and ideological controversies that have during this century scarred other communities in Britain, though sometimes such controversies themselves might well have served as much to stimulate discussion and life. They represent perhaps, now as ever, an oasis of thought and of religious calm. The community has survived virtually intact, and there is no reason why it should not so continue. It has never depended purely upon numbers, more upon its traditions of a living continuity with its past. The remembrance of that continuity, above all with the communities so brutally attacked in 1492, and so well evident in the circumstances of the emergence of a Sephardi congregation in London a century and a half later, will without doubt carry the community forward and continue its contribution to the life of the Sephardi diaspora.

Notes on the Text

Select Bibliography

Sources of Illustrations

Index

Notes on the Text

CHAPTER ONE

1 For this and what follows, as well as the difficulties in drawing demographic conclusions from the available evidence, see L. Suárez Fernández, *Judíos Españoles en la Edad Media* (Madrid 1980), pp.96–100.
2 For the example of Jerez, see the excellent edition of the relevant documentation in M. González Jiménez and A. González Gómez, eds, *El Libro del Repartimiento de Jerez de la Frontera* (Cádiz 1980).
3 Y. Baer, *A History of the Jews in Christian Spain*, 2 vols (Philadelphia 1966), vol.i, pp.124–26, 164, 166, 362–64.
4 *Ibid.*, p.367; Philippe Wolff, 'The 1391 Pogrom in Spain. Social Crisis or Not?', *Past and Present*, no.50, pp.6–7.
5 For what follows I am greatly indebted to my research student, Philip Hersch, who kindly placed his M.Litt. thesis at my disposal: Philip Hersch, *Politics, Economics and Ethics in Thirteenth- and Fourteenth-Century Hispano-Jewish Society* (Edinburgh, M.Litt. thesis, 1991).
6 For both these quotations, *ibid.*, p.23.
7 On the Alconstantini family, see Baer, i, pp.105–6.
8 On the controversy, *ibid.*, pp.96–110.
9 On what follows and for an excellent account of Judah Halevi, see Haim Beinart, 'Yehuda Halevi y su Tiempo', in *1 Congreso internacional 'Encuentro de las Tres Culturas'* (Toledo 1983), pp.19–36.
10 See David Goldstein, trans. and ed., *The Jewish Poets of Spain, 900–1250* (Harmondsworth 1971), p.128.
11 For this extraordinary allegation, see the summary of the letter sent by the Ibn Hasdai brothers to the communities of Castile and Aragon in Baer, i, p.401.
12 Baer, i, pp.266–77.
13 *Ibid.*, p.244. These small towns were to figure prominently in the mystical and visionary movements of Christian Illuminists (*alumbrados*) of the very late fifteenth and early sixteenth centuries.
14 For this and what follows, see Baer, *op. cit.*, i, ch.vi.
15 Usually the 'Averroists' are associated with fifteenth-century conversos, sometimes on the implied assumption that they had been 'bad' Jews and when converted, were equally 'bad' Christians. However, there is plenty of evidence to suggest that 'Averroistic unbelief' existed among Old Christians as well.
16 See Fernando Díaz Esteban, 'La convivencia linguística del árabe, el hebreo y el romance reflejada en un documento del siglo XIV', in *I Congreso Internacional 'Encuentro de las Tres Culturas'* (Toledo 1983), pp.195–205.
17 On the translators and what follows, see G. Lemay, 'Dans l'Espagne du XIIe Siècle. Les Traductions de l'Arabe au Latin', *Annales E.S.C.*, xviii, (1963), pp.639–65; Moisés Orfali, 'Los Traductores Judíos de Toledo: Nexo entre Oriente y Occidente', in *II Congreso Internacional 'Encuentro de las Tres Culturas'* (Toledo 1985), pp.253–60.
18 On this and what follows on Mallorcan Jewish cartographers, see José M^A^. Millas Vallicrosa, 'Aportaciones Científicas de los Judíos Españoles a Fines de la Edad Media', in *Actas del I Simposio de Estudios Sefardíes* (Madrid 1970), pp.33–42.
19 See J.R.S. Phillips, *The Medieval Expansion of Europe* (Oxford 1988), p.219.
20 See E.W. Bovill, *The Golden Trade of the Moors* (2nd edn, Oxford 1970), pp.90–91.
21 Consulting any good book on the history of the Jews in Spain gives one an idea of the enormous importance of the *responsa*. For this particular example, see A. MacKay, 'Las cortes de Castilla y León y la historia monetaria', in *Las Cortes de Castilla y León en la Edad Media*, i (Valladolid 1988), pp.375–426, which gives a Spanish translation of R. Isaac ben Sheshet's *Responsum* on pp.418–19.
22 See Margherita Morreale, 'The Vernacular Scriptures in Spain', in *The Cambridge History of the Bible*, ii, *The West from the Fathers to the Reformation*, ed. G.W.H. Lampe (Cambridge 1969), pp.465–91.
23 See Ron Barkai, 'Las tres culturas en la cronografía judía (siglo XII)', in *I Congreso internacional 'Encuentro de las tres culturas'* (Toledo 1983), pp.337–47 (p.347).
24 Alfonso X, O Sabio, *Cantigas de Santa María*, ed. Walter Mettmann (Coimbra 1959–72), 4 vols, gives the texts of the poems but not the illustrations. The miniatures corresponding to the stories are reproduced in J. Guerrero Lovillo, *Las Cántigas. Estudio arqueológico de sus miniaturas* (Madrid 1949). For what follows, see V. Hatton and A. MacKay, 'Anti-Semitism in the *Cantigas de Santa María*', *Bulletin of Hispanic Studies*, lx (1983), pp.189–99.
25 *Ibid.*, pp.195–96; A. MacKay, 'The Hispano-Converso predicament', *T.R.H.S.*, 5th Series, 35 (1985), pp.159–79 (pp. 161–2).
26 Baer, *op. cit.*, i, pp.152–53; J. Cohen, *The Friars and the Jews: The Evolution of Medieval Anti–Judaism* (Ithaca and London 1982), pp.108–22.
27 Baer, *op. cit.*, ii, pp.158–62.
28 Hersch, *op. cit.*, ch.3; M. Barber, 'Lepers, Jews and Moslems: The Plot to Overthrow Christendom in 1321', *History*, 66 (1981), pp.1–17; A. MacKay,

'Faction and Civil Strife in late Medieval Castilian Towns', *Bulletin of the John Rylands University Library of Manchester*, 72 (1990), pp.119–31.
29 On Samuel Halevi, see Baer, *op. cit.*, i, pp.362–64. On what follows on the synagogue he built in Toledo, see F. Cantera Burgos, *Sinagogas Españolas* (Madrid 1955), pp.65–149.
30 See *Encyclopedia Judaica*, ed. C. Roth and G. Wigoder (Jerusalem 1971–2), *s.v.* 'Blood Libel' and 'Host, desecration of; A. MacKay, 'The Lord of Hosts' in *Essays on Hispanic Themes in Honour of Edward C. Riley*, ed. J. Lowe and Philip Swanson (Edinburgh 1989), pp.41–50.
31 On the fate of the Jews during the civil war see the brief study of J. Valdeón Baruque, *Los Judíos de Castilla y la Revolución Trastámara* (Valladolid 1968).
32 See P. Wolff, 'The 1391 Pogrom in Spain', pp. 4–18.
33 A. MacKay, 'Popular Movements and Pogroms in Fifteenth-Century Castile', *Past and Present*, no.55 (1972), pp.33–67.

CHAPTER TWO

1 F. Cantera-Millás, *Las inscripciones hebraicas de España* (Madrid 1956); S. Edmonds, 'A Note on the Art of Joseph ibn Hayyim', *Studies in Bibliography and Booklore* xi, 1–2 (1975–76), 24–40; H. Graetz, *A History of the Jews* (London 1899); A. Marx, *Studies in Jewish History and Booklore* (New York 1944).
2 Eleazar Gutwirth, 'The Jews in 15th-century Castilian Chronicles', *Jewish Quarterly Review* (April 1984), no.4, 379–96. The Jewish accounts are analyzed in my 'The Bible and Medieval Jewish Historiography', (Paper delivered at the EAJS Troyes meeting 1990, forthcoming). Some additional details on the Jewish reactions to 1391 may be found in my *Social Tensions Within Fifteenth-Century Hispano–Jewish Communities* (University of London 1978 Ph.D. Thesis), chapter 1.
3 Y. Baer, *A History of the Jews in Christian Spain* (Philadelphia 1966) vol.ii, ch.10, p.95ff. For Valencia see the articles by Dánvila and Chabás cited in F. Baer, *Die Juden im Christlichen Spanien* i (Berlin 1929) p.1088.
4 An example of Christian vernacular anti-Jewish polemic in fifteenth-century Spain is discussed in Eleazar Gutwirth, 'Maestre Juan el Viejo and his Tratado (Madrid MS)', *Proceedings Ninth World Congress of Jewish Studies*, B (Jerusalem 1986), 129–34. See also E. Marin, *La Ley* (Madrid 1989).
5 On fifteenth-century Hispano–Jewish polemicists see e.g. Eleazar Gutwirth, 'History and Apologetics in XVth c. Hispano–Jewish Thought, *Helmantica*, vol.35, no.107 (1984) 231–42; Eleazar Gutwirth, 'Actitudes judías hacia el cristianismo: Ideario de los traductores hispano–judíos del latín', *Actas Segundo Encuentro de las Tres Culturas* (Toledo 1985), 189–96.
6 Eleazar Gutwirth, 'Caste, Class and Magic: Witches and Amulets amongst the Jews of Late Medieval Spain' (Catalan) in *La Cabala* (Barcelona 1989), 85–99.
7 V.Y. Yahalom in *Galut Ahar Golah* (Jerusalem 1988) and my review article in *Peamim* 41, 1990, 156ff. See also Eleazar Gutwirth, 'Fragments of a Judeo–Spanish Ballad from the Geniza' (Hebrew), *Jerusalem Studies in Folklore* 5–6 (1984), 71–83.
8 Eleazar Gutwirth, 'Religion, Historia y las *Biblias Romanceadas*', *Revista Catalana de Teologia* 13/1 (1988), pp.115–34; Eleazar Gutwirth, 'An Unknown Medieval Aljamiado Manuscript of Gnomic Verse' in *Colloquium Hierosolymitanum Litterae Judaeorum in Terra Hispanica*, Hebrew University, Jerusalem (1984).
9 On the assumptions of Celestina criticism see P.J. Smith, 'Violence and Metaphysics', *Michael* xi (1989); Eleazar Gutwirth, 'Fernán Díaz de Toledo y los Judíos', *Homenaje . . . F. Pérez Castro* (Madrid: CSIC, 1986), 229–34.
10 On the common literary motifs see for example Eleazar Gutwirth, 'The "World Upside Down" in Hebrew', *Orientalia Suecana*, 30 [(1981) 1983], 141–47. On Profayt Duran see Eleazar Gutwirth, 'Religion and Social Criticism in Late Medieval Roussillon: An Aspect of Profayt Duran's Activities; *Michael* xii (1991), 135–56.
11 See Eleazar Gutwirth, 'Actitudes judías hacia el cristianismo: Ideario de los traductores hispano-judíos del latín', *Actas Segundo Encuentro de las Tres Culturas* (Toledo 1985), 189–96.
12 See Eleazar Gutwirth, 'The Jews in 15th-century Castilian Chronicles', *Jewish Quarterly Review* [(April 1984) 1986] lxxxiv, no.4, pp.379–96 and Eleazar Gutwirth, 'The Expulsion of the Jews from Spain and Jewish Historiography', *Jewish History: Festschrift C. Abramsky* (ed. A. Rapoport-Albert), London 1988, 141–61.
13 Abraham Saba, *Seror Ha-Mor* (Venice edn) f109 verso; and E. Marín, *La Ley* (Madrid 1989).
14 For the text in Hebrew *aljamía* see Y. Baer, *Die Juden im Christlichen Spanien* ii (Berlin 1936), no.287, pp.280–98; Y. Moreno Koch, *Las Taqqanot de Valladolid* (Salamanca 1988). For an analysis of their content within the context of Castilian centralizing tendencies in the fifteenth century see Eleazar Gutwirth, 'Trends towards centralization in XVth-c. Castilian Jewish Communities' (Hebrew), *Teudah* 4 (1986), 231–46.
15 Y. Baer, *History*, p.250.
16 Y. Baer, *Die Juden* ii, pp.286, 292, 307.
17 Eleazar Gutwirth, 'El comercio hispano-magrebí y los judíos (1391–1444)', *Hispania*, xlv (1985), 199–205; Eleazar Gutwirth, 'Elementos étnicos e históricos en las relaciones judeo-conversas en Segovia', *Jews and Conversos* (ed. Y. Kaplan), Jerusalem 1985, 83–102.

18 On Abraham Seneor see Eleazar Gutwirth, 'Abraham Seneor: Social Tensions and the Court-Jew', *Michael* xi (1989), 169–229.

CHAPTER THREE

1 Aspects of the theme of the present chapter are studied in more detail in Henry Kamen, 'The Mediterranean and the expulsion of Spanish Jews in 1492', *Past and Present*, 119, May 1988. The reactions of Machiavelli and other contemporaries are summarized by Yitzhak Baer, *Historia de los judíos en la España cristiana*, trans. José Luis Lacave, 2 vols, Madrid 1981, ii, 651–4. I cite the Spanish edition because its bibliography, by Lacave, is the most up-to-date.
2 The well-publicized views of Meyer Kayserling and others, that the discovery of America (by a Columbus who was secretly Jewish) enabled Jews to flee there, is based on intriguing but circumstantial evidence, and has not been supported by scholars.
3 See Jonathan Israel, *European Jewry in the age of Mercantilism 1550–1750*, Oxford 1989, pp.7–10.
4 Baer's view of the decree as an unprecedented act – 'a great and terrible novelty in those days', ii, 649 – overlooks the growing pressure against Jews both in southern Castile and in other European states, a typical case being Provence, see Danièle Iancu, *Les Juifs de Provence (1475–1500)*, Aix 1986.
5 I have been unable to consult Benjamin Gampel, *The last Jews on Iberian soil: Navarrese Jewry 1479–1498*, Berkeley 1989.
6 Benzion Netanyahu, *Don Isaac Abravanel*, Philadelphia 1968.
7 The image is e.g. in Meyer Kayserling, *História dos Judeus em Portugal*, São Paulo 1971, p.110: 'não só queria exterminar completamente a raça hebréia, mas também procurava conquistar os regentes dos outros Estados para sua politica odiosa'.
8 Pilar León Tello, *Judíos de Toledo*, 2 vols, Madrid 1979, i, 347. The king seems to have sent similar letters to all the nobility; see for example the almost identical letter to the conde de Belchite, dated 31 March 1492, in M.A. Motis Dolader, 'La expulsión de los judíos aragoneses' in the volume *Destierros Aragoneses*, Saragossa 1988, p.104.
9 Baer, ii, 646.
10 For an introduction to the extensive literature see Henry Kamen, *Inquisition and Society in Spain in the sixteenth and seventeenth centuries*, London 1985; the standard work is Henry Charles Lea, *History of the Inquisition of Spain*, 4 vols, New York 1906–8.
11 For some figures, see Kamen, *Inquisition*, p.42. The interconnection of the Jewish and converso problems is underlined in Angus MacKay, 'Popular movements and pogroms in fifteenth-century Castile', *Past and Present*, 55, May 1972.
12 Jaume Vicens Vives, *Ferran II i la ciutat de Barcelona 1479–1516*, 2 vols, Barcelona 1936, i, 382.
13 Netanyahu has argued convincingly that Jews did not accept affinity with the religion of the conversos: see his *The Marranos of Spain from the late XIVth to the early XVIth century, according to contemporary Hebrew sources*, 2nd edn, New York 1973. This view is the opposite of that held by some Jewish scholars, notably Baer and H. Beinart; see Kamen, *Inquisition*, pp.27–8.
14 H. Graetz, 'La police de l'Inquisition d'Espagne à ses débuts', *Boletín de la Real Academia de la Historia*, xxiii, 1893, pp.383–90; I. Baer, *Die Juden im christlichen Spanien: Urkunden und Regesten, vol. ii: Kastilien/Inquisitionsakten*, Berlin 1936, i, p.912, doc.563.
15 For opposition see Kamen, *Inquisition*, chap.4.
16 E. Cantera Montenegro, 'El apartamento de judíos y mudejares en las diócesis de Osma y Sigüenza a fines del siglo XV', *Anuario de Estudios Medievales*, 1987, vol.17, 501–10.
17 In Orense (Galicia) the city tried to put the decree into effect, but nine years later Christians were still living within the assigned *aljama* and Jews outside, a situation that the crown explicitly tolerated; Luis Suárez Fernández, *Documentos acerca de la expulsión de los judíos*, Valladolid 1964, doc.126.
18 For the expulsions, see Fidel Fita, 'Nuevos datos para escribir la historia de los judíos españoles: la Inquisición en Jérez de la Frontera', *Boletín de la Real Academia de la Historia*, xv (1889), pp.313–32; Luis Suárez Fernández, *Documentos*, p.41; H. Sancho de Sopranis, 'Contribución a la historia de la judería de Jérez de la Frontera', *Sefarad*, xl (1951), pp.349–70. Baer believes that the expulsions occurred, ii, 571–2.
19 Stephen Haliczer, 'The Castilian urban patriciate and the Jewish expulsions of 1480–92', *American Historical Review*, 78, February 1973. Haliczer is unable to cite any examples to back his thesis that the conversos in the towns of Castile were the chief influence behind the decision to expel.
20 Benzion Netanyahu, 'The primary cause of the Spanish Inquisition', in A. Alcalá, ed., *The Spanish Inquisition and the inquisitorial mind*, Boulder 1987. Netanyahu's own opinion, as expressed in 1968 (*Abravanel*, p.46 [the first edn was in 1953]), seems to coincide with those of the scholars he discusses: he affirmed that the crown desired an 'entrenchment of the absolutist regime' and 'the exploitation of the vast fortunes of the Jews'; but his views appear to have changed since then.
21 The relevant works are J.A. Llorente, *Histoire Critique de l'Inquisition d'Espagne*, 4 vols, Paris 1817; L. von Ranke, *The Ottoman and Spanish Empires in the sixteenth and seventeenth centuries*, Philadelphia 1945, trans. from the German version of 1827; K.J. von Hefele, *The life and times of Cardinal Ximenes*, London 1885.

22 For the administration of Jews in Castile, see Suárez Fernández, pp.13ff; I. Baer, *Die Juden.*
23 José Amador de los Ríos, *Historia social, política y religiosa de los judíos en España y Portugal*, 3 vols, Madrid 1875–6.
24 The author who did most to disseminate the thesis of religious unity, however, was the young Menéndez y Pelayo, in terms that scarcely bear repetition. (Marcelíno Menédez y Pelayo, *Historia de los Heterodóxos españoles*, edn of 8 vols, Madrid 1963, iv, 287.) He refers to 'the generous impulse of the Catholic Kings, who preferred the religious unity of their realms to any interest of state'.
25 E.g. the suggestive but quite undocumented verdict of Vicens Vives that the expulsions of 1492 'eliminated from the social life of Castile the only groups capable of giving an impulse to early capitalism, snuffed out the prosperity of many towns and realized an enormous quantity of wealth, most of which was used to finance the foreign policy of the Catholic Kings while the rest was frittered away in the hands of the aristocracy'. (J. Vicens Vives, *Aproximación a la historia de España* [first edn, 1952], Barcelona 1976 edn, p.103.)
26 Both cited in Kamen, *Inquisition*, p.147.
27 *Ibid.*, p.31.
28 *Ibid.*, p.36.
29 Juan Blázquez Miguel, *Inquisición y Criptojudaismo*, Madrid 1988, suggests that possibly twice as many conversos were tried by the Inquisition as historians have supposed.
30 Baer, for example, assumes it was a decree of expulsion and leaves no doubts about it: 'on the 31 July 1492,' he says apocalyptically, 'the last Jew left the country'. (Baer, *Historia*, ii, 650.)
31 Translated from text as given in Motis Dolader, *La expulsión de los judíos de Zaragoza*, Saragossa 1986, pp.201–5, from a version in Arxiu de la Corona de Aragó, Barcelona, section Real Cancillería reg. 3569 f.130v. There were slightly different texts of the decree, depending on the recipient, Suárez Fernández, doc.177, prints a text addressed to the city and see of Burgos; the text in Motis, taken from the registers of the crown of Aragon, is inexplicably directed to the city and see of Toledo.
32 A view shared by an expert on the subject: 'the decree', states Motis, *Zaragoza*, p.77, 'was intended not to expel the Jews but to eliminate the Jewish faith'.
33 Andrés Bernáldez, *Memorias del reinado de los Reyes Católicos*, edn of Madrid 1962, chap. cxii.
34 'The prescribed places of embarkation were too remote to be reached within the allotted time, and resort to the adjacent Iberian and North African realms was prohibited. The edict was virtually an order for forcible conversion': R.B. Merriman, *The Rise of the Spanish Empire in the Old World and the New, vol.II: the Catholic Kings*, New York 1918, p.96.
35 A. Domínguez Ortiz and B. Vincent, *Historia de los Moriscos*, Madrid 1978, p.24–5.
36 Jerónimo de Zurita, *Historia del rey Don Hernando el Catholico*, 6 vols, Saragossa 1610, i, 9v.
37 Juan de Mariana, *Historia de España*, Biblioteca de Autores Españoles, xxi, Madrid 1872, bk 26, chap.i.
38 Luís de Páramo, *De origine et progressu Officii Sanctae Inquisitionis*, Madrid 1598, título 2, chap.6, p.165.
39 The opinion of Fernando Coutinho, bishop of Silves, is cited in several authors. My reference is from M. Kayserling, *História dos Judeus em Portugal*, p.113.
40 All cited in Baer, *Historia*, ii, pp.790–1.
41 For a fuller discussion see Kamen, 'The Mediterranean'.
42 M.A. Motis Dolader, 'La conversión de judíos aragoneses a raiz del edicto de expulsión', in the volume *Encuentros en Sefarad*, Madrid 1987, pp.224–5.
43 Israel, *European Jewry*, p.24, who has looked at the European rather than at the Iberian context, prefers the figure of 200,000 Jews in Iberia on the eve of the expulsion, which represents over three per cent of the population, a proportion unjustified by any existing document or tax census. Equally unacceptable – since both unlikely and undocumented – is the estimate by Netanyahu (*Marranos*, appendix E, 'The number of the Marranos in Spain') that Jews were three per cent and Marranos a further seven, adding up to a semitic population in 1492 of one tenth of Spain's population, or some 600,000 in all. See also note 49.
44 Suárez Fernández, doc.239.
45 José Hinojosa Montalvo, 'Solidaridad judía ante la expulsion; contratos de embarque, Valencia 1492', *Saitabi*, xxxiii (1983), pp.105–24.
46 See the discussion in Kamen, 'The Mediterranean', p.40.
47 Israel, *European Jewry*, in the first edition (1985) of his book states that 100,000 Spanish Jews fled to the Ottoman empire, but in his second edition reduces this figure to 50,000. Since no evidence has so far emerged of Spanish Jews fleeing to Ottoman territory in 1492, even this figure is unacceptable.
48 In his splendid study of two volumes, for example, Baer devotes only five pages to it. (Baer, *Historia*, ii, 646–50.)
49 The various estimates are considered in Kamen, 'The Mediterranean', p.44.
50 It is unlikely that the 'many' conversos, 'men of standing in the Church, the administration and finance', who are stated by J.H. Elliott, *Imperial Spain*, Harmondsworth 1970, p.109, to have left the country along with the Jews in 1492, can be shown to exist, since no available source appears to mention them.
51 Cited in Kamen, 'The Mediterranean', p.49.
52 Haim Beinart, *Conversos on Trial. The Inquisition in Ciudad Real*, Jerusalem 1981.

53 A. Domínguez Ortiz, *Los Judeoconversos en España y América*, Madrid 1971, p.43.
54 Cited in *ibid.*, *Los conversos de origen judío después de la expulsión*, Madrid 1955, p.30, n.14.
55 G.A. Bergenroth, ed., *Calendar of State Papers, Spain, vol.i*, London 1862, repr. 1969, pp.51, 164–5. Henry VII pleased the prior by telling him he would 'punish soundly any Jew or heretic found in his realms'. Santa Cruz also wrote back poisonous reports on the then Spanish ambassador, De Puebla, a known converso.
56 In Sicily, it seems, the Jews were not expelled but for the most part accepted conversion; see Eliyahu Ashtor, *The Jews and the Mediterranean economy, 10th–15th centuries*, London 1983, p.241.
57 See references in Kamen, 'The Mediterranean', pp.40, 47.
58 Suárez Fernández, doc.242.
59 R.B. Merriman, p.92.
60 Vicens Vives, *Aproximación*, p.103.
61 Elliott, *Imperial Spain*, pp.109, 123.
62 Cf. Kamen, *Inquisition*, pp.31, 36, 147, 260.
63 For example, Ruth Pike has underlined the role of conversos in the trade of America: *Aristocrats and Traders, Sevillan Society in the Sixteenth Century*, Cornell 1971.
64 Martin Carrillo, abbot of Montearagón, *Annales y memoriales cronológicas*, Madrid 1620, p.382v.
65 Motis Dolader, *Zaragoza*, pp.146–81.
66 Pilar León Tello, *Judíos de Toledo*, map facing p.368 of vol.i.
67 F. Cantera Burgos and C. Carrete Parrondo, 'La judería de Buitrago', *Sefarad*, xxxii, 1972, pp.3–87.
68 Speaking of an earlier epoch, but in words that have since been borrowed and misapplied by others, a distinguished scholar with few pretensions to specialization in economic history made the daring claim that 'the history of Spain was built on the basis of a Jewish economy', a claim for which not the slightest historical evidence existed but which encouraged non-historians to lend credence to this extravagant view. (Américo Castro, *España en su historia. Cristianos, Moros y Judíos*, Buenos Aires 1948, p.489.) It was typical of Don Américo that he went on to attack any contradiction of his statement based on archival work, with the rounded assertion that 'the history of Spain needs much less archival research than people say'.
69 Manuel Serrano y Sanz, *Orígenes de la Dominación Española en América*, vol.xxv of Nueva Biblioteca de Autores Españoles, Madrid 1918.
70 The trading confraternity called the 'Corredores del Veinte' in 1492 consisted by its constitution of fourteen Christian members and six Jews; see Motis Dolader, *Zaragoza*, pp.100–06.
71 *Ibid.*, p.122.
72 *Ibid.*, p.56.
73 Manuel F. Ladero Quesada, 'Apuntes para la historia de los judíos y los conversos de Zamora en la edad media (siglos XIII–XV)', *Sefarad*, 1988, fasc. i, p.46. The author gives no evidence for dislocation but says, fairly enough, that he has the impression that it occurred.
74 Full text in Motis, pp.230–3.
75 J. Gómez-Menor Fuentes, 'Un judío converso de 1498: Diego Gómez de Toledo y su proceso inquisitorial', *Sefarad*, xxxiii, 1973; Motis Dolader, in *Encuentros en Sefarad*, p.239. In Atienza (Guadalajara) a returnee in November 1492 was not only given back all his property but also all debts due to him were declared to be in force again; F. Cantera Burgos and C. Carrete Parrondo, *Las juderías medievales en la provincia de Guadalajara*, Madrid 1975, p.205.
76 What follows is drawn from the contribution by Bruno Anatra in *La Sardegna medioevale e moderna*, vol.x of the *Storia d'Italia* edited by G. Galasso, Turin 1984, pp.337–40.
77 Benito de Peñalosa, *Libro de las cinco excelencias del Español que despueblan a España*, Pamplona 1629, p.35v.
78 The document is cited in A. Rodriguez Villa, 'Los judios españoles y portugueses en el siglo XVII', *Boletín de la Real Academia de la Historia*, 49, 1906, p.99.

CHAPTER FOUR

1 On the riots and conversions see: H. Beinart, 'The Jews in Spain', in *The Jewish World*, edited by Elie Kedourie, London 1979, pp.165–66. A converso problem exists to some extent to this day in Mallorca and Belmonte, a village in the region of Tras-os-Montes in Portugal.
2 Born approximately in 1350; died in 1419. A driving force in conversions (see also chapter 2, p.47), Ferrer influenced Rabbi Samuel Halevi of Burgos to convert, and also took part in the Tortosa Disputation of 1413–14; he was adviser to Anti-Pope Benedict XIII (1394–1417). On Samuel Halevi (= Pablo de Santa Maria, Bishop of Burgos), see below.
3 See Y. Baer, *Die Juden im christlichen Spanien* ii, Berlin 1936, pp.263–72. (= Baer, *JchS*). See also on the Cortes ruling in 1480, further below.
4 See *Memorial de diversas hazañas*, edited by J. de Mata Carriazo, Madrid 1941, pp.xxxi–xxxii.
5 See J. Vives, *Concilios visigóticos e hispano-romanos*, Barcelona-Madrid 1943, p.29, no.65.
6 See Baer, *JchS* ii, p.18: ut nullus Iudaeis, nullus nuper renatus, habeat mandamentum super nullum christianum in Toleto nec in suo territorio. See also H. Beinart, *Conversos on Trial*, Jerusalem 1981, p.6, no.16 (= Beinart, *Conversos*).
7 See E. Benito Ruano, 'El Memorial contra los conversos del bachiller Marcos Gracía de Mora', *Sefarad* 17 (1957), pp.314–57. Marcos García wrote his memorandum while in prison after the uprising of Sarmiento was quelled. He was most probably the 'Spiritus rector' of the Sentencia-Estatuto.

8 Edited by Manuel Alonso, Madrid 1943. It contains in appendices memoranda written in defence of the conversos.
9 Edited by N. López Martínez and V. Paroaño Gil, Burgos 1957. Juan de Torquemada had Jewish ancestry.
10 Marcos García de Mora calls him by his Jewish name: Moshe Hamomo.
11 *Instrucción del Relator para el Obispo de Cuenca a favor de la nación hebrea.* See M. Alonso (n.8), *ibid.*
12 See L. Serrano, *Los conversos Pablo de Santa María y Alonso de Cartagena*, Madrid 1942; F. Cantera Burgos, *Alvar García de Santa María*, Madrid 1952.
13 He used a play of words: *maleficium* and *beneficium.* See Alonso, *ibid.*, pp.323ff.
14 See H. Pflaum, REJ 86 (1928), pp.131–50; Y. Baer, *A History of the Jews in Christian Spain* ii, Philadelphia 1966, pp.280–81 (= Baer, *History);* N. López Martínez, *Los judaizantes castellanos y la Inquisición en los tiempos de los Reyes Católicos*, Burgos 1954, pp.383–87.
15 *Concionero de Juan Alfonso de Baena*, edición critica por José Maria Azáceta, vols 1–3, Madrid 1966; F. Cantera Burgos, *Sefarad* 27 (1967), pp.71–111.
16 *Cancionero de Juan Fernández de Ixar*, estudio y edición critica por J. Ma. Azáceta, vols 1–3, Madrid 1956.
17 On Rodrigo de Cota see F. Cantera Burgos, *El poeta Ruy Sánchez Cota (Rodrigo Cota) y su familia de judíos conversos*, Madrid 1970; on Anton de Montoro see *Antonio de Montoro, cancionero*, edición preparada por F. Cantera Burgos y C. Carrete Parrondo, Madrid 1984.
18 Incunabula impression printed in Nuremberg in 1485. This was not the first impression of the book.
19 For a detailed analysis see: Beinart, *Conversos*, pp.9–20.
20 See Beinart, *ibid.*, p.12.
21 See M. Lunenfeld, *The Council of the Santa Hermandad*, Coral Gables (Fl), 1970.
22 See Baer, *History* ii, p.332ff.
23 See Beinart, *Conversos*, p.187ff.; on the corregidor's power see M. Lunenfeld, *Keepers of the City*, Cambridge 1987.
24 See Beinart, *Conversos*, pp.105–95 and bibliography there on the various evaluations of the Inquisition and reasons for its foundation.
25 See H. Beinart, 'The Living Quarters of the Jews in Spain during the 15th Century and the Order of Separation' (in Hebrew), *Zion* 51 (1986), pp.61–85.
26 The Court functioned till 1485.
27 See H. Beinart, *Carta's Atlas of the Jewish People in the Middle Ages* (in Hebrew), Jerusalem 1981, map 101 (p.78).
28 For a detailed discussion see F. Cantera Burgos, *Sefarad* 4 (1944), pp.295–348.
29 See his *Lumen Dei ad revelationem gentium*, recently translated by Luis A. Díaz y Díaz as *Luz para conocimiento de los gentiles*, Madrid 1979. There was a controversy between him and Alonso de Espina, who favoured strict measures for the conversion of Jews and the treatment of conversos who lapsed into their old ways and habits. On Alonso de Oropesa, *ibid.*, pp.21–25.
30 Perhaps alluding to the fact that Alonso de Espina was himself of converso descent.
31 See H. Beinart, *Los Reyes Católicos y sus pragrámaticas sobre oficios públicos y reales*, Estudios Mirandeses 8 (1988), pp.37–60.
32 Andrés Bernáldez, *Memorias del reinado de los Reyes Católicos*, edición y estudio M. Gómez Moreno–J. de Mata Carriazo, Madrid 1962, chapter 44.
33 See H. Beinart, *Records of the Trials of the Spanish Inquisition in Ciudad Real*, vols i–iv, Jerusalem 1974–85; *idem, Conversos, passim.*
34 See Baer, *JchS*, i, p.911. This order was sent to the communities of Calatayud, Tarazona, Huesca, and Daroca among others.
35 See H. Beinart, *Jewish Witnesses for the Prosecution of the Spanish Inquisition*, Essays in Honour of Prof. Ben Beinart, Cape Town 1978, pp.37–46.
36 See H. Beinart, *The Judaizing Movement in the Order of San Jeronimo in Castile*, Scripta Hierosolymitana 7 (1961), pp.167–92.
37 See for instance the trial of Sancho de Ciudad, inhabitant of Ciudad Real: Beinart, *Records* 1, p.1ff.
38 See *ibid.*, the trial of Mari Díaz, la Cerera, p.40ff.
39 See H. Beinart, 'La Inquisición española y la expulsión de los judíos de Andalucía', in *Jews and Conversos, Studies in Society and Inquisition* (ed. by Y. Kaplan), Jerusalem 1985, pp.103–23.
40 The town authorities came later to an arrangement with the Jews who did not return. They settled in nearby localities. See H. Beinart, 'The Expulsion of the Jews from Valmaseda' (in Hebrew), *Zion* 46 (1981), pp.39–51.
41 It was carried out only in 1492. See further below.
42 For the full text see N. López Martínez, *Los judaizantes castellanos y la inquisición en tiempo de Isabel la Católica*, Burgos 1954, pp.391–404.
43 The play was an Incunabula printing. See *Revista de Archivos, Bibliotecas y Museos* 30 (1926), p.409ff.
44 For a detailed description and analysis see: Baer, *History* ii, pp.398–423.
45 See H. Beinart, 'The Jews in Spain', in *The Jewish World*, edited by E. Kedourie, London 1979, p.167.
46 In Saragossa it was promulgated on 29 April 1492.
47 There is a confusion between the use of the names in various documents of the period.
48 See M. Bataillon, *Erasmo y España*, 2nd edn,

Mexico 1966, p.17 and Reg. s.v.
49 For the document see: L. Suárez Fernández, *Documentos acerca la expulsión de los judios*, Valladolid 1964, pp.487–89. While leaving, properties fell in their value; often a house was exchanged for a mule or a donkey.
50 For the order see: J. Amador de los Ríos, *Historia social, política y religiosa de los judíos de España y Portugal* (reprint), Madrid 1960, pp.1009–10.
51 See I. Tishby, *Messianism in the Time of the Expulsion from Spain and Portugal* (in Hebrew), Jerusalem 1985, *passim.*
52 See *Alpha Betha d'Ben Sira*, ed. J. Steinschneider, letter 21; M. Kasher, *Tora Shelema* 7, Parashat Vayigash, New York, 1946, pp.1163 (in Hebrew).
53 For more details see H. Beinart, *Zion* 48 (1983), pp.241–73.
54 Her file is not extant.
55 See Y.H. Yerushalmi, *The Lisbon Massacre of 1506 and the Royal Image in the Shebet Yehudah*, Cincinnati 1976. Among those who left was Shlomo Ibn Verga, the author of *Shebet Yehuda.*
56 See H. Beinart, 'Converso Emigration from Spain in the 15th to 17th Centuries' (in Hebrew), *Scritti in Memoria di Umberto Nahon*, Jerusalem 1978, pp.63–106.
57 See I.S. Revah, *REJ* (NS) 17 [108] (1958), pp.128–35.
58 Enrique was 27 years old. Diogo da Silva was appointed Archbishop of Braga.
59 See H. Beinart, 'The Spanish National Inquisition outside the Borders of Spain', *Proceedings of the Fifth World Congress of Jewish Studies*, vol.ii, Jerusalem 1967, pp.118–72 (in Hebrew).
60 On Ancona see: I. Sonne, *Mi-Paulo ha-Revii ad Pius ha-Khamishi*, Jerusalem 1954, p.30ff. On Venice see P.C. Ioly Zorattini, *Processi del S. Uffizio di Venezia contra Ebrei e Giudaizzante*, vols ii–x, Florence 1980–89.
61 See H. Beinart, note 56. On 8 December 1573 all Jews were ordered to leave his dominion.
62 There is no estimate of their numbers in Spain; however, their number was much higher there than in Portugal.
63 See Beinart, above note 56; R. Feingold, 'The "New Christian Problem" in Portugal 1601–1625' (in Hebrew), *Zion* 54 (1989), pp.379–400.
64 See H. Kellenbenz, *A participação de Compania de Judeus na conquista holandesa de Pernambuco*, Universidad Federal de Paraiba 1966. This venture ended in 1654 when the Portuguese reconquered the region. The remainder of them fled and settled in New Amsterdam (the later New York). This was also the beginning of settlement in Dutch holdings in the Caribbean Islands and South America.
65 See H. Beinart, 'The Jews in the Canary Islands: A Re-evaluation', *Transactions of the Jewish Historical Society of England* 25 (1977), pp.48–86. See also chapter nine.
66 See A. Glaser, 'Portuguese Sermons at Auto-da-fés', *Studies in Bibliography and Book-Lore* 2 (1955), pp.53–96; *Idem*, 'Invitation to Intolerance', *HUCA* 27 (1956), pp.327–86.
67 See H. Beinart, *Moroccan Jews in Spain early in the 17th Century*, Salo W. Baron Jubilee Volume (Hebrew Part), Jerusalem 1975, pp.15–39.
68 The chair was founded in 1314.
69 See H. Beinart, 'The Proselyte Lope de Vera y Alarcón and his death as a Martyr as Yehuda the Believer', *Beorach Mada*, Aharon Mirsky Jubilee Volume (in Hebrew), Lod 1986, pp.31–56.
70 See the Book of Esther 2:10.
71 See H. Beinart, *The Sephardi Heritage*, vol.i, edited by R. Barnett, London, pp.467–70.
72 See J. Caro Baroja, *Los judíos en la España Moderna y Contemporanea*, vol.ii, Madrid 1962, pp.420–22 and Reg. s.v.
73 See H. Beinart, 'The Trials of Jacob Cansino and his son Abraham by the Court of the Inquisition in Murcia' (in Hebrew), *Zion* 55 (1990), pp.341–45. He and his son Abraham were fined 400 gold ducats as a penalty. The tractates were confiscated.
74 See H. Beinart, *The New Jewish Settlement in Spain, Background, Reality and Evaluation*, Jerusalem 1969, p.13ff. (in Hebrew).
75 See Angela S. Selke, *The Conversos of Majorca*, Jerusalem 1986.

CHAPTER FIVE

1 There are different approaches among modern scholars as to the possible influence of the expulsion on the emergence of Jewish historiography in the sixteenth century: see Joseph Hayyim Yerushalmi, *Zakhor, Jewish History and Jewish Memory*, New York 1989, pp.57–75 who argues in favour of such an influence versus Robert Bonfil, 'How Golden Was the Age of the Renaissance in Jewish Historiography?', *History and Theory, Beiheft 27, Essays in Jewish Historiography*, Wesleyan University 1988, pp.78–102, who attributes the renaissance of Jewish historiography to the influence of the Italian ambiance.
2 It would be interesting to compare the bibliography concerning the possible impact of the destruction of the Temple on the subsequent Jewish literature to the model offered by scholars in the case of the expulsion. It is of great importance to mention that at least in the case of the ancient trauma, it is very difficult to prove the existence of a messianic literature generated by the event of the destruction. See Baruch M. Bockser, 'Rabbinic Responses to Catastrophe: From Continuity to Discontinuity', *Proceedings of the American Academy for Jewish Research*, vol.50 (1983), pp.37–61; Robert Goldenberg, 'Early Rabbinic Explanations of the Destruction of Jerusalem', *Journal of Jewish Studies* vol.xxxiii (1982) = *Essays in Honour of Yigael Yadin*, eds G. Vermes and J. Neusner, pp.517–25; Anthony J. Saldarini, 'Varieties of Rab-

binic Destruction of the Temple', *Society of Biblical Literature, 1982 Seminar Papers*, ed. K.H. Richards, Scholars Press, Atlanta 1982, pp.437–58.
3 This view was expounded in several instances by Gershom Scholem, see below notes 5, 7, 8 and the more elaborate treatment of this hypothesis in Rachel Elior, 'Messianic Expectations and the Spiritualization of Religious Life in the Sixteenth Century', *Revue des Etudes Juives* vol.cxlv (1986), pp.35–49.
4 See Ariel Toaff, 'The Jewish Communities of Catalonia, Aragon and Castile in 16th-Century Rome', eds A. Toaff–S. Schwarzfuchs, *The Mediterranean and the Jews: Banking, Finance and International Trade (XVI–XVIII Centuries)*, Bar-Ilan University Press, Ramat-Gan 1989, pp.249–70.
5 See e.g. his *Major Trends in Jewish Mysticism*, New York 1967, pp.244–51; *idem*, *The Messianic Idea in Judaism*, New York 1972, pp.41–48. See also below notes 7–8.
6 See e.g. Isaiah Tishby, *Messianism in the Time of the Expulsion from Spain and Portugal*, The Zalman Shazar Center for Jewish History, Jerusalem 1985, pp.52–54 (Hebrew); Joseph Dan, *Jewish Mysticism and Jewish Ethics*, University of Washington Press, Seattle–London 1986, pp.76–79; Elior, 'Messianic Expectations' (note 3 above), especially p.48 where she mentions 'the acute messianic expectations that motivated the majority of the changes in the religious life in the sixteenth century'. Compare below note 9.
7 *Explications and Implications, Writings on Jewish Heritage and Renaissance*, Am Oved Publishers, Tel Aviv 1975, p.205 (Hebrew), translated in a more concise form in his *The Messianic Idea in Judaism*, p.41. See also *Explications*, p.201.
8 *Kabbalah*, Keter Publishing House, Jerusalem 1974, p.68.
9 They include some of the writings of Rabbi Abraham ben Eliezer ha-Levi; the anonymous *Sefer Kaf ha-Qetoret*, which was described by Scholem as if it were in its entirety an eschatological writing (*Major Trends*, p.248), while in fact the role of this element in the general scheme of the book is much more modest; the anonymous *Sefer Galiya Razza*; some hints in the writings of Rabbi Shlomo Molkho and some small fragments spread in the works of Rabbi Abraham Sabba and Joseph ibn Shraga. Altogether, this material constitutes no more than a very small percentage of the huge kabbalistic literature.
10 The single outstanding exception is the controversy concerning the semikhah in Safed; see Jacob Katz, *Halakhah and Kabbalah*, The Magnes Press, Jerusalem 1984, pp.213–36 (Hebrew).
11 This seems to be the case in the poetry of North Africa since the sixteenth century, as Prof. Joseph Shitrit has kindly informed me.
12 On Abravanel's view of messianism see Tishby, *Messianism* (note 6 above), pp.19–20; Benzion Netanyahu, *Don Isaac Abravanel, Statesman & Philosopher*, Philadelphia 1972, pp.195–247 and below note 70.
13 See note 6 above.
14 See my preface to A.Z. Aeshkoly, *Jewish Messianic Movements*, Mossad Bialik, Jerusalem 1987, 2nd edn, p.23 (Hebrew).
15 Aeshkoly, *ibid.*, p.271; Tishby, *Messianism* (note 6 above), p.73.
16 This is the view of e.g. Isaac Baer; see my forthcoming preface to A.Z. Aeshkoly, *The Story of David ha-Reuveni*, Mossad Bialik, Jerusalem 1991, 2nd edn (Hebrew).
17 See above the quotation from Scholem, in Tishby, *Messianism* (note 6 above), p.52, and my remarks as to the abuse of the term 'movement', in the preface to Aeshkoly, *Jewish Messianic Movements* (note 14 above), p.11.
18 'Hope against Hope – Jewish and Christian Messianic Expectations in the Late Middle Ages' in *Exile and Diaspora*, eds A. Mirsk, A. Grossman, Y. Kaplan, Jerusalem 1991, pp. 185–202.
19 See an up-to-date survey on this figure in the preface of Gershom Scholem – Malakhi Beit-Arie, eds, to ha-Levi's *Ma'amar Meshare Qitrin* (Jewish National & University Press/Arno Press, Jerusalem/New York 1977) (Hebrew); Ira Robinson, 'Messianic Prayer Vigils in Jerusalem in the Early Sixteenth Century', *Jewish Quarterly Review*, vol.lxxii (1981), pp.32–42; Moshe Idel, 'On Mishmarot and Messianism in Jerusalem in the 16th–17th Centuries', *Shalem* vol.5 (1987), ed. Joseph Hacker, pp.83–90 (Hebrew).
20 *Major Trends in Jewish Mysticism*, p.247.
21 Cf. Moshe Idel, 'Inquiries in the Doctrine of *Sefer ha-Meshiv*', *Sefunot* NS vol.2 (17) (1983), p.202 (Hebrew).
22 See my preface to Aeshkoly, *Jewish Messianic Movements* (note 14 above), pp.24–26.
23 See his various messianic epistles. The role of hope, in addition to, or even in contrast to despair, in the emergence of the messianic consciousness is worth a detailed study; see meanwhile, Moshe Idel, 'The Beginning of Kabbala in North Africa? – A Forgotten Document by R. Yehuda ben Nissim ibn Malka', *Pe'amin*, vol.43 (1990), pp.8–12 (Hebrew).
24 *Explications and Implications* (note 7 above), pp.204–05.
25 On Abulafia's messianism see Abraham Berger, 'The messianic Self-Consciousness of Abraham Abulafia – A Tentative Evaluation', *Essays on Jewish Life and Thought Presented in Honor of Salo Wittmayer Baron*, New York 1959, pp.55–61; M. Idel, *Studies in Ecstatic Kabbalah*, State University of New York Press, Albany 1988, pp.45–61.
26 'The Messiah of the Zohar', *The Messianic Idea in Jewish Thought*, The Israel Academy of Science and Humanities, Jerusalem 1982, pp.89–118 (Hebrew).
27 See Idel, preface to Aeshkoly, *Jewish Messianic*

Movements (note 14 above), pp.17–19.
28 *Ibid.*, and also Idel, 'Inquiries' (note 21 above), pp.193–204.
29 See Rivka Schatz, 'Gnostic Literature as a Source of Shlomo Molkho', ed. Joseph Dan, *Early Jewish Mysticism*, Jerusalem 1987, pp.235–67 (Hebrew); *idem*, 'Lines for the Image of the Political-Messianic Effervescence After the Expulsion from Spain', *Daat* vol.xi (1983), pp.53–66 (Hebrew).
30 Cf. Scholem, *Major Trends* (note 5 above), pp.244–86, especially pp.250, 261.
31 Scholem, *The Messianic Idea in Israel* (note 5 above), pp.41–48.
32 *Ibid.*, pp.43–44.
33 *Ibid.*, pp.44–46; *Major Trends*, pp.260–61.
34 *Major Trends*, p.260. See also Elior, 'Messianic Expectations' (note 3 above), p.48.
35 That the concept of *Zimzum* was already in existence before the expulsion from Spain is a fact recognized even by Scholem, but he was inclined to downplay its importance in order to allow a greater impact of the historical event on the course of the development of Kabbalah. In a forthcoming Hebrew study devoted to this issue, I have collected the extant discussions on the *Zimzum* written by Spanish kabbalists in Spain and my conclusion is that it is very difficult to find significant changes in this concept in the sixteenth-century Kabbalah.
36 See Moshe Idel, *Kabbalah: New Perspectives*, Yale University Press, New Haven/London 1988, p.265.
37 In my opinion there is more than one centre of gravitation in the Lurianic Kabbalah; no less important than the eschatological one is the ritualistic focus, which was strengthened by a theurgical interpretation of the significance of the commandments; and an apotropaic one, which regarded the disclosure of this type of Kabbalah as a function of the augmentation of evil; Lurianic Kabbalah is, according to this view, a system that is efficacious in order to counteract the demonic. See Moshe Idel, 'One from a Town, Two from a Clan: The Question of the Diffusion of Lurianic Kabbalah and Sabbateanism: A Reexamination', *Pe'amim* 44 (1990) pp.5–30 (Hebrew).
38 See Bernard D. Septimus, 'Tahat Edom velo Tahat Ishmael', *Zion* vol.xlvii (1982), pp.103–11.
39 See Georges Vajda, 'Passages Anti-Chrétiens dans *Kaf ha-Qetoret*', *Revue de l'Histoire des Religions*, vol.cxlviii (1980), pp.45–58; Moshe Idel, 'The Attitude to Christianity in *Sefer ha-Meshiv*', *Immanuel*, vol.xli (1981), pp.77–95; Tishby, *Messianism* (note 6 above), pp.59–66.
40 See Idel, *ibid.*, p.82.
41 Joseph R. Hacker, 'On the Intellectual Character and Self-Perception of Spanish Jewry in the Late Fifteenth Century', *Sefunot* NS vol.ii (17) (1983), pp.49–50, 52–56 (Hebrew).
42 On the Kabbalah of this author see Melila Helner, 'Transmigration of Souls in the Kabbalistic Writings of R. David ibn Zimra', *Pe'amim*, vol.xliii (1990), pp.16–50 (Hebrew).
43 See my preface to the facsimile edition of *Sefer Zaphnat Pa'aneah* of Rabbi Joseph Al-Ashqar (Misgav Yerushalaim, Jerusalem 1991) pp.21–33 (Hebrew).
44 Gershom Scholem, *Chapters in the History of the Literature of Kabbalah*, Jerusalem 1931, pp.69–86, 154–62.
45 Boaz Hus, 'The Theory of Sephirot in "Ketem Paz" by R. Shim'on Lavi', *Pe'amim* vol. xliii (1990), pp.51–84 (Hebrew).
46 See his introduction to *Sefer Minhat Yehudah*, Mantua 1558, fol. 2ab.
47 Moshe Idel, 'The Magical and Neoplatonic Interpretations of Kabbalah in the Renaissance', ed. Bernard D. Cooperman, *Jewish Thought in the Sixteenth Century*, Harvard University Press, Cambridge, Mass. 1983, pp.186–242.
48 *Idem*, 'Particularism and Universalism in Kabbalah: 1480–1650' (forthcoming); 'Major Currents in Italian Kabbalah between 1560 and 1660', *Italia Judaica*, vol.ii, Rome 1986, pp.243–62.
49 *Idem*, 'Between the View of Sefirot as Essence and Instrument in Kabbalah in the Renaisssance', *Italia* vol.iii (1982), pp.89–102 (Hebrew).
50 *Idem*, 'The Study Program of Rabbi Yohanan Alemanno', *Tarbiz*, vol.xlviii (1979), pp.330–31 (Hebrew).
51 See Ephraim Gottlieb, *Studies in the Kabbalah Literature*, ed. Joseph Hacker, Tel Aviv 1976, pp.404–12 (Hebrew); Hava Tirosh-Rotschild, 'Sefirot as the Essence of God in the Writings of David Messer Leon', *Association of Jewish Studies Review*, vol.vii–viii (1982/3), pp.409–25.
52 See e.g. *Minhat Yehudah*, fol. 98ab.
53 *Ibid.*, fol. 97b.
54 Cf. Idel, 'The Study Progress' (note 50 above), pp.330–31.
55 See, for the time being, Alexander Marx, 'Le Faux Messie Ascher Leimlein', *Revue des Etudes Juives*, vol.lxi (1911), pp.136–38.
56 See the studies mentioned above, note 48, and from another point of view Moshe Idel, 'Jewish Magic from the Renaissance Period to Early Hasidism', eds J. Neusner, E.S. Frerichs, P.V. McCracken Flesher, *Religion, Science and Magic, In Concert and in Conflict*, Oxford University Press, New York 1989, pp.82–117.
57 The Byzantine centre of Kabbalah, of utmost importance in the 14th and 15th centuries, still requires a separate study to establish its particular spiritual physiognomy.
58 See Roland Goetschel, *Meir ibn Gabbay, Le discours de la Kabbale Espagnole* (Peeters, Leuven 1981).
59 Namely *Sefer Kaf ha-Qetoret*, cf. Idel, 'Inquiries' (note 21 above), pp.195–201.
60 Rachel Elior, *Galiya Razza* (Hebrew University, Jerusalem 1981), pp.7–14 (Hebrew); R.J. Zwi Werb-

lowsky, *Joseph Karo, Lawyer and Mystic* (The Jewish Publication Society of America, Philadelphia 1977); Idel, 'Inquiries' (note 21 above), *passim*.
61 See Scholem, *Major Trends* (note 5 above), p.141; Idel, *Studies in Ecstatic Kabbalah* (note 25 above), pp.122–25.
62 Scholem, *ibid*., pp.244–86; Werblowsky, *Joseph Karo* (note 60 above); Lawrence Fine, *Safed Spirituality*, Paulist Press, New York/Ramsay, Toronto 1984.
63 Idel, *Studies in Ecstatic Kabbalah* (note 25 above), pp.136–40.
64 *Ibid*., p.140.
65 See the studies mentioned in notes 42–44 above; compare, however, the view of Rachel Elior, 'The Kabbalists of Dra', *Pe'amim*, vol.xxiv (1985), pp.36–73 (Hebrew) who assumes that some more visionary forms of Moroccan Kabbalah were influenced by the Marabut phenomenon in North Africa.
66 See Menachem Kellner, *Dogma in Medieval Jewish Thought from Maimonides to Abravanel*, Oxford 1986, pp.83–195.
67 Though there is an extensive bibliography on this seminal author, the only comprehensive monographs on him are those of Harry A. Wolfson, *Crescas' Critique of Aristotle*, Harvard University Press, Cambridge, Mass. 1971; Aviezer Ravitzki, *Crescas' Sermon on the Passover and Studies in His Philosophy*, Israel Academies of Science, Jerusalem 1988 (Hebrew).
68 See Moshe Idel, 'Kabbalah and Ancient Philosophy in the Writings of Isaac and Yehudah Abravanel', in *The Philosophy of Leone Ebreo*, eds Menahem Dorman, Zeev Levi, Hakkibutz ha-Meuhad Publishing House, 1985, pp.75–76 (Hebrew).
69 Cf. Moshe Idel, 'The Magical and Theurgic Interpretation of Music in Jewish Sources from the Renaissance to Hassidism', *Yuval*, vol.iv (1982), pp.42–45 (Hebrew).
70 On the relationship between expulsion and the thought of Abravanel see Isaac Baer, 'The Messianic Movement in Spain in the Period of the Expulsion', *Zion* vol.i (1933), pp.31–77 (Hebrew) and note 12 above.
71 See Shaul Regev, 'Messianism and Astrology in the Thought of Rabbi Isaac Abravanel', *Assufot* vol.i (1987), pp.169–87 (Hebrew).
72 On the philosophy of this author, writing immediately after the expulsion, see Sarah Heller-Wilensky, *The Philosophy of Isaac Arama in the Framework of Philonic Philosophy*, The Bialik Institute and Devir Publishing House, Jerusalem, and Tel Aviv 1956 (Hebrew).
73 Regev, *ibid*., p.179 note 45.
74 Leone Ebreo's thought has been analyzed in several studies; see above note 68; T.A. Perry, *Erotic Spirituality: The Integrative Tradition from Leone Ebreo to John Donne*, Alabama 1980; Arthur Leslie, 'The Place of the *Dialoghi d'Amore* in Contemporaneous Jewish Thought', in *Ficino and Renaissance Neoplatonism*, eds Konrad Isenbichler and Olga Z. Pulgiese, Toronto 1988, pp.69–86; Shlomo Pines, 'Medieval Doctrines in Renaissance Garb? Some Jewish and Arabic Sources of Leone Ebreo's Doctrines', ed. Cooperman, *Jewish Thought* (note 47 above), pp.365–429.
75 See e.g. Beinart's 'The Movement of the Prophetess Ines in Puebla de Alquisir', *Tarbiz*, vol.li (1982), pp.633–58 or 'The Conversos of Halia and the Movement of the Prophetess Ines', *Zion*, vol.liii (1988), pp.31–52 (Hebrew). On the whole question of conversos see now the excellent collection of studies edited by Josef Kaplan, *Jews and Conversos, Studies in Society and the Inquisition*, The Magnes Press, Jerusalem 1985.
76 See my preface to Aeshkoly's *Story of David ha-Reuveni* (note 16 above).
77 *Ibid*.
78 Gershom Scholem, 'On the History of the Kabbalist Rabbi Jacob Zemah and his Literary Activity', *Qiriat Sefer*, vol.xxvi (1950), pp.185–94; *ibid*., vol.xvli (1951), pp.107–10 (Hebrew).
79 See Scholem, *Kabbalah* (note 8 above), pp.396–400.
80 On the accusations of Karaism in the seventeenth century see Moshe Idel, 'Differing Conceptions of Kabbalah in the Early 17th Century', *Jewish Thought in the Seventeenth Century*, eds Isadore Twersky and Bernard Septimus, Harvard University Press, Cambridge, Mass. 1987, pp.148–49.
81 Though it is not an unknown assumption, the affinity between the Marranos and Sabbateanism was downplayed in the recent explanation of the acceptance and diffusion of Sabbateanism, as it was accepted in the school of G. Scholem.
82 On the importance of the rupture in the historiography of Scholem see Ivan Marcus, 'Beyond the Sefardi Mystique', *Orim*, vol.i (1985), pp.36, 46–47.
83 See above notes 5, 7.
84 R.N. Bellah, 'Religious Evolution', ed. R. Robertson, *Sociology of Religion, Selected Readings*, Harmondsworth 1969, p.266.
85 *Ibid*.
86 Cf. Gershom Scholem, *Sabbatai Sevi, The Mystical Messiah*, tr. R.Y. Zwi Werblowski, Princeton University Press, Princeton 1973.
87 Gershom Scholem, *On the Kabbalah and its Symbolism*, tr. Ralph Manheim, Schocken Books, New York 1969, pp.2–3.
88 See especially Elior, 'Messianic Expectations' (note 3 above), p.48, quoted above note 6.

CHAPTER SIX

1 Juan de Mariana, *Historia General de España*, (*BAE*, 30–31, 2 vols, Madrid 1950), i, pp.156, 359.
2 *Ibid*., i, p.256.
3 See Henry Kamen, 'The Mediterranean and the Expulsion of Spanish Jews in 1492', *Past and*

Present, 119 (1988), pp.30–55, for a revision downwards of the numbers expelled: 40,000–50,000 in a population of 5.2 million. See also the present book, chapter 3.
4 Luis Suárez Fernández, *Documentos acerca de la expulsión de los judíos* (Valladolid 1964), p.487.
5 Stephen Haliczer, *Inquisition and Society in the Kingdom of Valencia, 1478–1834* (Berkeley and Los Angeles 1990), pp.50–1.
6 Ricardo García Carcel, *Herejía y sociedad en el siglo XVI. La Inquisición en Valencia 1530–1609* (Barcelona 1980), pp.140–55; Jaime Contreras, *El Santo Oficio de la Inquisición de Galicia, 1560–1700* (Madrid 1982), pp.65–80; Haliczer, *Inquisition and Society in the Kingdom of Valencia*, p.208.
7 Haim Beinart, *Conversos on Trial: The Inquisition of Ciudad Real* (Jerusalem 1981), p.23. See also the present book, chapter 4.
8 Benzion Netanyahu, *The Marranos of Spain from the Late XIVth to the Early XVIth Century* (New York 1966), p.3; see also Ricardo García Carcel, *Orígenes de la Inquisición española. El tribunal de Valencia, 1478–1530* (Barcelona 1976), pp.195–99.
9 Julio Caro Baroja, *Los judíos en la España moderna y contemporánea* (3 vols, Madrid 1962), i, p.298.
10 Haliczer, *Inquisition and Society in the Kingdom of Valencia*, pp.211–12.
11 *Ibid.*, pp.212–17.
12 Beinart, *Conversos on Trial*, pp.84–100.
13 García Carcel, *Orígenes de la Inquisición Española*, p.170.
14 Bartolomé Bennassar, ed., *L'Inquisition espagnole, XV*[e]*–XVI*[e] *siècle* (Paris 1979), pp.20, 34.
15 Catherine Brault-Noble and Marie-José Marc, 'La répression des minorités', Bennassar, *L'Inquisition espagnole*, pp.153–55.
16 Haliczer, *Inquisition and Society in the Kingdom of Valencia*, p.230.
17 Jean-Pierre Dedieu, *L'Administration de la foi: L'Inquisition de Tolède XVI*[e]*–XVIII*[e] (Madrid 1989), pp.51–55, 230–48.
18 Bennassar, *L'Inquisition espagnole*, pp.29–30.
19 Gustav Henningsen, *The Witches' Advocate: Basque Witchcraft and the Spanish Inquisition* (Reno, Nevada 1980), pp.388–89.
20 Jaime Contreras and Gustav Henningsen, 'Forty-four Thousand Cases of the Spanish Inquisition (1540–1700)', Gustav Henningsen and John Tedeschi, eds, *The Inquisition in Early Modern Europe: Studies on Sources and Method* (DeKalb 1986), pp.118–19; see also Stephen Haliczer, *Inquisition and Society in Early Modern Europe* (London 1987), pp.1, 3.
21 Albert Sicroff, *Les controverses des statutes de pureté de sang en Espagne du XV au XVIII siècle* (Paris 1960), pp.42–58, 80–92, 250–82; Henry Kamen, *Inquisition and Society in Spain in the Sixteenth and Seventeenth Centuries* (London 1985), pp.119–20.
22 Kamen, *Inquisition and Society*, pp.123–24.
23 Sicroff, *Les controverses des statutes de pureté de sang*, p.203.
24 Quoted by Haliczer, *Inquisition and Society in Early Modern Europe*, p.10; see also Kamen, *Inquisition and Society*, pp.127–32; Patrick Williams, 'A Jewish Councillor of Inquisition? Luis de Mercado, the Statutes of *Limpieza de sangre* and the Politics of Vendetta (1598–1601)', *Bulletin of Hispanic Studies*, 67 (1990), pp.253–64.
25 J.H. Elliott, *The Count-Duke of Olivares. The Statesman in an Age of Decline* (New Haven and London 1986), pp.10–11.
26 Haliczer, *Inquisition and Society in the Kingdom of Valencia*, pp.121–23, 235–42; they were a very small minority, six out of seventy in Haliczer's sample of Valencia inquisitors.
27 Jonathan I. Israel, *European Jewry in the Age of Mercantilism 1550–1750* (Oxford 1985), pp.24–25.
28 Caro Baroja, *Los judíos en la España moderna y contemporánea*, i, p.221.
29 Rafael Carrasco, 'Preludio al "siglo de los portugueses". La Inquisición de Cuenca y los judaizantes lusitanos en el siglo XVI', *Hispania*, 47, 166 (1987), pp.503–59.
30 James Boyajian, *Portuguese Bankers at the Court of Spain* (New Brunswick, N.J., 1983), pp.2–13.
31 John Lynch, *Spain under the Habsburgs* (2nd edn, 2 vols, Oxford 1981), ii, pp.62–66.
32 Caro Baroja, *Los judíos en la España moderna y contemporánea*, ii, pp.115–30.
33 Quoted by Elliott, *The Count-Duke of Olivares*, p.11.
34 Kamen, *Inquisition and Society*, p.225; Boyajian, *Portuguese Bankers*, p.40.
35 Boyajian, *Portuguese Bankers*, pp.44, 133–80.
36 *Ibid.*, pp.104–8.
37 Rafael de Lera García, 'Venta de oficios en la Inquisición de Granada (1629–1644)', *Hispania*, 48, 170 (1988), pp.909–62, see especially p.939.
38 Contreras and Henningsen, 'Forty-four Thousand Cases of the Spanish Inquisition (1540–1700)', pp.120–22.
39 Brault-Noble and Marc, 'La répression des minorités', Bennassar, *L'Inquisition espagnole*, p.156.
40 Boyajian, *Portuguese Bankers*, p.118.
41 *Ibid.*, p.148.
42 Israel, chapter eight (present book) and *European Jewry in the Age of Mercantilism*, pp.154–60; Bennassar, *L'Inquisition espagnole*, p.162.
43 Quoted by Haliczer, *Inquisition and Society in Early Modern Europe*, p.15.
44 Kamen, *Inquisition and Society*, pp.229–31.
45 Lynch, *Spain under the Habsburgs*, ii, pp.121–22, 184, 194–95, 213; Boyajian, *Portuguese Bankers*, pp.122–24; Harry E. Cross, 'Commerce and Orthodoxy: A Spanish Response to Portuguese Commercial Penetration in the Viceroyalty of Peru, 1580–

1640', *The Americas*, 35 (1978), pp.151–67.
46 Seymour B. Liebman, *The Jews in New Spain: Faith, Flame and Inquisition* (Coral Gables, Florida 1970), and 'The Great Conspiracy in New Spain', *The Americas*, 30 (1973), pp.18–31; J.I. Israel, *Race, Class and Politics in Colonial Mexico, 1610–1670* (Oxford 1975), pp.200–46.
47 Joaquin Pérez Villanueva and Bartolomé Escandell Bonet, eds, *Historia de la Inquisición en España y América*, vol.I (2nd edn, Madrid 1984), pp.1386, 1396.
48 Caro Baroja, *Los judíos en la España moderna y contemporánea*, iii, pp.91–92, 111.
49 Haliczer, *Inquisition and Society in the Kingdom of Valencia*, pp.233–34, 332.
50 Caro Baroja, *Los judíos en la España moderna y contemporánea*, iii, p.133.
51 Haliczer, *Inquisition and Society in the Kingdom of Valencia*, pp.233, 242.
52 Kamen, *Inquisition and Society*, pp.233–34.
53 Henry Swinburne, *Travels through Spain in the Years 1775 and 1776* (London 1779), pp.68–69.
54 Joseph Townsend, *A Journey through Spain in the Years 1786 and 1787* (2nd edn, 3 vols, London 1792), ii, pp.341–55; iii, 83–84.
55 *Ibid.*, iii, p.139.
56 Richard Herr, *The Eighteenth-Century Revolution in Spain* (Princeton 1958), p.386.
57 Caro Baroja, *Los judíos en la España moderna y contemporánea*, iii, pp.43–44.
58 Pérez Villanueva and Escandell Bonet, *Historia de la Inquisición*, p.1274; see also John Lynch, *Bourbon Spain 1700–1808* (Oxford 1989), pp.254–61, 287–90.
59 'Instrucción Reservada', 8 July 1787, in Conde de Floridablanca, *Obras originales del conde de Floridablanca y escritos referentes a su persona*, ed. A. Ferrer del Río (*BAE*, 59, Madrid 1952), pp.217–18.
60 'Representación a Carlos IV sobre lo que era el Tribunal de la Inquisición', 1798, *Obras de Jovellanos* (*BAE*, 87, Madrid 1956), pp.333–34, 413.
61 Herr, *The Eighteenth-Century Revolution in Spain*, pp.379–80; Pérez Villanueva and Escandell Bonet, *Historia de la Inquisición*, pp.1319–32.
62 *Diarios*, 11 April 1797, *Obras de Jovellanos* (*BAE*, 85, Madrid 1956), p.421.
63 José Toribio Medina, *Historia del Tribunal del Santo Oficio de la Inquisición de Lima (1569–1820)* (2nd edn, 2 vols, Santiago de Chile 1952), ii, pp.202, 237–39.
64 Guillermo Lohmann Villena, 'Manuel Lorenzo de Vidaurre y la Inquisición de Lima', *Mar del Sur*, 18 (1951), pp.104–13.
65 M.L. Pérez Marchand, *Dos etapes ideológicas del siglo XVIII en México a través de los papeles de la Inquisición* (Mexico 1945), pp.122–24; José Toribio Medina, *Historia del Tribunal del Santo Oficio de la Inquisición en México* (rev. edn, Mexico 1952), pp.371–92, 342–49.
66 Pérez Villanueva and Escandell Bonet, *Historia de la Inquisición*, p.1367.
67 Raymond Carr, *Spain 1808–1939* (Oxford 1966), p.170: Peter Janke, *Mendizabal y la instauración de la monarquía constitucional en España (1790–1853)* (Madrid 1974), pp.8, 232–33.
68 Benjamin Disraeli, *Coningsby, or the New Generation* (London 1989), pp.232–37.
69 Quoted by Caro Baroja, *Los judíos en la España moderna y contemporánea*, iii, p.189.
70 *Ibid.*, iii, p.193.
71 Carr, *Spain 1808–1939*, pp.605–7.
72 Isidro González García, 'El problema del racismo y los judíos en el fascismo italiano y su incidencia en el gobierno de Burgos en el año 1938', *Hispania*, 47, 165 (1987), pp.309–35.
73 Raanan Rein, 'La negativa israelí: las relaciones entre España y Israel (1948–49)', *Hispania*, 49, 172 (1989), pp.659–88.
74 Adolfo de Castro, *The History of the Jews in Spain* (Cambridge 1851).
75 José Amador de los Ríos, *Estudios históricos, políticos y literarios sobre los judíos en España* (Madrid 1848).
76 John Lynch, 'Menéndez Pelayo as a Historian', *Bulletin of Hispanic Studies*, 33, 4 (1956), pp.187–201.
77 Marcelino Menéndez Pelayo, *La Ciencia Española* (2 vols, Madrid 1933), i, p.97.
78 Menéndez Pelayo to Valera, 17 October 1887, *Epistolario de Valera y Menéndez y Pelayo* (Madrid 1946), p.408; *Historia de los heterodoxos españoles* (8 vols, Santander 1946–48), ii, p.471, iv, p.109.
79 Américo Castro, *The Structures of Spanish History* (Princeton 1954), pp.421–30, 532, 540.
80 Salvador de Madariaga, *The Fall of the Spanish American Empire* (London 1947), pp.245–83.
81 García Carcel, *Origenes de la Inquisición española*.

CHAPTER SEVEN

1 For a general history of the Ottoman empire, see Stanford J. Shaw and Ezel K. Shaw, *History of the Ottoman Empire and Modern Turkey*, 2 vols (Cambridge 1976–77).
2 The latest study of Byzantine Jewry is Steven Bowman, *The Jews of Byzantium, 1204–1453* (Tuscaloosa 1985). A general overview of the history of the Jews in the first century of the Ottoman empire is in Moïse Franco, *Essai sur l'histoire des Israélites de l'Empire ottoman depuis les origines jusqu'à nos jours* (Paris 1897), pp.27–35. See also Mark A. Epstein, *The Ottoman Jewish Communities and their Role in the Fifteenth and Sixteenth Centuries* (Freiburg 1980), pp.19–52.
3 For a study of the *dhimma* and the relationship of Islam with other religions, see Bernard Lewis, *The Jews of Islam* (Princeton, New Jersey 1984), pp.3–66.

4 The best and most thorough study of the *sürgün* as it applied to the Jews is in Joseph Hacker, 'The *Sürgün* System and Jewish Society in the Ottoman Empire during the 15th–17th centuries' in Aron Rodrigue, *Ottoman and Turkish Jewry: Community and Leadership* (Bloomington, forthcoming).

5 See Aryeh Shmuelevitz, *The Jews of the Ottoman Empire in the late Fifteenth and the Sixteenth Centuries* (Leiden 1984), p.31.

6 Eliyahu Capsali, *Seder Eliyahu Zuta*, 2 vols, ed. Aryeh Shmuelevitz (Jerusalem 1975–77), ii: p.218. This chronicle was originally compiled in Crete in 1523. The English translation of this statement is in Jacob Barnai, 'On the History of the Jews in the Ottoman Empire' in Esther Juhasz (ed.), *Sephardi Jews in the Ottoman Empire: Aspects of Material Culture* (Jerusalem 1990), p.19.

7 Cited from Immanuel Aboab, *Nomologia o discursos legales* (Amsterdam 1629) in *Encyclopedia Judaica*, s.v. 'The Ottoman Empire'.

8 Lewis, *The Jews of Islam*, pp.118–23.

9 See Mark A. Epstein, 'The Leadership of the Ottoman Jews in the Fifteenth and Sixteenth Centuries' in Benjamin Braude and Bernard Lewis, eds, *Christians and Jews in the Ottoman Empire*, 2 vols (New York 1982), i: pp.101–15.

10 For a study of the Romaniote Ioannina community, see Rae Dalven, *The Jews of Ioannina* (Philadelphia 1990).

11 There is a large literature on the internal structure and leadership of the Sephardi communities of the Ottoman empire in this period, as well as on their relationship with the authorities. See for example Joseph Hacker, 'The Jewish Community of Salonica from the Fifteenth to the Sixteenth Century (Ph.D diss., The Hebrew University of Jerusalem 1978) (in Hebrew); Leah Bornstein-Makovetsky, 'The Jewish Communal Leadership in the Near East from the End of the Fifteenth Century through the Eighteenth Century' (Ph.D diss., Bar Ilan University 1978) (in Hebrew); and Joseph Nehama, 'The Jews of Salonica in the Ottoman Period' in Richard D. Barnett and Walter M. Schwab, eds, *The Western Sephardim* (Grendon, Northants 1989), pp.203–42.

12 On Haim Nahum and his policies see Esther Benbassa, 'Haim Nahum Effendi, dernier Grand Rabbin de l'Empire ottoman (1908–1920): Son rôle politique et diplomatique' (Thèse de doctorat d'état ès lettres, Université de Paris III, 1987); *idem*, *Un Grand Rabbin sépharade en politique, 1892–1923* (Paris 1990).

13 See Amnon Cohen, *Jewish Life under Islam: Jerusalem in the Sixteenth Century* (Cambridge, Mass. 1984), and Joseph Hacker, 'Jewish Autonomy in the Ottoman Empire: Its Scope and Limits' in Shmuel Almog, Yisrael Bartal, Michael Graetz *et al.*, eds, *Transition and Change in Modern Jewish History. Essays in Honor of Shmuel Ettinger* (Jerusalem 1987), pp.349–88 (in Hebrew).

14 See Cecil Roth, *Dona Gracia of the House of Nasi* (Philadelphia 1948) and *idem*, *The House of Nasi: The Duke of Naxos* (Philadelphia 1948).

15 Daniel Rodriguez was also known as Daniel Rodriga. On his activities, see Benjamin Ravid, 'An Autobiographical Memorandum by Daniel Rodriga, *inventore* of the *scala* of Spalato' in Ariel Toaff and Simon Schwarzfuchs, eds, *The Mediterranean and the Jews: Banking, Finance and International Trade (XVI–XVIII Centuries)* (Ramat Gan 1989), pp.189–214.

16 For a general discussion of mercantilism and the Jews of Europe, see Jonathan Israel, *European Jewry in the Age of Mercantilism, 1550–1750*, 2nd edn (Oxford 1989).

17 There is a large literature on the Salonica textile industry. For the latest interpretation, see Simon Schwarzfuchs, 'Quand commença le déclin de l'industrie textile des Juifs de Salonique' in Toaff and Schwarzfuchs, eds, *The Mediterranean and the Jews*, pp.215–36.

18 For a general overview of the economic activities of the Ottoman Sephardim in this period, see Eliezer Bashan, 'The Rise and Decline of the Sephardi Communities in the Levant: The Economic Aspects' in Barnett and Schwab, eds, *The Western Sephardim*, pp.349–88.

19 A recent important article that studies the intellectual life of Ottoman Jewry in this period is Joseph Hacker, 'The Intellectual Activity of the Jews of the Ottoman Empire during the Sixteenth and Seventeenth Centuries' in Isadore Twersky and Bernard Septimus, eds, *Jewish Thought in the Seventeenth Century* (Cambridge, Mass. 1987), pp.95–135. See also the present book, chapter five.

20 For some interpretations of the decline, see Lewis, *The Jews of Islam*, pp.166–70; Traian Stoianovich, 'The Conquering Balkan Orthodox Merchant', *Journal of Economic History* 20 (1960), pp.234–313; William H. McNeill, 'Hypotheses Concerning Possible Ethnic Role Changes in the Ottoman Empire in the Seventeenth Century' in Osman Okyar and Halil Inalcik, eds, *Social and Economic History of Turkey* (Ankara 1980).

21 The most comprehensive work on this episode is Gershom Scholem, *Sabbatai Sevi: The Mystical Messiah* (Princeton, New Jersey 1973).

22 On the *Me-am Loez*, see Michael Molho, *Le Meam Loez, encyclopédie populaire du sépharadisme levantin* (Salonica 1945).

23 There is a very large literature on Judeo-Spanish. The language also is known as Ladino. For an overview, see David Bunis, *Sephardic Studies: A Research Bibliography incorporating Judezmo Language, Literature and Folklore, and Historical Background* (New York 1981).

24 For a discussion of the reforms and the Jews, see Aron Rodrigue, *French Jews, Turkish Jews: The Alliance Israélite Universelle and the Politics*

of Jewish Schooling in Turkey (Bloomington 1990), pp.25–35.
25 *Ibid.*
26 For a discussion of the usage of the term, see Benjamin Braude, 'Foundation Myths of the *Millet* System' in Braude and Lewis, eds, *Christians and Jews*, i: pp.69–88.
27 Shaw and Shaw, *History of the Ottoman Empire*, ii: p.113.
28 There is a large literature on the Alliance. For two books that treat the organization's activities as a whole, see André Chouraqui, *Cent ans d'histoire: L'Alliance Israélite Universelle et la renaissance juive contemporaine (1860–1960)* (Paris 1960) and Aron Rodrigue, *De l'instruction à l'émancipation: Les enseignants de l'Alliance Israélite Universelle et les Juifs d'Orient, 1860–1939* (Paris 1989).
29 For an overview of the Alliance's work among the Sephardim of Turkey, see Rodrigue, *French Jews, Turkish Jews.*
30 The economic history of the region is studied in Charles Issawi, *The Economic History of Turkey, 1800–1914* (Chicago 1980). See also Vedat Eldem, *A Study on the Economic Circumstances of the Ottoman Empire* (Ankara 1970) (in Turkish).
31 Itshac Emmanuel, 'Los Jidios de Salonique' in David Recanati, ed., *Zikhron Saloniki*, 2 vols (Tel Aviv 1972–86), i: pp.19–26. See also Paul Dumont, 'La structure sociale de la communauté juive de Salonique à la fin du dix-neuvième siècle', *Revue Historique*, no.263 (April–June 1980), pp.351–93.
32 The Judeo-Spanish press is catalogued in Moshe D. Gaon, *The Ladino Press: A Bibliography* (Jerusalem 1965) (in Hebrew). On the Judeo-Spanish press and literature as vehicles of modernization, see Esther Benbassa, 'Processus de modernisation en terre sépharade' in Shmuel Triagno, ed., *La Société juive à travers les ages* (Paris, forthcoming).
33 See Rodrigue, *French Jews, Turkish Jews*, pp.86–90.
34 See Esther Benbassa, 'Zionism in the Ottoman Empire at the End of the 19th and the Beginning of the 20th Century', *Studies in Zionism* 11 (1990), pp.127–40; Rodrigue, *French Jews, Turkish Jews*, pp.121–44.
35 For a discussion of the myths that surround this issue, see Elie Kedourie, 'Young Turks, Freemasons, and Jews', *Middle Eastern Studies* 7 (January 1971), pp.89–104.
36 See Jacob Barnai, 'Blood Libels in the Ottoman Empire from the Fifteenth to the Nineteenth Centuries' in Shmuel Almog, ed., *Antisemitism through the Ages* (Oxford 1988), pp.189–94.
37 Archives of the French Foreign Ministry, Nouvelle Série, Turquie, vol.138, letter from the Alliance Central Committee, 30 December 1912.
38 Archives of the Alliance, Grèce, I.C. 49, 12 November 1912.
39 Archives of the Alliance, Grèce, I.C. 51, 12 November 1912.

CHAPTER EIGHT

1 For the statistics of Portuguese New Christian settlement in Antwerp during the sixteenth century, see I.S. Revah, 'Pour l'histoire des marranes à Anvers: recensement de la "Nation Portugaise" de 1571 à 1666' in *Revue des Etudes Juives*, 4th ser. vol.ii (cxxii) (1963), pp.123–47; and Hans Pohl, *Die Portugiesen in Antwerpen (1567–1648). Zur Geschichte einer Minderheit* (Wiesbaden 1977), pp.63–68.
2 S. Seeligmann, 'Het marranen-probleem uit oekonomisch oogpunt', *Bijdragen en Mededeelingen van het Genootschap voor Joodsche Wetenschap in Nederland* iii (1925); see also Jonathan I. Israel, *European Jewry in the Age of Mercantilism, 1550–1750* (revised edn, Oxford 1989), pp.63–64.
3 H.P. Salomon, 'A Copy of Uriel da Costa's *Examen dos Tradicõens Phariseas* located in the Royal Library of Copenhagen', in *Studia Rosenthaliana. Journal for Jewish Literature and History in the Netherlands* xxiv (1990), pp.153–68.
4 On the role of Lopes Suasso, Machado and Pereira in the Glorious Revolution of 1688, see Harm den Boer and Jonathan I. Israel, 'William III and the Glorious Revolution in the Eyes of Amsterdam Sephardi Writers', in Jonathan I. Israel (ed.), *The Anglo-Dutch Moment. Essays on the Glorious Revolution and its World Impact* (Cambridge 1991), pp.339–42.

CHAPTER NINE

1 A.M. Hyamson, *The Sephardim of England: a history of the Spanish and Portuguese Community, 1492–1951* (London 1951); V.D. Lipman, 'Sephardi and other Jewish immigrants in England in the 18th century' in A. Newman (ed.), *Migration and Settlement* (London 1970); *Bevis Marks Records*, i (ed. L.D. Barnett, Oxford 1940).
2 D.S. Katz, *Philo-Semitism and the Re-admission of the Jews to England, 1603–55* (Oxford 1982); E.R. Samuel, 'The Re-admission of the Jews to England in the light of English economic policy', *Trans. Jew. Hist. Soc.* 31 (1990), pp.153–70; A.S. Diamond, 'The Community of the Resettlement, 1656–80', *Trans. Jew. Hist. Soc.* 24 (1975), pp.134–50.
3 Diamond, 'Community'; H. Pollins, *Economic History of the Jews in England* (Oxford 1982).
4 Hyamson, *Sephardim.*
5 Pollins, *Economic History*; G. Yogev, *Diamonds and Coral: Anglo-Dutch Jews and Eighteenth-Century Trade* (Leicester 1978); L.S. Sutherland, 'Samson Gideon: eighteenth-century Jewish financier' in A. Newman (ed.), *Politics and Finance in the Eighteenth Century* (London 1984).
6 *Bevis Marks Records*, i; Hyamson, *Sephardim.*
7 Sutherland, 'Samson Gideon'; M. Woolf, 'Joseph Salvador 1716–76', *Trans. Jew. Hist. Soc.* 21 (1968),

pp.104–37; T.M. Endelman, *The Jews of Georgian England* (Philadelphia 1979).
8 T.M. Endelman, *Radical Assimilation in English Jewish History, 1656–1945* (Bloomington 1990).
9 The anniversary of Sir Moses Montefiore's birth and death stimulated a wide literature. Sonia and V.D. Lipman, *The Century of Moses Montefiore* (Oxford 1985) provides the widest coverage.
10 A. Newman, *The Board of Deputies, 1760–1985; a brief survey* (London 1986).
11 Endelman, *Radical Assimilation.*
12 *Bevis Marks Records*, iii (ed. G.H. Whitehall, London 1973).

Sources of Illustrations

Numbers refer to pages

AMSTERDAM, Rijksmuseum 172 (bottom), 173 (top)
Universiteitsbibliotheek 172 (top)

AVILA, Archivio Historico Provincial 97

COPENHAGEN, Royal Library 32 (bottom left)

THE HAGUE, Mauritshuis 173 (bottom left)

JERUSALEM, Central Zionist Archives 174 (bottom)

LISBON, National Gallery 99 (top)

LONDON, British Library 28 (top), 29, 32 (bottom right), 90 (top left), 98 (top right), 103
National Portrait Gallery 174 (top)
Spanish and Portuguese Jews Congregation 175

MADRID, El Escorial 99 (bottom)
Palacio de Liria 25, 26 (top), 26 (centre), 26 (bottom), 27
Prado 100–101, 104 (top), 104 (bottom)

OXFORD, Bodleian Library 28 (bottom)

PARIS, Alliance Israélite Universelle 102 (bottom)
Bibliothèque Nationale 32 (top), 169, 171 (top left)

PRAGUE, Jewish Museum 99 (left)

TEL-AVIV, Museum of Jewish Diaspora 171 (bottom)

WASHINGTON D.C., Library of Congress 176

WOLFENBÜTTEL, Herzog August Bibliothek 173 (bottom right)

Photo MAS, Barcelona 25, 30, 31 (top), 31 (left), 31 (right), 98 (bottom), 99 (top right and bottom), 100–101

Select Bibliography

The literature on the expulsion has grown rapidly in the last twenty years. The reader will find further references on specialized topics in the bibliographies of many of the books cited below. Where the same work is relevant to more than one chapter it has been allowed to appear more than once.

CHAPTER ONE

J. Amador de los Ríos, *Historia social, política y religiosa de los judíos de España y Portugal*, 3 vols, Madrid 1875; published in one volume, Madrid 1960.
Y. Baer, *A History of the Jews in Christian Spain*, 2 vols, Philadelphia 1966.
A. MacKay, 'Popular Movements and Pogroms in Fifteenth-century Castile', *Past and Present*, no.55 (1972), pp.33–67.
A.A. Neumann, *The Jews in Spain: Their Social, Political and Cultural Life during the Middle Ages*, 2 vols, Philadelphia 1944.
L. Suárez Fernández, *Judíos españoles en la Edad Media*, Madrid 1980.
J. Valdeón Baruque, *Los judíos de Castilla y la revolución Trastámara*, Valladolid 1968.
P. Wolff, 'The 1391 Pogrom in Spain. Social Crisis or Not?', *Past and Present*, no.50 (1971), pp.4–18.

CHAPTER TWO

Y. Baer, *Die Juden im christlichen Spanien* i, Berlin 1929, II 1936.
—*A History of the Jews in Christian Spain*, Philadelphia 1966, ch.v, p.424ff.
E. Gutwirth, 'European Reactions to the Expulsions of the Jews from Spain', forthcoming.
—'The Jews in 15th-century Castilian Chronicles', *Jewish Quarterly Review* [(April 1984) 1986] lxxxiv, no.4, pp.379–96.
—'The Expulsion of the Jews from Spain and Jewish Historiography', *Jewish History: Festschrift C. Abramsky* (ed. A. Rapoport-Albert), London 1988, pp.141–61.
—'Abraham Seneor: Social Tensions and the Court-Jew', *Michael* xi (1989), pp.169–229.
Y. Haker, 'New Chronicles on the Expulsion of the Jews from Spain, its Causes and Effects' (Hebrew), *Zion* 44 (1979), pp.201–28.
S.H. Haliczer, 'The Castilian Urban Patriciate and the Jewish Expulsions of 1492', *American Historical Review*, 78/1 (1973), pp.35–58.
M. Kriegel, 'La prise d'une decision: l'expulsion des juifs d'Espagne en 1492', *Revue Historique* 260 (1978), pp.49–90.
M.A. Motis Dolader, 'Estudio de los objetos litúrgicos de las sinagogas zaragozanas embargados por la corona en el año 1492', *Aragón en la Edad Media: Estudios de Economía y Sociedad* iv, 4 (1984), pp.211–51.
—*La expulsión de los judíos de Zaragoza*, Saragossa 1986.
—'Los judíos de Magallón (Zaragoza) a fines del siglo XV y su expulsión', *Cuadernos de Estudios Borjanos* xvii–xviii (1986), pp.141–248.
—*La expulsión de los judíos del reino de Aragón*, Saragossa 1990.

CHAPTER THREE

Y. Baer, *Die Juden im christlichen Spanien: Urkunden und Regesten, vol. ii: Kastilien/Inquisitionsakten*, Berlin 1936.
—*Historia de los judíos en la España cristiana*, trans. José Luis Lacave, 2 vols, Madrid 1981.
Haim Beinart, *Conversos on Trial. The Inquisition in Ciudad Real*, Jerusalem 1981.
Andrés Bernáldez, *Memorias del reinado de los Reyes Católicos*, edn of Madrid 1962.
F. Cantera Burgos and C. Carrete Parrondo, 'La judería de Buitrago', *Sefarad*, xxxii, 1972, pp.3–87.
José Hinojosa Montalvo, 'Solidaridad judía ante la expulsión: contratos de embarque, Valencia 1492', *Saitabi*, xxxii (1983).
Henry Kamen, 'The Mediterranean and the expulsion of Spanish Jews in 1492', *Past and Present*, 119, May 1988.
Pilar León Tello, *Judíos de Toledo*, 2 vols, Madrid 1979.
M.A. Motis Dolader, *La expulsión de los judíos de Zaragoza*, Saragossa 1986.
Benzion Netanyahu, *Don Isaac Abravanel*, Philadelphia 1968.
Luis Suárez Fernández, *Documentos acerca de la expulsión de los judíos*, Valladolid 1964.

CHAPTER FOUR

Y. Baer, *Die Juden in christlichen Spanien*, vols i–ii, Berlin 1929–36 (reprinted 1970 by Gregg International Publishers).
—*A History of the Jews in Christian Spain*, vols i–ii, Philadelphia 1961–66.
H. Beinart, *Conversos on Trial*, translated from the Hebrew by Y. Guiladi, Jerusalem 1981.
H.C. Lea, *A History of the Inquisition of Spain*, vols i–iv, Philadelphia 1906–07.
B. Llorca, *La Inquisicion en España*, 2nd edn, Barcelona 1946.
E. Schaefer, *Beiträge zur Geschichte des spanischen Protestantismus und der spanischen Inquisition im*

16ten Jährhundert, Gütersloh 1902.
E. van der Vekené, *Bibliographie der Inquisition*, Hildesheim 1963.

CHAPTER FIVE

H. Hillel Ben-Sasson, ed., *A History of the Jewish People*, Cambridge, Mass. 1976, pp.612–45.
Benzion Netanyahu, *Don Isaac Abravanel, Statesman & Philosopher*, The Jewish Publication Society of America 1972.
Gershom Scholem, *Sabbatai Sevi, The Mystical Messiah, 1626–1676*, tr. R.J. Zwi Werblowsky, Princeton 1973, pp.1–102.
R.J. Zwi Werblowsky, *Joseph Karo, Lawyer and Mystic*, The Jewish Publication Society of America, Philadelphia 1977.
H.J. Yerushalmi, *Zakhor, Jewish History and Jewish Memory*, New York 1989.

CHAPTER SIX

Angel Alcalá, ed., *The Spanish Inquisition and the Inquisitorial Mind*, New York 1987.
Haim Beinart, *Conversos on Trial: The Inquisition in Ciudad Real*, Jerusalem 1981.
Bartolomé Bennassar, ed., *L'Inquisition espagnole (XVᵉ–XIXᵉ siècle)*, Paris 1979.
Juan Blázquez Miguel, *La Inquisición en Albacete*, Albacete 1985.
—*La Inquisición en Castilla – La Mancha*, Madrid 1986.
—*Inquisición y criptojudaismo*, Madrid 1988.
James Boyajian, *Portuguese Bankers at the Court of Spain*, New Brunswick, N.J. 1983.
Julio Caro Baroja, *Los judíos en la España moderna y contemporánea*, 3 vols, Madrid 1962.
Rafael Carrasco, 'Preludio al "siglo de los portugueses". La Inquisición de Cuenca y los judaizantes lusitanos en el siglo XVI', *Hispania*, 47, 166 (1987), pp.503–59.
Paulino Castañeda and Pilar Hernández, *La Inquisición de Lima (1570–1635)*, vol.i, Madrid 1989.
Harry E. Cross, 'Commerce and Orthodoxy: A Spanish Response to Portuguese Commercial Penetration in the Viceroyalty of Peru, 1580–1640', *The Americas*, 35 (1978), pp.151–67.
Jean-Pierre Dedieu, *L'Administration de la foi: L'Inquisition de Tolède XVIᵉ–XVIIIᵉ*, Madrid 1989.
Antonio Domínguez Ortiz, *Los judeoconversos en España y América*, Madrid 1971.
Ricardo García Carcel, *Orígenes de la Inquisición española: El tribunal de Valencia, 1478–1530*, Barcelona 1976.
—*Herejía y sociedad en el siglo XVI: La Inquisición en Valencia 1530–1609*, Barcelona 1980.
Stephen Haliczer, *Inquisition and Society in the Kingdom of Valencia 1478–1834*, Berkeley and Los Angeles 1990.
—ed., *Inquisition and Society in Early Modern Europe*, London 1986.
Gustav Henningsen and John Tedeschi, *The Inquisition in Early Modern Europe: Studies on Sources and Method*, DeKalb 1986.
Jonathan I. Israel, *European Jewry in the Age of Mercantilism 1550–1750*, Oxford 1985.
—*Race, Class and Politics in Colonial Mexico, 1610–1670*, Oxford 1975.
Henry Kamen, *Inquisition and Society in Spain in the Sixteenth and Seventeenth Centuries*, London 1985.
Seymour B. Liebman, *The Jews in New Spain: Faith, Flame and Inquisition*, Coral Gables, Florida 1970.
John Lynch, *Bourbon Spain 1700–1808*, Oxford 1989.
Joaquín Pérez Villanueva and Bartolomé Escandell Bonet, eds, *Historia de la Inquisición en España y América*, vol.i, 2nd edn, Madrid 1984.
Albert Sicroff, *Les controverses des statutes de pureté de sang en Espagne du XV au XVIII siècle*, Paris 1960.
José Toribio Medina, *Historia del Tribunal del Santo Oficio de la Inquisición de Lima (1569–1820)*, 2nd edn, 2 vols, Santiago de Chile 1952.
—*Historia del Tribunal del Santo Oficio de la Inquisición en México*, rev. edn, Mexico 1952.
Patrick Williams, 'A Jewish Councillor of Inquisition? Luis de Mercado, the Statutes of *limpieza de sangre* and the Politics of Vendetta (1598–1601)', *Bulletin of Hispanic Studies*, 67 (1990), pp.253–64.

CHAPTER SEVEN

Esther Benbassa, *Un grand rabbin sépharade en politique, 1892–1923*, Paris 1990.
Benjamin Braude and Bernard Lewis, eds, *Christians and Jews in the Ottoman Empire*, 2 vols, New York 1982.
Mark A. Epstein, *The Ottoman Jewish Communities and their Role in the Fifteenth and Sixteenth Centuries*, Freiburg 1980.
Moise Franco, *Essai sur l'histoire des Israélites de l'Empire ottoman depuis les origines jusqu'à nos jours*, Paris 1897.
Abraham Galanté, *Histoire des Juifs de Turquie*, 9 vols (reprint), Istanbul 1985.
Bernard Lewis, *The Jews of Islam*, Princeton 1984.
Aron Rodrigue, *De l'instruction à l'émancipation. Les enseignants de l'Alliance israélite universelle et les Juifs d'Orient 1860–1939*, Paris 1989.
—*French Jews, Turkish Jews: The Alliance Israélite Universelle and the Politics of Jewish Schooling in Turkey, 1860–1925*, Bloomington 1990.
—ed., *Ottoman and Turkish Jewry: Community and Leadership*, Bloomington, forthcoming.
Aryeh Shmuelevitz, *The Jews of the Ottoman Empire in the late 15th and 16th Centuries*, Leiden 1984.

CHAPTER EIGHT

Israel Adler, *Musical Life and Traditions of the Portuguese Jewish Community of Amsterdam in the Eighteenth Century*, Jerusalem 1974.

Herbert I. Bloom, *The Economic Activities of the Jews of Amsterdam in the 17th and 18th Centuries*, 1937; repr. Port Washington, New York 1969.

I.S. Emmanuel and S.A. Emmanuel, *A History of the Jews of the Netherlands Antilles*, 2 vols, Cincinnati 1970.

Mozes H. Gans, *The Memor Book*, Baarn 1971.

Jonathan I. Israel, *The Dutch, the Spanish Monarchy and the Jews, 1585–1713*, London 1990.

—'The Amsterdam Stock Exchange and the English Revolution of 1688', *Tijdschrift voor Geschiedenis* 103 (1990), pp.412–40.

—and Katz, D.S. (eds), *Sceptics, Millenarians and Jews*, Leiden 1990.

Yosef Kaplan, *From Christianity to Judaism. The Story of Isaac Orobio de Castro*, Oxford 1989.

—Henry Méchoulan and Richard H. Popkin (eds), *Menasseh ben Israel and his World*, Leiden 1989.

Richard H. Popkin, 'Menasseh ben Israel and Isaac La Peyrère', in *Studia Rosenthaliana* viii (1974), pp.59–63 and ii in *Studia Rosenthaliana* xviii (1984), pp.12–20.

Edgar R. Samuel, 'Manuel Levy Duarte (1631–1714): an Amsterdam merchant jeweller and his trade with London', *Transactions of the Jewish Historical Society of England* xxviii (1982), pp.11–31.

Daniel Swetschinski, 'An Amsterdam Jewish Merchant-Diplomat: Jeronimo Nunes da Costa alias Moseh Curiel (1620–1697), Agent of the King of Portugal' in L. Dasberg and J.N. Cohen (eds), *Neveh Ya'akov. Jubilee Volume presented to Dr Jaap Meijer on the Occasion of his seventieth birthday*, Assen 1982, pp.3–30.

Arnold Wiznitzer, *The Jews of Colonial Brazil*, New York 1960.

Gedalia Yogev, *Diamonds and Coral: Anglo-Dutch Jews and Eighteenth-Century Trade*, Leicester 1978.

CHAPTER NINE

Bevis Marks Records, vol.i (ed. L.D. Barnett) Oxford 1940; vol.iii (ed. G.H. Whitehill) London 1973.

A.S. Diamond, 'The Community of the Resettlement, 1656–1680', *Trans. Jew. Hist. Soc.* 24 (1975), pp.134–50.

T.M. Endelman, *The Jews of Georgian England*, Philadelphia 1979.

—*Radical Assimilation in English Jewish History, 1656–1945*, Bloomington 1990.

A.M. Hyamson, *The Sephardim of England; a history of the Spanish and Portuguese Jewish Community, 1492–1951*, London 1951.

D.S. Katz, *Philo-Semitism and the Re-admission of the Jews to England, 1603–1655*, Oxford 1982.

V.D. Lipman, 'Sephardi and other Jewish immigrants in England in the 18th century' in A. Newman, ed., *Migration and Settlement*, London 1970.

Sonia and V.D. Lipman, *The Century of Moses Montefiore*, Oxford 1985.

A. Newman, *The Board of Deputies, 1760–1985; a brief survey*, London 1986.

J. Picciotto, *Sketches of Anglo-Jewish History*, 2nd edn edited by I. Finestein, London 1956.

H. Pollins, *Economic History of the Jews in England*, London 1982.

E.R. Samuel, 'The Re-admission of the Jews to England in the light of English economic policy', *Trans. Jew. Hist. Soc.* 31 (1990), 153–70.

L.S. Sutherland, 'Sampson Gideon: eighteenth-century Jewish financier' in A. Newman (ed.), *Politics and Finance in the Eighteenth Century*, London 1984.

M. Woolf, 'Joseph Salvador, 1716–1786', *Trans. Jew. Hist. Soc.* 21 (1968), pp.104–37.

G. Yogev, *Diamonds and Coral: Anglo-Dutch Jews and Eighteenth-Century Trade*, Leicester 1978.

Index

Numbers in italic refer to pages on which illustrations are found.